The Holy Spirit and *Ch'i (Qi)*

Princeton Theological Monograph Series

K. C. Hanson, Charles M. Collier, D. Christopher Spinks,
and Robin Parry, Series Editors

Recent volumes in the series:

Sara M. Koenig
Isn't This Bathsheba?: A Study in Characterization

Aliou Cissé Niang
*Text, Image, and Christians in the Graeco-Roman World:
A Festschrift in Honor of David Lee Balch*

James L. Papandrea
Novatian of Rome and the Culmination of Pre-Nicene Orthodoxy

Susan Marie Smith
*Christian Ritualizing and the Baptismal Process:
Liturgical Explorations toward a Realized Baptismal Ecclesiology*

Nico Vorster
*Created in the Image of God:
Understanding God's Relationship with Humanity*

John J. Bombaro
*Jonathan Edwards's Vision of Reality: The Relationship of God
to the World, Redemption History, and the Reprobate*

Paul G. Doerksen
*The Church Made Strange for the Nations:
Essays in Ecclesiology and Political Theology*

Jennifer R. Ayres
Waiting for a Glacier to Move: Practicing Social Witness

The Holy Spirit and *Ch'i (Qi)*

A Chiological Approach to Pneumatology

Koo Dong Yun

*PICKWICK *Publications* · Eugene, Oregon

THE HOLY SPIRIT AND *CH'I (QI)*
A Chiological Approach to Pneumatology

Princeton Theological Monograph Series 180

Unless otherwise noted, Scripture quotations are taken from the Holy Bible, New
International Version®, NIV®. Copyright © 1973, 1978, 1984, 2011 by Biblica,
Inc.™ Used by permission of Zondervan. All rights reserved worldwide.

Pickwick Publications
An Imprint of Wipf and Stock Publishers
199 W. 8th Ave., Suite 3
Eugene, OR 97401

www.wipfandstock.com

ISBN 13: 978-1-978-1-61097-181-2

Cataloguing-in-Publication data:

Yun, Koo Dong.

The Holy Spirit and *ch'i (qi)* : a chiological approach to pneumatology /
Koo Dong Yun.

xviii + 170 pp. ; 23 cm. Includes bibliographical references and index.

Princeton Theological Monograph Series 180

ISBN 13: 978-1-978-1-61097-181-2

1. Holy Spirit. 2. Qi (Chinese philosophy). 3. Christianity and other religions.
I. Title. II. Series.

BT121.3 .Y86 2012

Manufactured in the U.S.A.

For Three Generations of Hyo (Filial Piety)
Rev. Young Min and Yeon Hyang Yun
Mr. Anason and Isu Pak
Mijeong and Koo Dong Yun
Kristian Hyo and Justice Mia Yun

Contents

Acknowledgments

IN THIS BOOK, I HAVE TRIED TO WRITE A POSTCOLONIAL CONTEXTUAL pneumatology that is congenial to the East Asian soil from a "chiological" perspective. Like any other pneumatology, it contains its own limitations and biases, rooted in its particular, communal horizon. In this sense, I am not trying to construct a *theologia perennis* that pretends to be a universal truth at all times and in all places.

I, as an individual, exist in a particular community and various relationships. In this regard, this book has been a communal work. It would have been impossible devoid of others' support, help, and constructive critical remarks. Many people contributed to the making of this book. To begin with, I want to thank my friends at Bethany University in California. Special thanks go to the members of the School of Theological Studies: Professor Daniel Albrecht, Terance Espinoza, and Steve Chandler. I am also grateful to the students and colleagues of Bethany University who have listened to me discussing the issues in this book, especially President Lewis Shelton, Dean Tim Powell, and Dr. Morris Barenfus.

Many people also read and commented on the manuscript at different stages. Professor David Nah at Bethel Seminary and Paul Chung at Luther Seminary provided many critical comments from the inception of this book project. My former Teaching Assistant Justin D'Agostino read and edited the manuscript, and my current Teaching Assistant Brianna Wright helped me with the bibliography.

I would like to thank the following professors who have inspired and helped me in shaping my personal theology: Donald Gelpi, Ted Peters, Veli-Matti Kärkkäinen, Jürgen Moltmann, George Lindbeck, and Harvey Cox.

Special thanks to the first generation of Asian-American theologians who laid the foundation on which I can stand, especially Sang Hyun Lee, Andrew Sung Park, Anselm Min, and Peter Phan.

In terms of technical and library support, I would like to thank the following persons: Bill Meng, Anna Temple, and Carol Atwood.

I am grateful to Pickwick Publications (Princeton Theological Monograph Series). Special thanks go to Dr. Charlie Collier, who provided timely advice and feedback. I also want to thank other editors who supported this project: Diane Farley, Christian Amondson, and Jim Tedrick. In addition, Patrick Harrison truly helped me to improve the quality of this book.

I want to express my gratitude to the global circle of my friends: Samuel Cheon at Hannam University (South Korea), Jae-Hyun Kim, Deberniere Torrey, Richard Israel, Frank Macchia, Amos Yong, and Sang-Ehil Han. Especially, I am thankful to Professor Tao Feiya, who invited me to Shanghai University (China) in the winter of 2009 so that I had a chance to share part of chapter 3 and 5 in front of premier Chinese scholars.

The earliest version of chapter 5 was published as "Pneumatological Perspectives on World Religions: The Holy Spirit and Ch'i" in Paul Chung et al., *Asian Contextual Theology for the Third Millennium* (Eugene: Pickwick Publications, 2007). This portion of the chapter is used by permission of Wipf and Stock Publishers.

Most of all, without the sacrificial support from my family, I could not have completed this book. I thank God everyday for my wife Mijeong and two children, Kristian and Justice. Mijeong has stood by me in every situation with her love and encouragement. Kristian and Justice bring me joy each day.

Koo Dong Yun
Santa Cruz, California
April 10, 2011

Introduction

LIVING IN THE POSTMODERN AND POSTCOLONIAL ERA, MANY ASIAN scholars have attempted to write "contextual" theologies that are relevant and culturally-sensitive to the Asian soil. Some Asian theologians in the past have deployed exclusive and countercultural models (e.g., the Sri Lankan Ajith Fernando and the Indian Ravi Zacharias) as they are defined by Stephen Bevans in *Models of Contextual Theology*. These two models more or less disclose "anti-culturalism" and are disrespectful of indigenous cultures. H. Richard Niebuhr would have labeled these as "Christ against Culture." On the other hand, many liberal mainline Asian theologians have uncritically endorsed pluralism by overemphasizing commonality between Christianity and other religious faiths (e.g., Stanley Samartha and C. S. Song). In opposition to the countercultural and exclusive models, I argue that the *sangjeok* dimension of the Holy Spirit—that is formal and archetypal—is present and active in all cultures and religions. And against the pluralistic and anthropological models, I claim that the *muljeok* dimension of the Spirit—that is material and categorical—is mainly revealed and normatively embodied through Christianity.

Since I am constructing a postmodern, postcolonial, and postfoundational pneumatology that is congenial to the East Asian soil, the chiological pneumatology in this monograph does not pretend to be universal, totalitarian, absolute, and totally objective. Hans-Georg Gadamer correctly pointed out that there is no pure objectivity and "prejudice" is part of being human.[1] I am writing a contextual pneumatology that stems from a particular community and horizon,[2] which

1. Michael Griffin, "Some Fusions and Disfusions of Horizon in a Gadamerian Reading of *A Passage To India,*" *Literature & Theology* 12, no. 2 (June 1998) 172–73. Also, see Hans-Georg Gadamer, *Truth and Method,* 2nd rev. ed., trans. Joel Weinsheimer and Donald Marshall (New York: Continuum, 1989) 276–77.

2. I speak of four senses regarding the word *horizon*: 1) literal, 2) epistemological, 3) ontological, and 4) communal. The "communal" horizon is synonymous with a community or tradition. For more information on this, see Koo Dong Yun, *Baptism in the*

bears its own biases and advantages. I am a Korean-American Christian, so I write theology in this particular, limited horizon. As I concede my limitation and bias, as well as advantage, in my theology, I want to see more Western theologians avowing their limitation and bias. In the past, many European and American thinkers influenced by Orientalism and Colonialism devalued, "demonized" or "satanized" indigenous non-Western religions. While European theologies stood objective, neutral, sound, rationalistic, and superior, non-Western theologies and religions stayed barbaric, exotic, primitive, and inferior. Well, time has changed. It is no longer either the West or the East. In this globalized society, both Eastern and Western theologians, avowing our limitations and biases, need to come to the table of dialogue and share with one another what we have found in our experiences and others' experiences, as well as what we have found in the Bible and cultures. In this regard, this book calls for a global and ecumenical dialogue resulting in mutual transformation and mutual illumination. Hopefully, in the end, we will find some common ground on which we, as sisters and brothers of the one universal family, can stand together.

In the first chapter of this book, I apply a "chiological" approach to the doctrine of the Holy Spirit. First and foremost, the chiological approach conceives the essence of the reality as *ch'i* (Chinese 氣, Korean 기),[3] and the form of *ch'i* is *change*. *Ch'i* is not only the essence of all natural objects but also the essence of *Tao* and *I* (the Ultimate Reality or the Divine). In this regard, the chiological approach underscores the continuity and affinity of all beings including natural and divine beings. As a result, the chiological approach in the Christian horizons descries more of the immanence of God.

Since this *ch'i* is constantly changing, moving, and transforming, the *I Ching* describes the Ultimate/Absolute Reality as *Change* (C. 易, K. 역) Change manifests itself in the process of "changes." This view stands against the Greek-Augustinian-Aquinas' substance metaphysical paradigm. This paradigm within the Western tradition construed the ultimate reality of God as *ousia* in Greek and *substantia* in Latin. For

---

Holy Spirit: An Ecumenical Theology of Spirit Baptism (Lanham, MD: University Press of America, 2003) 147–48.

3. For Romanizing Chinese words, I primarily employed the Wade-Giles system because most traditional books I used utilized this system, unless another transliteration is so common and demanded. Also, hereafter, "C." stands for Chinese; "K." stands for Korean; "J." stands for Japanese.

Augustine, this substance is unchangeable, invisible, and eternal, and Aquinas too depicts his God as the fullness of being, as pure act, devoid of becoming and mutability. The chiological approach teaches that "change" antecedes "substance" and "essence." Moreover, *ch'i* itself as a moving force is also "change."

Second, the chiological approach is "synthetic" as defined by Stephen Bevans. The 'synthetic' model remains both/and, and dialectical insofar as it tries to maintain a perfect balance between the experience of the past (i.e., Bible and Christian traditions) and the experience of the present context (i.e., current experience, culture, social location, and social change). The chiological approach embraces both the Judeo-Christian traditions as well as East Asian religious traditions (i.e., the *I Ching*, Taoism, Confucianism, Shamanism, and East Asian Buddhism). These do not have to be mutually-exclusive; instead, they may be mutually-transforming, mutually illuminating, and complimentary.

Third, the chiological approach remains "holistic" in light of both the breadth of revelation and epistemology. Our God is God of all peoples including people of *other* faiths and cultures. All life and breath originate from God (Gen 2:7). In this sense, all people are children and heirs of God who is not a racist (Rom 2:11) and loves all of his children. To this extent, our God has not neglected but has communicated with 'other' children, such as Chinese, Korean, and Japanese in East Asia. God's qualities have been revealed since the beginning of creation to all people via general revelation and Pneumatological cosmic presence (Rom 1:20). Hence, the chiological approach affirms God's action and revelation embedded and detected in East Asian cultures. In other words, God reveals Godself through the Bible as well as culture. In terms of epistemology, "knowing" (*episteme*) does not only involve "discursive thinking" (i.e. rationalism and Cartesian foundationalism). In this regard, the chiological approach remains *post-foundational* in ways that "knowing" consists of three elements: 1) *Ji* (in Korean): Cognition, 2) *Jeong* (in Korean): "Emotuition" (emotion+intuition), and 3) *Che* (in Korean): Action or Praxis. As three elements cannot be separated, they constitute "one" whole.

The fourth foundation that characterizes the chiological approach is postcolonial. Postcolonialism truly commenced around the 1950s when the colonized nations fought for independence. Postcolonialism is regarded as a process of liberating natives from colonial imposition and domination that includes political, social, economic, intellectual

and cultural areas. The colonizers and Orientalists propagated the ideology that Western culture or religion was superior to those of Asians.
Thus, the colonizers imposed their languages, dress styles, discourses,
religions, and philosophies on indigenous Asian people. When possible,
the chiological approach wants to occlude colonialism and Orientalism
by retrieving or reinventing indigenous worldviews, vocabularies, discourses, theologies, and philosophies. Language and discourse do not
stay neutral; usually, they tend to favor the powerful and dominating.
With indigenous Asian terms and worldviews, the chiological approach
helps descry the neglected and "other" dimensions of God that have
been often despised by Western people.

Chapter 2 explicates the *I Ching* (*the Book of Change*) and its relevant teachings of *ch'i*. The *I Ching* is known as the most important single
work in Chinese history, and it still remains the most foundational work
in Chinese culture. Furthermore, no one can underestimate its influence
in Korea and Japan. It is believed that Taoism, Confucianism, and even
Shamanism to some degree found their roots in this book. Hence, it is
crucial to grasp the teachings of the *I Ching* in order to comprehend East
Asian cultures and religions. It is generally accepted that the *I Ching* has
been compiled by many authors in three stages from 2000 to 500 BCE.
According to Chinese tradition, the first stage began with the legendary
ruler Fu Hsi (ca. 2000 BCE), who was credited for the linear symbols of
the *I Ching*. In this first stage, eight trigrams were produced. The second
stage began with King Wen of the Chou dynasty (ca. 1150 BCE), who
brought forth 64 hexagrams. The third stage formulated the Ten Wings
(*Shih I*) mainly by Confucius and his disciples.

Chapter 2 also introduces the trinitarian principle in the *I Ching*. A
hexagram comprises 6 lines. The two bottom lines describe the condition
of Earth; the two middle lines portray the condition of Humanity; the
top two lines depict the condition of Heaven. In addition, in the *I Ching*,
the essence of *I* (Change), *T'ai-chi*, and *Tao* is *ch'i*, which is a Chinese
counterpart to the English term *Spirit*. The original *ch'i* is the source of
all beings, whereas *li* remains differentiated and specific activities of the
original, creative *ch'i*.

Chapter 3 analyzes six East Asian philosophers' constructs of *ch'i*.
First, Mencius (371–289 BCE) understood *ch'i* as the psychophysical
energy that united moral, physical, and spiritual entities. Like many of
his contemporaries, Mencius assumed that the universe is made of *ch'i*

with its various densities: The grosser *ch'i* became the earth, and the lighter *ch'i* became the sky. Humans consist of both kinds. Interestingly, Mencius also saw *ch'i* as breath. Second, Chou Tun-yi (1017–1073 CE), one of the founding figures of Neo-Confucianism, is best known for his Diagram of the Great/Supreme Ultimate (*T'ai-chi T'u*). Another name of the Great Ultimate is the Ultimateless (*Wu-chi*). The Great Ultimate begot the yin and yang, which in turn begot the five material forces that are water, fire, wood, metal, and earth. Basically, the interaction between yin and yang produces and reproduces a myriad of things. In general, Chou is credited for introducing the apposition of *li* (Principle) and *ch'i* to Neo-Confucianism. *Li* belongs to the sphere of the Great Ultimate whereas *ch'i* pertains to the realm of the yin and yang. Chu Hsi took up the apposition further. Third, Chang Tsai (1020–1077 CE) expatiated upon the concept of *ch'i* further. For him, *ch'i* was synonymous with the Great Void (*T'ai-hsü*), which was the equivalent of the Great Ultimate. In another place, he insisted that *ch'i* was the original substance of the Great Void. Basically, he endorsed *ch'i* monism. When *ch'i* condensed, it became visible objects; when *ch'i* dispersed, it became invisible objects; when *ch'i* lost shape, it returned to the Great Void.

The fourth East Asian philosopher of we will explore is Chu Hsi (1130–1200 CE), who was a complicated dualist. For Chu, *li* remained the substance or essence of Tao or the Great Ultimate. *Li* stayed ontologically prior to *ch'i*. *Li* belonged to the metaphysical world that is "above shapes"—*hsing erh shang,* while *ch'i* pertained to the material world that is "within shapes"—*hsing erh hsia.* One, however, should remember that Chu's separation between *li* and *ch'i* belongs to the *ontological* world, not the *existential, material* world with shapes. The fifth East Asian philosopher is Yi Yulgok (1536–1584 CE). Neo-Confucianism truly blossomed in Korea, wherein Yulgok, for many, was known as the best Korean Neo-Confucian scholar. He clarified and meliorated the relation between *li* and *ch'i* in a highly complicated way. On the whole, his position on *li* and *ch'i* was labeled as "not one and not two": They can be neither separated nor mix together. He spoke of the two aspects of *li*: 1) the original *li* that was undifferentiated and purely good, and 2) the moving *li* (riding on *ch'i*) that generated a myriad of things in the concrete world. Also, influenced by Chu Hsi, Yulgok taught that *T'ai-chi* consisted of *li*, not *ch'i*. The sixth East Asian philosopher whom I chose is Kaibara Ekken (1630–1714 CE), a Japanese Neo-Confucianist. He called for a monism of *ch'i*, which united all things including both form and matter. Unlike Yi Yulgok and Chu Hsi, *ch'i*, for Ekken, was the essence or substance of both "above shapes" and "within shapes." He opposed Chu Hsi's bifurcation of *li* and *ch'i*. In fact, Ekken taught that even the Great Ultimate (*T'ai-chi*) consisted of *ch'i* in contrast to Chu Hsi's and Yulgok's view that *li* is the substance of the Great Ultimate.

Chapter 4 starts with the pneumatologies of two leading European theologians in the twentieth century, namely, Karl Barth and Wolfhart Pannenberg, and it ends with a chiological response to these pneumatologies. To begin with, Pannenberg objects to the traditional Christian theory of "relation of origin": "God the Father" is the source of the trinity. The Father begets the son; the Spirit proceeds from the Father. This one-way-flow of the trinity undermines and subordinates the other two persons of the trinity: the Son and the Holy Spirit. Accordingly, Pannenberg endorses the trinitarian origin. Moreover, he calls for "mutual dependence" in the intratrinitarian relationships. For Pannenberg, the Spirit is not only the essence of God but also the dynamic field. On the other hand, Barth elucidates God the Father as the source or origin of the trinitarian relation and of creation. In view of the trinitarian terminology, Barth deploys "3 modes of 1 being," which tends to be modalistic, whereas Pannenberg's tends to be tritheistic because he more or less speaks of three subjects. Another critical point of Barth's pneumatology is that the Spirit is the essence of the Godhead.

In the *I Ching*, *ch'i*—the Chinese equivalent of "Spirit"—is regarded as the essence of *I* (Change), *Tao*, and *T'ai-chi*. Furthermore, the original *ch'i* is understood as the source of all beings. In view of the Ultimate Reality that are categorized as God, *I*, *Tao*, and *T'ai-chi*, the Reality Itself is not knowable according to the *I Ching*. Even *ch'i*-in-itself remains inscrutable although the original, primal *ch'i*—when it is embodied in *li* (Principle)—becomes scrutable. Pannenberg and Barth, however, acceded to the notion that the immanent trinity to some extent becomes accessible via the economic trinity.

Chapter 5 begins with the pneumatologies of Jürgen Moltmann and Stanley Samartha, two of the world's premier theologians. Moltmann speaks of the Spirit of Father and the Spirit of the Christ: The former is the Spirit of the Creation, and the latter is the Spirit of Redemption, although both of them continue to be one and the same Spirit. The redemptive Spirit works on salvation of all human beings; on the contrary, the creative Spirit penetrates in all things that include plants, animals, and even earth. In light of the creative Spirit, the works and presence of the Spirit in other cultures and religions are clearly ratified. The premier Asian theologian Stanley Samartha not only confirms the works of the Spirit in other faiths but also provide some criteria for discerning "spirits." Some of the biblical criteria are freedom, boundlessness, new relationships, and new communities. Moreover, he adds ethical and inward dimensions of the Spirit's presence. Next, I expatiate on the Shamanic roots of Chinese religions, especially its influence on Taoism. Shamanism was very active even at the beginning of the Chou dynasty (1122–256 BCE). After that, I introduce a commonality between Moltmann's creative Spirit and Taoism's material *ch'i*: both of them penetrates in existents. Finally, I use the chiological approach in order to understand world religions better. The thrust of my argument is this: From the *sangjeok* viewpoint that is *formal* and *archetypal,* the Holy Spirit is present in all cultures and religions. On the other hand, from the *muljeok* viewpoint that is *material* and *particular,* the Holy Spirit is mainly revealed and categorically embodied through Christianity.

1

The Chiological Approach to the Holy Spirit

EVERY THEOLOGY IS A *contextual* theology that stems from a particular culture and horizon. To suggest some examples, there are *black* theology, *German* theology, *Korean* theology, *minjung* theology, *feminist* theology, and *liberation* theology. Whenever my family gathers together for a special occasion, theological debates take place. My father, an ordained Presbyterian minister, often inculcates that the most foundational doctrine of Christianity is *hyo* (K. 효 *hyo*, C. 孝 *hsiao*)[1] by quoting the fifth commandment of the Decalogue. For him, Jesus Christ is the ultimate embodiment of *hyo* who obeyed His Father (God the Creator) and volunteered to die on the Cross for His Father. The central point of Christianity is to obey the Heavenly Father (God) and the earthly father (human father). In the face of this, I accuse him of being a "Confucianized Christian." He often reminds me of being an "Americanized" and "individualistic" Christian because I overemphasize individual salvation. Then, I realize that although we worship the same Christian God, my father and I focus on different aspects of God in dissimilar contexts.

In this book, I strive to construct a contextual pneumatology that is congenial to East Asian soil, although part of me has already been *Americanized* having lived many years in the United States. To write a contextual pneumatology with a distinctively Asian flavor necessitates a sound theological methodology relevant to the East Asian context. After only a few days of research, it did not take me long to realize that the best Chinese translation of the biblical term "Spirit/spirit"[2] (*ruach*

1. Hereinafter, "K." stands for Korean; "C." stands for Chinese.

2. *Ch'i* (*Ki* in Korean and Japanese) is the Chinese counterpart to the English word "Spirit/spirit." For more information on this, see section "The Holy Spirit as *Ch'i*: The Holy Spirit, Spirit, spirit(s)" below.

1

and *pneuma*) ought to be *ch'i* (C. 氣), a term which encompasses such a variety of meanings as *spirit, force, material force, energy, vital energy, vapor, breath, and air.* Accordingly, I have endeavored to understand the Spirit from this *ch'i* perspective, and called this the "chiological approach." Thus, chapter 1 is an expatiation of the chiological approach utilizing four foundational categories: 1) *ch'i*, 2) synthesis, 3) (w)holism, 4) postcolonialism.

The Essence of Reality as *Ch'i*

The Ultimate Reality

What is the *Ultimate Reality* beyond which there is nothing? By "the Ultimate Reality" I mean the Source or the Creator of all things and beings. All things come from this Ultimate Reality, and all things including human beings return to this. This Ultimate Reality is the One who is behind and within all religions,[3] albeit our human concepts or notions of this may have been limited, tainted and infected. The Ultimate Reality remains both *transcendent and immanent.* As the *transcendent* Reality, it cannot be contained in any human systems and any human languages that are culturally and socially constructed. Taoists call this "the unnamable, eternal Tao."[4] Many human symbols are used to describe the transcendent Ultimate Reality as the Mystery, the Divine, the Void, and the Ultimateless. John Hick calls this the Real and the Divine that is the center, source, or goal of all religions. Although no human has *direct, immediate* access to the Real, many religious persons *experience* the Real with their particular historical and cultural categories. Moreover, no human can fully understand the Real-in-itself—the *noumenon* in the Kantian sense, so one can only understand the *phenomenon* of the Real.[5] Humans can only describe the Real in symbols, metaphors, and myths. In this regard, humans can only experience the Real "as" something. We portray

---

3. See Eph 4:6, which states, "*One* God and *Father of all*, who is *over* all and *through* all and *in* all." Italics are mine. This One God is "over" all—alluding to transcendence of God; this one is "through" and "in" all—alluding to immanence of God.

4. Chapter one of *Tao Te Ching* states, "The Tao that can be told [named] is not the eternal Tao. The name that can be named is not the eternal Name. The unnamable is the eternally real." This translation is from Stephen Mitchell's Tao Te Ching (New York: Harper Perennial, 2006).

5. John Hick, *An Interpretation of Religion: Human Responses to the Transcendent* (New Haven: Yale University Press, 1989) 235–36.

the Real as Father, Mother, Spirit, Way, Force, and so forth. Furthermore, the Real (or the Ultimate Reality) is symbolized both as personal beings (e.g., Father, Mother, Shiva, or Krishna), and as impersonal beings (e.g., Force, Way, Emptiness, Void, or Heaven).[6] The other side of the Ultimate Reality stays *immanent* insofar as it is present in our universe and nature. It is present in all things and all beings. This Ultimate Reality resides not only in living beings such as humans and animals but also inanimate beings such as trees, rocks, and even in soil and air.

Yahweh and *Theos* (God) are the two main Judeo-Christian names (or symbols) of this one *Ultimate Reality*. Both Judaism and Christianity practice monotheism. The *Shema* teaches, "The Lord our God, the Lord is *one*" (Deut 6:4). This one God created the universe (Gen 1:1) and all people (Gen 1:27). Furthermore, this *one God* is the *Father of all people* that include American, Chinese, Korean, and even nonbelievers.[7] Hence, Ephesians 4:6 states, "One God and *Father of all*, who is over all and through all and in all." Although some conservative scholars argued that the phrase "Father of all" applies only to Christian believers,[8] I think a more sound interpretation of the phrase refers to all creatures that include all peoples and animals. Ernest Best argues that the phrase "of all" (Greek *pantōn*) can be either neuter or masculine. When it is the masculine, it speaks of believers in the church. When neuter, it stands for the cosmos. Best, however, favors the neuter: "In the end it is probably better to give 'all' a neuter meaning throughout with the sense, 'one creator God and Father who governs the cosmos, works through it and present in it.'"[9] First Corinthians 8:6 also supports the view that this one God is

---

6. Paul Knitter, *Introducing Theologies of Religions* (Maryknoll, NY: Orbis, 2002) 117.

7. See Veli-Matti Kärkkäinen, *The Doctrine of God: A Global Introduction* (Grand Rapids: Baker Academic, 2004) 39–42. The idea of the fatherhood of God in the Old Testament is rare, but as we move into the New Testament, we see a proliferation of the term *Father*. In numerous occasions, Jesus addressed God as *abba*, and asked his disciples to do so. The usage of the term *Father* in the NT increased over the years. In Mark, the earliest Gospel, we only see four references, whereas in Matthew, we see more than thirty references. John, written later than Mark and Matthew, contains more than 120 references.

8. See E. K. Simpson and F. F. Bruce, *Commentary on the Epistles to the Ephesians and the Colossians,* The New International Commentary on the New Testament (Grand Rapids: Eerdmans, 1973) 90.

9. Ernest Best, *A Critical and Exegetical Commentary on Ephesians* (Edinburgh: T. & T. Clark, 1998) 371. See also Ralph P. Martin, *Ephesians, Colossians, and Philemon,* Interpretation: A Bible Commentary for Teaching and Preaching (Atlanta: John Knox, 1991) 48. It also favors the neuter meaning.

the Father of the cosmos that incorporates such beings as all humans and animals. It says, "Yet for us there is but *one God, the Father, from whom all things came and for whom we live;*[10] and there is but one Lord, Jesus Christ, through whom all things came and through whom we live." It is clear that this verse endorses the view that this one God is *the Father of all things in the cosmos.* Moreover, when Jesus spoke of God's Fatherhood in the Gospels, it meant the Fatherhood of all humanity, all peoples.[11]

As the Father of all humanity, both believers and nonbelievers, this one God (or the Ultimate Reality) has spoken and communicated not only with Jews and Christians but also with the "other" children such as native East Asians and Africans, for whom Jesus Christ also died for their salvation and loved them unconditionally despite their utmost rebellion (John 3:16; Rom 3:22–24). This one God does not show favoritism (Rom 2:11), and this is the God of both Jews and Gentiles, as well as both believers and nonbelievers (Rom 3:29). Since this one God has spoken to these other children, naturally there has been revelation of God in other people's cultures. This God's communication with all of God's children can be labeled as "General Revelation" (Rom 1:19–20). Moreover, since this God is also "in all" as the Spirit, careful human eyes will detect the pneumatological works and presence in nature and human cultures (Eph 4:6).

In the traditional Western world, they often use the word *God (theos)* to describe this. In the pluralistic East Asian context, the Ultimate Reality is translated with numerous words, such as *T'ai-chi* (the Great Ultimate), *Wu-chi* (the Ultimateless), *Shang-ti* (the Lord on High), *T'ien-chu* (the Lord of Heaven), and *Ha-na-nim* or *Ha-neu-nim* (the Lord of Heaven in Korean). In *the I Ching,* known as *the Book of Change(s),* the terms *I* (Change) and *Tao* (the Way) are frequently deployed in order to depict the Ultimate Reality.

The Translation of "God" into Chinese and Korean

How do we translate "God," the ultimate reality of Christianity (i.e., *Yahweh* or *Theos*), into Chinese? There was a great debate in the 19th century in China regarding this name of "God." Two main groups argued against each other. The first group, mainly led by many American mis-

---

10. Italics are mine.

11. Ernest Best, *Critical and Exegetical Commentary on Ephesians,* 370.

sionaries, preferred the term *Shen* (神), which denotes the whole class of Gods. The other group, led by many English missionaries, wanted to call "God" *Shang-ti* (上帝), denoting "the Lord/Sovereign on High."[12]

There is another Chinese term that has been deployed to refer to God, namely, *T'ien* (天) or Heaven. According to Yu-lan Fung, both terms Heaven (*T'ien*, 天) and God (*Ti*, 帝) (or *Shang-ti*—the Supreme God) have been frequently used by Chinese before Confucius' time in the *Shu Ching* (Book of History) and *Shih Ching* (Book of Odes), *Tso Chuan*, and *Kuo Yü*. In these writings, one sees frequent references to Heaven and God, and numerous references speak of an "anthropomorphic" *Shang-ti*—personal God. From this we can deduce the doctrine that *Shang-ti* (the literal translation means "Supreme Emperors") is the highest and supreme authority, who presides over an elaborate hierarchy of spirits (*shen* 神). This group of *shen* (spirits) stayed secondary to *Shang-ti*, to whom they paid allegiance. This ancient religious belief of the common people of China had existed since early times.[13]

As each Chinese word possesses numerous meanings, the ideogram *T'ien* also contains at least 5 meanings. In the first place, it refers to a material or physical *T'ien* or sky as in opposition to the physical earth. The next meaning signifies "fate" (*ming* 命), over which a person has no control. Another meaning of this Chinese character is "nature" that includes all things in the universe. This Chinese word also denotes the highest moral principle of the universe. This moral understanding of *T'ien* can be seen in the *Chung Yung* (Doctrine of Mean). The fifth meaning of this Chinese word denotes God (*Shang-ti*) or Supreme deity. Hence, when a Chinese person speaks of *T'ien* (Heaven), this Heaven also refers to an anthropomorphic *T'ien*—a personal God. Even during the Ming dynasty (1368–1643 CE), the Chinese words *T'ien* and *Shang-ti* were used in order to describe God; however, Pope Clement XI, in 1704 banned the use of these terms.[14] Later, Roman Catholics in East

12. Cf. Max Weber, *The Religion of China: Confucianism and Taoism,* trans. Hans Gerth (New York: The Free Press, 1951) 20–25. According to Weber, Chinese of antiquity conceived *Shang-ti* as both the Heaven itself (impersonal) and the King of Heaven (personal). In Chinese philosophy, the "personal" god or deity eventually vanished from the 12th century. Thereafter, the "impersonal" conception of deity procured the upper hand especially in the official cult.

13. Yu-lan Fung, *A History of Chinese Philosophy* (Princeton: Princeton University Press, 1952) 2:30–31.

14. Paul Chung, *Constructing Irregular Theology: Bamboo and Minjung in East Asian Perspective* (Leiden: Brill, 2009) 107–8.

Asia started to employ the term *T'ien-chu* (the Lord of Heaven) in order to demarcate their name of God from the names of traditional Chinese religions.

This debate regarding translating the name of God also took place among early Protestant missionaries in Korea. H. G. Underwood (1859–1916), who was one of the first Presbyterian missionaries to Korea, preferred the Korean term *shin* (Korean 신, Chinese 神, *shen*) at the beginning of his missionary work in Korea. Shortly thereafter, some confusion arose among indigenous Koreans because the Korean word *shin* also denoted *gui-shin* (demons). Accordingly, Underwood started using *Cham-shin* (true God) and *Sang-je* (*Shang-ti* in Chinese).[15] In contrast to Underwood, many of his English contemporary missionaries in Korea were using the traditional Korean term *Hananim* (Korean 하나님). At first, Underwood thought *Ha-na-nim* was a name of a gentile idol. Later, his view was shifted in that he saw many positive elements in the indigenous Korean culture including traditional Korean religions. As a result, he accepted the indigenous Korean term *Hananim,* which came from the Korean shamanistic soil.[16] Etymologically speaking, there are at least two different interpretations of the term *Hananim,* which is the combination of the two words: 1) *hana,* and 2) *nim. Nim* denotes "lord" or "master," but the etymological origin of the word *hana* is trickier. Some scholars postulate that *hana* comes from the root word *haneul* (meaning heaven or *sky* in Korean) as many names of God in Siberian and Central Asian Shamanism speak of "Sky" or "Heaven."[17] Others inculcate that the root

15. See Choe Byeong-heon, *Seongsan Myeong Gyeong,* Korean Christian Classics Series IV, trans. Deberniere Torrey (Seoul, Korea: KIATS, 2010) 15–96. Choe Byeong-heon (1856–1927) was one of the first Korean Methodist pastors and theologians. Choe was the author of *Seongsan Myeong Gyeong* (1922), which was a reprint of his original work, entitled *Syeongsan Yuramgui* (1907). In *Seongsan Myeong Gyeong,* one of the first Korean Protestant apologetics, a dialogue takes place among four men: 1) Jindo, 2) Wongak, 3) Baegun, and 4) Sin Cheon-ong, respectively representing Confucianism, Buddhism, Esoteric Daoism, and Christianity. At the end of the book, all of them decide to convert into Christianity. In this work, Choe's approach opposes the fundamentalistic exclusive view and pluralistic relativistic view. One should note a pivotal fact of this book that Christianity supplements Confucianism with such concepts as grace, heavenly citizenship, eternal life, and the merciful and intimate God. Another pivotal point is that the "Sovereign on High" (C. *Shang-ti,* K. *Sang-je*) of Confucianism is equated with the Christian God. In other words, Christianity fulfilled what was lacking in Confucianism.

16. Chung-su Seol, "Studies on H. G. Underwood's Understanding of *Ha-na-nim,*" PhD diss., Beijing University, 2009.

17. Mircea Eliade, *Shamanism: Archaic Techniques of Ecstasy,* trans. Willard Trask (London: Routledge & Kegan Paul, 1964) 9.

word of *hana* is also *hana*—literally meaning "one." On the basis of this etymology of *hana*, two different translations of *Hananim* arose: 1) the One and Only Lord, 2) the Lord of Heaven. Either way, this name refers to the One Sovereign God.

Just like the Christian God, *I* (Change) and Tao remain continuously inscrutable or mysterious, but they also manifest themselves in various ways so that humans can have access to these divine/ultimate realities. For example, the Judeo-Christian God was revealed via the Scriptures and the Christ event. While Tao in Taoism, in part, reveals itself through nature, *I* (Change) in the *I Ching* becomes manifest through *ch'i* (the dynamic movement) and *li* (the universal principle).

In order to derive the essential nature of the Christian God, Christians often speak of the attributes and properties of God on the basis of general and special revelation, although almost all of us avow the mysterious side of God that transcends human understanding and language. Nonetheless, the Christian God we worship continuously wants to communicate with humans and reveal Godself so that we worship the proper God, not idols.

God as Spirit/Ch'i

Regarding the query about the essence of God, John 4:24 says, "God is *spirit* (pneuma), and his worshipers must worship in spirit and truth." Not only the essence of God is understood as spirit, but Jesus Christ is also depicted as the Spirit: "Now the Lord is the *Spirit* (pneuma), and where the Spirit of the Lord is, there is freedom" (2 Cor. 3:17).

Both Wolfhart Pannenberg and Karl Barth argue that the very essence of God is Spirit. In volume 1 of *Systematic Theology*, Wolfhart Pannenberg regards the essence of God as Spirit: "The essence of God is indeed Spirit."[18] In addition, he speaks of Spirit as a dynamic force field. Moreover, this Spirit is the love that unites the Father and the Son. Barth, in volume I/1 of *Church Dogmatics*, describes the essence of God as the Spirit too. Barth writes, "The event of revelation has clarity and reality on its subjective side because *the Holy Spirit*, the subjective element in this event, *is of the essence of God Himself.*"[19] Also, this Spirit refers to the

---

18. Wolfhart Pannenberg, *Systematic Theology*, vol. 1, trans. Geoffrey W. Bromiley (Grand Rapids: Eerdmans, 1991) 429.

19. Karl Barth, *Church Dogmatics*, I/1:466. Italics are mine.

common element which enables the true fellowship among the persons of the Godhead.

A parallel understanding that *God is Spirit/spirit* is easily found in the *I Ching*, where *I* (Change) represents the Ultimate Reality. The *I Ching* regards *ch'i* as the essence (or substance) of *I* and Tao.[20] The term *I Ching* consists of the two Chinese ideograms. The ideogram *Ching* (經) denotes a book or thread, and the other ideogram *I* (易) means *change(s)*. No distinction between singular and plural exists in the old Chinese character, and also no distinction is made between upper cases and lower cases. I personally favor the word *Change*[21] with the upper case and singular when *I* refers to the absolute and ultimate reality; however, I sometimes utilize the plural *changes* with a lower case, referring to the manifestations of *I* (Change) in various stages.[22] So the better translation of *I Ching* is *the Book of Change*. At any rate, the ideogram *I* (易) is the combination of the two radicals: 1) the sun (日) and 2) the moon (月). The sun exemplifies the primary symbol of yang *ch'i*; the moon is the primary symbol of yin *ch'i*. In this sense, *I* (the Great Ultimate in the *I Ching*) remains the unity of yin and yang *ch'i*. Thus, the essence of *Change* is *ch'i*. Regarding this point, the later Neo-Confucian scholar Chang Tsai averred that *ch'i* was identical with the Great Void (C. *T'ai-hsü* 太虛, K. *Tae-heo* 태허)[23] that was a synonym of the Great/Supreme Ultimate (*T'ai-chi*) in Chang Tsai's natural philosophy.[24] In other words, Chang also conceived *ch'i* as the essence of the Great Void, that is, the ultimate reality.

Although there is no exact English word for the Chinese word *ch'i* (氣), various terms are rendered to describe this Chinese word, such as *spirit, energy, vital energy, force, material force, vapor, breath, and air*.[25] Without difficulty, one can see many similarities between the biblical

20. Chung-Ying Cheng, "*Li* and Ch'i in the I Ching: A Reconsideration of Being and Non-being in Chinese Philosophy, *Journal of Chinese Philosophy* 14 (1987) 11–12.

21. I also did not make use of a definite article before "Change" because Ancient Chinese did not have definite articles.

22. Jung Young Lee, *Embracing Change: Postmodern Interpretations of the I Ching from a Christian Perspective* (Scranton, PA: University Press of Scranton Press, 1994) 41.

23. Hereafter, "C." stands for Chinese; "K." stands for Korean.

24. Chang Tsai, *Correct Discipline for Beginners,* quoted in *Sources of Chinese Tradition: From Earliest Times to 1600,* vol. 1, comp. WM. Theodore DE Bary and Irene Bloom (New York: Columbia University Press, 1999) 687.

25. JeeLoo Liu, *An Introduction to Chinese Philosophy: From Ancient Philosophy to Chinese Buddhism* (Oxford: Blackwell, 2006) 6.

word *Spirit* (*ruach, pneuma*) and the Chinese word *ch'i*. In other words, the essences of both God (the ultimate reality in Christianity) and *I* (the ultimate reality in the *I Ching*) are seen as Spirit/*ch'i* (the Chinese translation for "Spirit"). This view of the essence of God as Spirit/*ch'i* in part ratifies my thesis in chapter 5 that the Cosmic Holy Spirit has been present in all cultures and religions in terms of its *form and pattern* (C. 象, K. 상) while the *material*, concrete dimension (C. 物 *wu*, K. 물 *mul*) of the Spirit of Christ was missing in traditional East Asian religions (e.g., Taoism, Confucianism, and Shamanism).

Not only the essence of God or Change is Spirit/*ch'i*, but all the visible and invisible objects in the *I Ching* also consist of *ch'i*. *Ch'i* remains the source and substance of all beings. For instance, the grosser and heavier *ch'i* comprises the earth, and the more refined and lighter *ch'i* constitutes the sky. Human beings are the combination of both kinds of *ch'i*. Moreover, the essence of trees is *ch'i*. When *ch'i* condenses, it becomes a visible thing, and when *ch'i* disperses, it becomes an invisible thing. When *ch'i* loses completely its form and shape, it returns to the Great Void or the Great Ultimate (*T'ai-chi*). This East Asian view of *ch'i* brings forth a *chiological (ch'i+ology) approach* that views the essence of all beings as *ch'i*.

Ch'i is constantly changing, moving, and transforming. That is why the *I Ching* sees *I* (Change) as the ultimate reality. The dynamic act of change is the metaphysical reality of yin and yang *ch'i*. In this sense, Change (*I*) is the most fundamental 'stuff' from which other beings emerge. Logically speaking, Change precedes being (*ontos*), and Change produces beings. In this regard, "changeology" takes priority over ontology.

This view of change as the ultimate reality stands against the Greek-Augustinian-Aquinas's substance metaphysics. This substance metaphysics of the Western tradition construed the ultimate reality of God as *ousia* in Greek and *substantia* in Latin. Augustine portrays God as a substance that is unchangeable, invisible, and eternal.[26] Furthermore, the God of Aquinas remains immutable and cannot go through any change.[27] Accordingly change belongs to the realm of accident, not substance. As

---

26. St. Augustine, *On the Trinity*, in *A Select Library of the Nicene and Post-Nicene Fathers* (Grand Rapids: Eerdmans, 1956) 3:89.

27. Ted Peters, *God as Trinity: Relationality and Temporality in Divine Life* (Louisville: Westminster/John Knox, 1993) 30–31.

a result, both Augustine and Aquinas brought forth the immutable God. While this Western Christian God, the ultimate reality, stays immutable, *I* (Change) and Tao—the ultimate reality in the *I Ching*—constantly changes, moves, and transforms itself.

In sum, the chiological approach not only regards the essence of the ultimate reality or the absolute (e.g., God, Change, or Tao) as *ch'i*, but even the essence of all existence is also construed as *ch'i*. In the Bible and Western theologies, one can easily find a parallel of the view that the essence of the ultimate reality is *ch'i* or Spirit. For instance, John 4:24 states that God is spirit, and Karl Barth and Wolfhart Pannenberg construed the essence of God as "Spirit."[28] As I indicated above, the best Chinese translation of the English word Spirit/spirit[29] is *ch'i*. While the chiological approach underscores the continuum between *ch'i* of humans and that of Change (or Tao), many Western Christian theologians (e.g., Karl Barth) have highlighted the discontinuity between the "spirits" of human beings and the "Spirit" of God. In this respect, the chiological approach has many advantages in elucidating the immanence of God or the ultimate absolute reality in nature.

The Holy Spirit as Ch'i: *The Holy Spirit, Spirit, or Spirit(s)*

Most modernists underscored "sameness" or "universality" among objects and cultures whereas Postmodernists tend to stress "difference" or "particularity" among them. Concerning the relationship between the Holy Spirit and *ch'i*, postmodernists by and large highlight differences between the two, while modernists draw attention to affinities between the two. The chiological approach accepts both affinities and differences between the Spirit and *ch'i*. In other words, the chiological approach acknowledges some common ground between the two.

What kinds of commonalities can we find between the Holy Spirit and *ch'i*? To begin with, both the Spirit and *ch'i* have been present everywhere and at all times. Both of them manifest themselves in both personal and impersonal categories. In John 14:26, Jesus Christ speaks of the Holy Spirit as the Advocate—a person. In Matthew 3:16, the Spirit of God was descending like a dove and lighting on Jesus. The Wisdom

---

28. Chapter 4 elucidates Barth's and Pannenberg's pneumatologies in detail.

29. Many early manuscripts of the New Testament did not distinguish upper and lower cases.

of Solomon 12:1 states, "Thy immortal Spirit is in all things." Moreover, Job 33:4 says, "The Spirit of God has made me and the breath of life gives me life." Hence, the Spirit of God is in all things, both in personal and impersonal beings. According to chapter 43 of the *Tao Te Ching*, *ch'i* also penetrated into all existing entities. As the Spirit of God manifested herself as both personal and impersonal beings, *ch'i* also embodied itself as both personal and impersonal beings. One step further, *ch'i* is the essence of all existents.

Another commonality which I find between the Holy Spirit and *ch'i* is the connotation of "wind." The Hebrew word *ruach* and the Greek *pneuma* are translated as "wind" or "breath." Ruach finds its etymological origin in *air* that manifests itself both as (1) wind in nature, and (2) breath in living beings. As the wind, the Spirit blows where it wills (John 3:8), and the Spirit came down like a wind (Acts 2:2). In the *I Ching* (Book of Change), *sun*—one of the eight trigrams—is produced via the interplay of yin *ch'i* and yang *ch'i*. Another name of *sun* (the 57th hexagram) is "wind," which is known for its penetrating power.[30] As wind, the material *ch'i* penetrates all existents.

Another commonality which one can find from both the Holy Spirit and *ch'i* is that of "breathing." Genesis 2:7 remarks, "Then the Lord God formed a man from the dust of the ground and breathed into his nostrils the breath of life, and the man became a living being." As the breath of life, the Spirit bestows life upon all living beings. The Spirit makes the living possible. In the Old Testament, God's breath is equated with the life-giving power (Gen 6:17; Num 16:22; Ps 104:29). In the New Testament, the Holy Spirit represents a life-giving power in the story of Jesus' birth (Matt 1:18–20; Luke 1:15, 35, 37). Tung Chung-shu, a prominent Chinese philosopher, elucidated *ch'i* as air to humans and water to fish. *Ch'i* is the life force of living creatures.[31] Moreover, Mencius also spoke of *ch'i* as breath.[32]

Another affinity that I find between the Spirit in the Bible and *ch'i* has to do with the concept of "vaporization." The Chinese word 氣 (*ch'i*) is a combination of two words: vapor and rice. Actually, *ch'i* portrays the

---

30. Richard Wilhelm and Cary Baynes, trans., *The I Ching or Book of Changes* (Princeton: Princeton University Press, 1977) 220–30.

31. Jung Young Lee, *The Trinity in Asian Perspective* (Nashville: Abingdon, 1996) 96–97.

32. D. C. Lau, trans., *Mencius* (London: Penguin, 2003) 2A:2, 32.

steam vapor rising out of a rice-cooking pot when heated. The Greek root *pneu-* for *pneuma* denotes a dynamic movement of air, and the Greek word *pnoē* (a derivative of *pneu-*) means steam and "evaporation."[33]

Not only do we see the common ground between the Holy Spirit and *ch'i*, but the Korean-American theologian Grace Kim also finds 'one' universal Spirit with 'many names' within various cultures, such as the Holy Spirit, *Ch'i, Prana,* and *Ha.* This one Spirit transcends culture, religion, and tradition. Both the Hebrew *Ruach* (e.g., Gen 2:7) and Chinese *ch'i* portray the "Spirit reality" as breath and life-force. Furthermore, understanding Spirit as breath is very common and is found in many other religions and cultures. To begin with the Hebrew view of *Ruach* as breath, some argue, finds its roots in ancient Egyptian and Mesopotamian civilizations. A similar idea is also found in the Koran. The word *nafas* means Allah's own breath. In Hinduism and Buddhism, the notion of *Prana* as "breath" and "life energy" shares affinities with the Christian notion of the Spirit. In Hawaii, the word *Ha* means breath. The Greeting "Aloha" can be translated as "meeting face to face (*alo*) of the breath of life (*ha*)," which is the sacred healing breath.[34]

One, however, cannot ignore differences between the Holy Spirit and *ch'i* (K. *ki*). In English, it is essential to distinguish between "spirit," "Spirit" and "the Spirit" due to its capitalization system. The original Greek of the New Testament, however, did not have upper cases and lower cases, and even its usage of the definite article was different from English. This presents some difficulties in distinguishing among the Spirit of God, human spirits, and other spirits such as evil spirits. Here are some ambiguous examples, such as Mark 14:38: "the spirit/Spirit is willing, but the flesh is weak," and John 4:23: "the true worshipers will worship the Father in the Spirit/spirit and in truth." Thus, in many cases, it is difficult to draw clear lines between the divine Holy Spirit and other spirits.[35]

It becomes more complicated when one translates the Spirit or spirit(s) into Chinese and Korean. To begin with both classical Chinese and Korean did not have their capitalization systems. They did not dis-

---

33. James D. G. Dunn, "Spirit, Holy Spirit" in Colin Brown, ed., *Dictionary of New Testament Theology,* vol. 3 (Grand Rapids: Zondervan Publishing, 1978) 689.

34. Grace Ji-sun Kim, "A Global Understanding of the Spirit," *Dialogue and Alliance* 21 (2007) 17–31.

35. Kirsteen Kim, *The Holy Spirit in the World* (Maryknoll, NY: Orbis, 2007) 12–16.

tinguish upper and lower cases. Moreover, many Chinese and Korean words can mean both singular and plural in English. For instance, the Chinese word *I* (C. 易) in the *I Ching* can be translated as both "change" and "changes." In terms of definite article, it is even more challenging. For example, Acts 1:5 states, "For John baptized with water, but in a few days you will be baptized in *the* Holy Spirit" (NIV).[36] But if we look at a Korean translation, we do not see "the"—definite article—in front of "Holy Spirit."

Then, many would raise these questions: "Why don't they distinguish lower cases form upper cases, as well as singular from plural?" "Why don't they make use of definite articles?" No one knows for sure, but one of logical answers is that both Korean and Chinese perhaps did not want to separate "the divine Spirit" from "human and natural spirits." As in the case of Karl Barth, many Western theologians want to separate human spirits from the divine Spirit, whereas East Asian thinkers observe and underscore the continuity and commonality between the two. To my surprise, even Paul Tillich tends to separate the divine Spirit (or Spiritual Presence) from a human spirit. Even when the divine Spirit breaks into the human and even when the divine Spirit grasps the human spirit, it still is the "human" spirit. It remains what it is; it does not become a divine Spirit.[37] On the contrary, according to the chiological approach of East Asia, *ch'i* is the essence of all beings including the absolute divine beings, and beneath all beings, *ch'i* remains the one unifying power.

The Chiological Approach as Synthetic

The second foundation of the chiological approach is "synthetic." In his pivotal book, entitled *Models of Contextual Theology*, Stephen Bevans introduces six models of contextual theology. The "synthetic" model is one of the six models in this book. Professor Bevans prefers the term "contextualization" over "indigenization" and "inculturation" because contextualization—as a broader term—includes and corrects the older terms such as indigenization and inculturation. Both indigenization and inculturation overvalued traditional cultures and ideologies, while "con-

---

36. *Italics are mine.*

37. Paul Tillich, *Systematic Theology*, vol. 3 (Chicago: The University of Chicago Press, 1963) 111–12.

textualization" critically reevaluates traditional, indigenous values and ideas and underscores the ever-changing dynamic nature of culture. The term "contextualization" in the theological context was first introduced in 1972.[38]

The first of the six models is named "countercultural." This model more or less resembles H. Richard Niebuhr's model "Christ against Culture" in his classic book *Christ and Culture*.[39] This model deeply *distrusts sanctity and revelational power of culture or context*. Traditional and indigenous cultures first need to be purified and weeded before the seeds of the Christian gospel can be planted. There is a sharp contrast between the culture of death and the gospel of life.[40]

Many verses in the Scriptures support this view. Johannine writings carry such a negative view of culture insofar as the *kosmos* (the world) is mostly viewed negatively in the Gospel of John, in which the word *kosmos* appears about 78 times. In John's Gospel, the *kosmos* mainly refers to the godless and rebellious world.[41] In the Letters of John, the world is clearly portrayed negatively, and the "world" signifies the whole society outside the church.[42] 1 John 2:15 states, "Do not love the world or anything in the world. If anyone loves the world, the love of the Father is not in him." This distrust of culture can also be found in some of the Pauline writings such as Rom 12:2 and 1 Cor 1:23. Out of many early Fathers of the church, Tertullian conveyed a classic example of the countercultural model.

This countercultural model, however, does not totally dismiss culture and context, without which communication cannot take place. Rather, it points out corrupted and tainted human elements of culture and context. It recognizes that all theological expressions and viewpoints stem from historically and culturally conditioned situations.[43] Hence, context and culture first need to be purified and critically evaluated so that the radically different gospel can be planted in a new soil. At any

38. Stephen B. Bevans, *Models of Contextual Theology* (Maryknoll, NY: Orbis, 2002) 26–27.

39. H. Richard Niebuhr, *Christ and Culture* (New York: Harper & Row, 1951) 45–82.

40. Ibid., 117.

41. F. F. Bruce, *The Gospel of John* (Grand Rapids: Eerdmans, 1983) 36–37.

42. Niebuhr, *Christ and Culture*, 48. See 1 John 2:2; 4:14.

43. Bevans, *Models*, 117.

rate, the main characteristic of this model is a sharp contrast between context/culture and the gospel of Christ.

The second model of contextual theology is "translation." This model is the most commonly utilized in engaging in contextual theology. The primary fidelity goes to "experience of the past" (i.e., the Scriptures and Christian tradition), and the secondary attention goes to "experience of the present" (context and present culture). It begins with the gospel message, and then moves into the context. Basically, the essential message of the gospel remains super-cultural or supra-contextual. It speaks of "the kernel" of the gospel that is surrounded by a nonessential cultural "husk." Methodologically speaking, this model first seeks an essential and supra-contextual message of the gospel, and then rewraps the essential message so that it fits into a new situation.[44]

"Translation," however, does not simply refer to the word-for-word literal interpretation, but it also involves the "dynamic-equivalence method" that centers on a translation of meanings, not just a translation of words and grammar.[45] For example, what is the best translation of the term *Holy Spirit*? In the past, Koreans have grappled with this inquiry, and they were divided into two main groups. One group promulgated the term *Seong-shin* (K. 성신); the other group deployed the term *Seong-lyeong* (K. 성령). I argue that both of these "literal" interpretations do not exemplify the best expression of the original biblical words, *ruach* and *pneuma*. I believe that a better Korean translation is the term *Seong-ki* (K. 성기), which is the combination of the two words: 1) *Seong*—meaning holy, and *ki* (氣, *ch'i* in Chinese)—meaning spirit, breath, energy, force, etc. I believe that the word *ki* provides a much better functional and dynamic equivalence of the term *Holy Spirit*. Therefore, in order to provide an accurate translation of a word, one should not only look into denotation, but also connotation. One step further, one should take account of a dynamic vitality of each word that goes through changes.

The third contextual model is "praxis." The praxis model elucidates the essence of Christianity in terms of "social change." Contextual theology does not primarily have to do translating or adapting the core gospel; rather, theologizing was chiefly construed as "doing theology." The foremost emphasis goes to action/practice. The prophetic tradition

44. Ibid., 37–40.

45. Charles H. Kraft, *Christianity in Culture: A Study in Dynamic Biblical Theologizing in Cross-Cultural Perspective* (Maryknoll: Orbis, 1979) 264–65.

in the Old Testament calls for not only words, but also action (Isaiah, Amos). James underlines the importance of one's action (James 1:22).[46] The Letters of John want to retrieve ethical dimensions of salvation.

Jon Sobrino, a theologian working in El Salvador, distinguishes Latin American Theology from European theology. European theology is grounded in the thoughts of Descartes and Kant calling for rationality and subjective responsibility. On the basis of rationality, they challenged authorities of the church. As a result, theology is understood in light of orthodoxy, namely, right thinking.[47] On the contrary, Latin American theology is rooted in the ideology of Karl Marx, insisting that "genuine knowledge" entails both right reason and action. Thus, Marx remarked, "The philosophers have only *interpreted* the world in various ways; the point is to *change* it."[48] In this regard, theology becomes much more than a cognitive, discursive enterprise; it has to do with liberating the poor and oppressed in the Two-Thirds world.

The transcendental model represents the fourth paradigm of contextual theology. Unlike other contextual models, this model starts with a human *subject*, who articulates on his or her religious experience. This model teaches that contextual theology does not start by analyzing one's social and historical context or by studying the essence of the gospel. Instead of beginning with the "out-there" objective reality, theologizing begins by critically examining one's subjective consciousness. Bernard Lonergan remarked, "Genuine objectivity is the fruit of authentic subjectivity."[49] In order to engage a proper theology, one needs to attend to one's transcendental subjectivity that naturally reaches toward truth.[50]

A subject is determined by context. In other words, every human subject is truly historically and culturally conditioned in terms of the *content of thought*. A human subject exemplifies a product of geographical, historical, social and cultural environment. So genuine contextual theology primarily has to do with the "contextualized subject," rather than the contextualized message of the gospel and Christian tradition.

---

46. Bevans, *Models,* 70–71.

47. Ibid., 71.

48. Karl Marx, *Theses on Feuerbach,* 11, in L. D. Easton and K. H. Guddat, eds. and trans., *Writings of the Young Marx on Philosophy and Society* (Garden City: Anchor Doubleday, 1967) 402.

49. Bernard Lonergan, *Method in Theology* (New York: Herder & Herder, 1972) 292.

50. Bevans, *Models,* 103–4.

Although there are diversity and difference in terms of the content of thought (e.g., images and concepts), a universal, transcultural commonality exists in terms of the subject's way of knowing (i.e., the basic cognitive operations).[51]

Another pivotal point of this model is the concept of "conversion." There is something which one cannot understand devoid of a complete change of mind, namely, conversion. Non-Christians cannot understand the Christian faith unless they enter the Christian horizon by means of conversion. Moreover, when a person undergoes a conversion, he or she endeavors to seek understanding of his or her religious experience, which is an essential piece of the transcendental method.

The anthropological model exemplifies the fifth of contextual theology. This model stands at the opposite end of the spectrum from the translation model. Whereas the translation model strives to preserve "Christian identity," this anthropological model chiefly tries to keep "cultural identity" of a person. From this perspective, the proper answer to the question, "Am I first a Christian or Korean?" is: I am first and foremost a "Korean," and only secondarily a "Christian."[52]

This model is labeled "anthropological" in two senses. In the first sense, it is anthropological in the way that it underscores the value and goodness of *anthropos,* the human person. It has such a high view of the human person to which God revealed Godself. The valid human experience is more or less equal to the other two *loci theologici,* namely, Scripture and tradition. In the second sense, this model incorporates the insights of the social science of anthropology, which tries to find God's presence in the web of human relationships and means (i.e., culture). By studying religious symbols and concepts of one's culture, we will bring out essential aspects of each religion.[53] In this regard, this model also has a very high view of culture, in which we find God's revelation. Accordingly, human nature and culture are deemed good and holy, so we find God's revelation in these two locations. To put it in another sentence, God's revelation is already given and present in indigenous cultures and original human nature.

This anthropological model bears a resemblance to H. Richard Niebuhr's model, "Christ of Culture," in which there is no tension be-

51. Ibid., 105.

52. Ibid., 54.

53. Ibid., 55.

tween Christ and culture. As a result, proponents of this model can maintain their loyalty to both Jesus Christ and important elements of their native cultures. Furthermore, there is no big chasm between the gospel of Jesus and one's indigenous traditional religions and cultures. For instance, for many Jewish Christians, Christianity was a fulfillment of Judaism and continuation of their religion.[54]

This anthropological model is excellently summarized by M. A. C. Warren's statement: "Our first task in approaching another people, another culture, another religion, is to take off our shoes, for the place we are approaching is holy. Else we may find ourselves treading on men's dreams. More serious still, we may forget that God was here before our arrival."[55] This view of Warren necessitates a different view of missions. Missionaries should not go to mission fields as "pearl merchants," who want to sell new Western products to natives. Instead, they should go as "treasure hunters," who want to find hidden treasures in new countries. Proponents of this model ratify the hidden God's grace in Christ in "other" cultures and religions.[56]

The sixth model of contextual theology is called "synthetic." Other names of this model are dialectical, dialogical, analogical, and conversational. This model is also known as a middle-of-the-road or both/and model. This is situated right in the middle of the spectrum of the six contextual models of Stephen Bevans.

The word *synthetic* has at least three senses. In the first place, it looks to a *synthesis* that endeavors to preserve a great *balance* between the experience of the past (i.e., Scripture, tradition), the experience of the present (i.e., personal and communal experiences, culture, social location, and social change), and other contexts (i.e., other religions and cultures). In the second sense, it reaches out to the other resources of the other contexts, such as the *I Ching, Tao Te Ching*, and *Mencius* in the East Asian context. Third, the word refers to the Hegelian dialectic that brings forth a new synthesis by putting a thesis and antithesis together, so that a new synthesis becomes acceptable to all standpoints.[57]

---

54. H. Richard Niebuhr, *Christ and Culture,* 83–86.

55. This statement appears in Warren's preface to John V. Taylor, *The Primal Vision* (London: SCM, 1963) 10.

56. Bevans, *Models,* 56–57.

57. Ibid., 89–90.

This model underscores the composite nature of both context and the Scriptures. The Korean culture in the twenty first century also evinces the composite make-up that includes traditional Korean elements (e.g., shamanism), Chinese elements (e.g., Taoism and Confucianism), American elements (e.g., democracy, American soldiers, and baseball), and Western Christianity. Even the Christian Bible itself is a composition of many ingredients. The Old Testament was originally the Hebrew Bible, and the New Testament, written in Greek, reflected mainly the Hellenistic culture. Even within the Old Testament, we see a "Priestly" writing, Yahwist writing, Elohist writing, and Deutronomic writing.[58] Even the New Testament comprises various writings and theologies, such as Pauline, Johannine, and Lukan.

This synthetic model calls for openness and dialogue because no single view sees the totality of truth. In fact, truth remains multidimensional, living, and moving. In this regard, David Tracy spoke of plurality and ambiguity of truth. Accordingly, it is much better to understand truth in terms of relation, conversation, and dialogue. Proponents of this model give a rebuff to the correspondence theory of truth that seeks a simple agreement between concept and reality. Truth is not something "out there," waiting to be captured. Instead, truth is conceived as a reality that emerges in authentic dialogue between women and men when they allow an open and honest conversation.[59]

This dialogical/conversational understanding of truth does not mean that anything goes or traditional formulations of faith are watered down. Genuine conversation also has some hard rules. One needs to say only what he or she means; one needs to say it as accurately as one can. One needs to listen to and respect what other people say. One needs to correct or defend one's opinion if challenged by conversation partners. One should be willing to change his or her view if the evidence points to the other way.[60] According to this synthetic model, theologizing is an exercise in genuine conversation and dialogue with others so that one's own cultural and religious identity emerges in this process. Hence, there

---

58. Koo Dong Yun, *Baptism in the Holy Spirit: An Ecumenical Theology of Spirit Baptism* (Lanham: University Press of America, 2003) 151.

59. Bevans, *Models*, 93.

60. David Tracy, *Plurality and Ambiguity: Hermeneutics, Religion, Hope* (New York: Harper & Row, 1987) 19.

is no contextual theology that is once-and-for-all thing, but it must be "ongoing."[61]

Chiological as Synthetic

The chiological approach endeavors to bring forth a new synthesis that keeps a great balance among the three key elements: 1) the experience of the past (i.e., the Bible and Christian tradition), 2) the experience of the present (i.e., personal and communal experiences, culture, social location, and social change), and 3) other contexts (i.e., other religions and cultures). For Christians, the Bible remains normative, and various Christian traditions have tried to clarify many crucial issues on the basis of biblical verses. Moreover, the Old Testament exemplifies a collection of personal and communal inspired experiences (or testimonies), and the New Testament consists of the multifarious inspired testimonies of the early stage of Christianity.

With respect to "the experience of the present," being a Korean to-date at the beginning of the 21st century comes with a composite identity. To be a Christian in the present Korean context means to have a Western Christian spirit, Taoistic body, Shamanistic gut or intuition, Confucian soul/mind, and Buddhistic karmic fate.[62] This composite Korean nature is also easily seen in popular culture. American hip hop music is a main ingredient of the Korean youth culture; baseball continues to be one of the most well-liked sports. Of course, South Korea is becoming more and more a "soccer nation" especially during the World Cup Finals. On the more traditional side, *Jeom* (shamanistic divination) or the activity of finding out one's fortune, still remains a major practice of most Koreans. Some Buddhist terms such as *Eop-bo* (karma) are part of daily language in South Korea. Culture is not static; it moves and goes through change. Hence, there is a radical difference between nineteenth-century Korea and twentieth-century Korea.

The term "other contexts" refers to wisdom derived from other cultures and religions, especially from East Asian religions. A foundational conviction of the chiological approach is that God is the God of all peoples, and this God has been communicating with all of God's people

---

61. Bevans, *Models*, 93–94.

62. Dai-wi Chung, "Christianity and the Religious World of East Asians: The Principle of Three Religions as One," in *Asian Contextual Theology for the Third Millennium*, ed. Paul Chung et al. (Eugene: Pickwick, 2007) 269–83.

because it is hard to imagine this loving God neglect God's own children at any moment of history. The chiological approach attends to these contents of God's general and pneumatological revelation in East Asia with careful and critical categories of the Christian gospel.

One main tool of the synthetic model is dialogue or conversation. In actuality, the chiological approach sees a "trilogue."[63] The three central poles of the trilogue are 1) the experiences of the past, 2) the experiences of the present, and 3) the experiences of other religions and cultures (other contexts). One can hear the voices of God not only in the Bible *materially*—specific and clear (C. 物 *wu*, K. 물 *mul*), but also in other religions and cultures *formally*—general and archetypal (C. 象 *hsiang*, K. 상 *sang*).[64] The *material side* of God's specific revelation via the Bible contains physical, tangible shape, whereas the *formal side* of God's general revelation via other cultures and religions remain vague, broad, and general, although this formal side still has some general shape. These three poles are not mutually exclusive; rather, they stay mutually complimentary and mutually transforming by creating a new synthesis that becomes more acceptable by more audiences. In the end, open and honest dialogue will bring forth a more refined and sound view of God.

Open and honest trilogue can produce a creative synthesis. For instance, John 4:24 states, "God is Spirit/spirit (*pneuma*)." Also, both Karl Barth and Wolfhart Pannenberg regard the essence of God as Spirit.[65] A similar understanding is also found in the *I Ching* (*the Book of Change*), which teaches that the essence of *I* (Change) and *Tao* is *ch'i*. As I mentioned before, the word *ch'i* can be translated as *spirit, energy, vital energy, force, vapor, and breath.* Thus, the Chinese word *ch'i* is the best translation of the English word *spirit.* The conspicuous Neo-Confucian Chang Tsai (1020–1077) viewed the essence of *T'aichi* (or the Great Void) as *ch'i*. The salient Japanese Confucian scholar Kaibara Ekken equated the essence of *T'aichi* (the Great Ultimate) is *ch'i* (*ki* in Japanese).[66] A synthetic statement of the above teaching is this: the essence of the ultimate reality

63. See Jürgen Moltmann, *Experiences of God,* trans. Margaret Kohl (Philadelphia: Fortress, 1980) 2–3. Moltmann also tells of a trilogue: 1) stories in the Bible, 2) personal stories, and 3) a whole number of different narratives.

64. See Yu-lan Fung, *A History of Chinese Philosophy,* 2:508.

65. Chapter 4 elaborates this idea in detail.

66. Kaibara Ekken, *The Philosophy of Ch'i: The Record of Great Doubts*, trans. Mary Evelyn Tucker (New York: Columbia University Press, 2007) 127.

(e.g., Christian God, *I, Tao, T'aichi*) is Spirit/*ch'i*. Both Spirit and *ch'i* are synonyms in this view. In this regard, the chiological approach stands against the postmodernists, including Michel Foucault, who disavow a supra-cultural and supra-contextual commonality shared by all religions and cultures. For instance, parents' love in general towards their children stays supra-cultural, although many differences lie in how this love is expressed in various cultures. Of course, on the other hand, this does not undermine the difference between the Christian God and *I* (or *Tao)*. While the Christian tradition underscored the transcendence of God, the *I Ching* and Taoism highlighted *the immanence of their ultimate reality* (or God). The concept of *ch'i* is much more naturalistic then the Spirit in Christianity. Once again, formally speaking, there is an overlap between the Spirit and *ch'i*, but what separates these two lies in the *muljeok* dimension (K. 물적, C. 物的) that is the *material side* of reality.

The Chiological Approach as Holistic

Holistic Epistemology

Many modern theologians strove to find the essence of theology in the sphere of cognition. Accordingly, they unduly highlighted noetic and discursive aspects of knowledge. By downplaying affective and praxis dimensions of knowing, the task of theology was limited to cognition. In this respect, many modern theologies became reductionistic in such a way that their frames of reference more or less precluded affective and volitional aspects of knowing. Against this "modern" reductionistic tendency, many "postmodernists" strove to retrieve a holistic (or wholistic) dimension of knowing.

In order to become more relevant to this postmodern context, I believe that Christians nowadays need to upgrade their epistemology (the study of knowledge). For the purpose of retrieving *a holistic epistemology*, it is a great idea to revisit pre-modern, ancient worlds. One can learn from Socratic intellectualism in the ancient Greek world that knowledge involves much more than just informational understanding. The simplistic definition of Socratic intellectualism is "to know is to do." In other words, if someone truly *knows* that smoking is harmful, she or he will not smoke again. Moreover, both Buddhism and Confucianism in general underscore practical and experiential dimensions of knowing. The Great twentieth-century theologian Karl Barth also endorses the holistic understanding of knowledge. Barth taught that the Greek words *ginosko* (to know) and *gnosis* (knowledge) in the New Testament did not merely refer to intellectual comprehension. These Greek words not only included an *informational* aspect, but also *affectional* and *volitional* aspects.[67]

The Old Testament books lack the notion that *the knowledge of God is simply speculative*; rather, it has to do with *acknowledgement, faith, obedience, behavior, and moral responsibility.* In this sense, the knowledge of God in the Old Testament stays *holistic.* The two Hebrew words *yada* and *da'at* are used most frequently with reference to knowledge. More than a thousand times, the root *yd'* appears in the Old Testament. These Hebrew words contain numerous connotations that can be divided into four families.[68]

First, the knowledge of God has to do with God's self-revelation. Human knowledge of God becomes possible when God initiates the process of self-disclosure. Regarding this point, Wolfhart Pannenberg states, "God can be known only if he gives himself to be known."[69] The self-revelation in the Old Testament transpires in a general way (Gen 4:6; 6:13), and in a special way with unique promises (e.g., Abraham and Moses).[70] Furthermore, God's self-revelation not only comes from "outside" but also from "within" via the *imago dei* (Gen 5:1f.). Only human beings were created in the image or likeness of God. In this sense, God revealed Godself universally in each human subject amid human rebellion.

Second, the knowledge of God in the Old Testament refers to the divine-human relationship or fellowship. One of the central themes of the biblical drama of redemption is relationship: 1) God and human beings, 2) between humans, and 3) humans and non-human life. Hosea portrays the knowledge of God as a personal relationship growing out of an encountering experience with God. The relationship between God

---

67. Karl Barth, *Church Dogmatics,* IV/3.1:183–85.

68. Steven B. Sherman, *Revitalizing Theological Epistemology: Holistic Evangelical Approaches to the Knowledge of God,* Princeton Theological Monograph Series 83 (Eugene: Pickwick Publications, 2008) 153–54.

69. Wolfhart Pannenberg, *Systematic Theology* trans. Geoffrey Bromiley (Grand Rapids: Eerdmans, 1991) 1:189.

70. Sherman, *Revitalizing,* 154.

and humans entails communication, respect, love, and complete trust in Yahweh.[71]

The third aspect of the knowledge of God in the Old Testament speaks of human obedience to God and ethics. Schmitz remarks, "In the wisdom literature, fear of Yahweh and knowledge of God are interchangeable terms."[72] Also, the knowledge of God includes doing rightly and justly (Isa 11:2; Jer 22:16). One step further, fear of Yahweh naturally results in departure from wickedness (Prov 3:7).[73]

Fourth, the knowledge of God in the Old Testament deals with God's salvific work toward Israel. Through God's deliverance from Egypt, the Israelites grew in the knowledge of God (Exod 7:5), and they realized once again that Yahweh was the only Power who can save them in times of trouble and foreign oppression. Yahweh's mercy and saving acts assured the fact that God was faithful and that Yahweh was Israel's God.[74]

Now, I want to explore the New Testament's understanding on knowledge. In the first Epistle of John, the Greek verb *ginosko* involves cognitive, relational, and volitional aspects. 1 John 4:8 remarks, "Whoever does not love does not *know* God, because God is love (NIV)." This verse shows the interconnection between "knowing" and "loving." Later, 1 John 5:2 elucidates how to *love* others, that is, by keeping God's commandments. No Christian can claim that she or he *knows* God devoid of loving others because the *ousia* (being or essence) of God is love.

The Greek verb *ginosko* in the New Testament often refers to experiential knowing. In Matt 1:25 and Luke 1:34, *ginosko* expresses an intimate union between a woman and man. Furthermore, the word *ginosko* in Matt 25:24, Mark 13:28, and Heb 10:34 stands much more than informational knowing. Another similar word *epiginosko,* meaning "to know fully," speaks of human participation in "kowning."

When we apply this holistic epistemology to the Christian faith, to know Jesus Christ does not simply mean intellectually consenting to the notion that Jesus Christ died for "me" on the cross. It entails affective and

71. Sherman, *Revitalizing,* 157.

72. E. D. Schmitz, "Knowledge, Experience, Ignorance," in *The New International Dictionary of New Testament Theology,* ed. and trans. Colin Brown (Grand Rapids: Zondervan, 1976), 396.

73. Sherman, *Revitalizing,* 160.

74. Ibid., 162–163.

moral conversions too.[75] Therefore, in order to theologize in the post-modern context, one needs a holistic epistemology that is more relevant to our culture at the beginning of the twenty-first century.

Ji-Jeong-Che Metaphysics and Epistemology

The subject of metaphysics deals with the question of reality: "What is there?" Monists argue that the reality only consists of *one* fundamental "stuff," out of which everything is made. For materialists, the single stuff comprises matter or body. For panpsychists, the single stuff refers to mind/soul. For neutral monists, the single stuff is neither material nor a mind-like thing, but a third potential substance that can become both. For physicalists, the fundamental stuff alludes to one sort of things studied in physical sciences, such as energy, forces, or fields.[76] In contrast to these monists, dualists speak of two fundamentally distinct and irreducibly different kinds of stuff, e.g., body and soul. The primary function of soul is to think, and the primary function of body is to be extended in space. Trichotomists claim that the reality consists of three irreducibly different kinds of stuff, namely, spirit, soul, and body.

As I mentioned before, the chiological approach understands the reality as *ch'i*, which is the essence of all beings including the divine, *I* (Change), *Tao*, or *T'ai-chi*. Regarding this understanding of the *I Ching*, Chung-ying Chen writes, "*I* (易) is *ch'i* (氣), and *hsing* (形) is *li* (理)."[77] In this regard, the chiological approach grounded in the *I Ching* more or less stands on *ch'i* monism. But *Ch'i* expresses itself in three modes: 1) *Ji*—cognition (C. *chih* 知), 2) *Jeong*—emotuition=emotion+intuition (C. *ch'ing* 情), and 3) *Che*—embodiment (C. *ti* 體). Each mode consists of one of three kinds of *ch'i*: 1) *sang* (C. *shang* 上)—top , 2) *jung* (C. *chung* 中)—middle, 3) *ha* (C. *hsia* 下)—bottom. *Ji* is constituted by *sang ch'i*; *Jeong* is constituted by *jung* chi; *Che* is constituted by *ha ch'i*.

---

75. For the topic of conversion, see Donald Gelpi, *The Conversion Experience: A Reflective Process of RCIA Participants and Others* (New York: Paulist, 1998) 24–30, and Koo Dong Yun, "Pentecostalism from Below: Minjung Liberation and Asian Pentecostal Theology," in *The Spirit in the World*, ed. Veli-Matti Kärkkäinen (Grand Rapids: Eerdmans, 2009) 106–9.

76. William James Earle, *Introduction to Philosophy* (New York: McGraw-Hill, 1992) 108–9.

77. Chung-Ying Cheng, "*Li* and Ch'i in the I Ching: A Reconsideration of Being and Non-being in Chinese Philosophy," *Journal of Chinese Philosophy* 14 (1987) 12. I inserted the classical Chinese words.

In a trigram of the *I Ching*, the bottom line (*ha*) represents the earth which consists of heavier, *ha ch'i*. The top line (*sang*) represents the sky or heaven which consists of lighter, *sang ch'i*. The middle line (*jung*) represents humanity which consists of in-between, *jung ch'i*. In the case of a hexagram (6 lines), the two bottom lines speaks of the condition of earth. The top two lines speak of the condition of heaven. The two middle lines depict the condition of humanity. This is a *triadic* understanding of *one* reality.[78] To put it in another way, there are three modes (*Ji-Jeong-Che*) within one unified reality.

This *Ji-Jeong-Che* view of reality also becomes applicable to the reality of God. The essence of God is Spirit/*ch'i* (John 4:24; 2 Cor 3:17). God the Father represents *Ji* (cognition); the Holy Spirit corresponds with *Jeong* (emotuition); Jesus Christ represents *Che* (embodiment). Jesus Christ is the concrete embodiment of the mind (God the Father). Analogous to Karl Barth's understanding of revelation, Jesus Christ is *the* revelation of the shape and action of God, the Creator/Father. The *Che* (Chinese *ti* 體), like many Chinese pictographs, has multiple meanings: body, shape, original substance, physical things, and action. In this Jesus Christ is the body, shape, and action of God the Creator. As the cognition (*Ji*), God the Father stays formless and shapeless, that is, "above/beyond shapes" (*hsing erh shang* 形而上). The Holy Spirit correspond with *Jeong* (C. *ch'ing* 情), which denotes feeling, love, kindness, passion, desire, etc. In this understanding of *Jeong*, the Holy Spirit is affection, love, desire of God. In this sense, when a person is filled with the Holy Spirit, she or he naturally expresses the qualities of the Spirit, such as love, joy, kindness (cf. Gal 5:22).

The *Ji-Jeong-Che* view not only applies to metaphysics but also to epistemology. This view brings forth a holistic epistemology in that "knowing" involves all the three modes. In order to "know" an object, generally in the U.S.A., we start by analyzing the object into smaller parts. Thereafter, we collect data and facts from our observations and experiences. Then, we interpret data and facts in order to deduce an in-

---

78. Cf. Charles Sanders Peirce, *Collected Papers,* ed. Charles Hartshorne and Paul Weiss, 8 vols. (Cambridge: Harvard University Press, 1931–1958) 1:25–26. Peirce also regards the reality as the three modes of being: *firstness, secondness,* and *thirdness.* The firstness refers to pure potentiality and qualities of a thing. The secondness signifies a brute force or fact or "thisness"—particularities. The thirdness speaks of the general laws, habits, and tendencies that react in a specific way. Interestingly, Karl Barth also conceives God as "three mode of one being."

ference, conclusion, or solution via conscious critical reasoning.[79] These deductive and inductive kinds of reasoning belong to the sphere of *Ji*—cognition.

Jeong also continues to be an indispensable part of knowing. *Jeong* (emotuition) includes affection, emotive thinking, abductive thinking, as well as unconscious and subconscious thinking.[80] There is not only "cognitive, critical" thinking in *Ji* but also "emotive" thinking in *Jeong.* For instance, when my son Kristian was three years old, I was listening to classical music as most Koreans do. All of sudden, he started crying. I was wondering why he was crying. Soon, I found out that it was engendered by this sad music. This is an example of emotive thinking. Human minds think both consciously and sub- or pre-consciously.

The *Ji-Jeong-Che* epistemology not only involves *Ji* and *Jeong* modes but also *Che* (Chinese *ti* 體), which also means action. The *Ji-Jeong-Che* epistemology includes orthodoxy (right belief)—*Ji,* orthopathy (right affection)—*Jeong,* and orthopraxy (right practice)—*Che.*[81] To come up with right knowledge or belief, a person has to engage in right affection and practice. In other words, each mode by itself cannot be compartmentalized; as a part of a whole, each mode cannot be separated. One's affection and practice also more or less determines one's belief and knowing. Many liberation theologians and Korean minjung theologians have emulated to retrieve praxis/action aspects of knowing. In this regard, Karl Marx averred that genuine knowledge entails both right thinking and action.

The Loci Theologici in the Ji-Jeong-Che Holistic Epistemology

The term *holistic* not only applies to the structure of knowing, but also to the *loci theologici,* that is, theological sources. Authentic theology first explores the testimonies in the Christian Bible, and then it incorporates the testimonies of the authentic voices of traditional Christianity, such as Paul, Augustine, Luther, Barth, and others. One main problem, however,

79. Richard Paul and Linda Elder, *Critical Thinking,* 2nd ed. (Upper Saddle River, NJ: Prentice Hall, 2006) xxiii–xxix.

80. For more information on affective and emotive aspects of thinking, see Donald Gelpi, *Experiencing God: A Theology of Human Emergence* (New York: Paulist, 1978) 85–99.

81. Steven Land, *Pentecostal Spirituality: A Passion for the Kingdom* (Sheffield, UK: Sheffield Academic Press, 1997) 122–81.

arises due to the fact that most traditional voices of Christianity have been dominated by the West with the general assumption that God has only spoken in the Bible and Western Christian culture. Grounded in the doctrine that God created all people—meaning God is the Father or Source of all people—it is hard for me to imagine that God as the Father did not communicate with all people, such as East Asians, before the arrival of Western Christian missionaries. In fact, most Christians have accepted this universal disclosure of God as general revelation.

When we accept the premise that God has spoken to these ancient East Asians, the next step is to find the contents of God's revelation and communication. In the first place, the chiological approach finds the contents of God's revelation in the *I Ching*, which has been serving the Chinese culture as the main source and foundation. Moreover, both Taoism and Confucianism are grounded in this book. The *I Ching* regarded the ultimate reality as Change (*I*) in contrast to Augustine's depiction of God as an unchanging substance.[82] But *the I Ching* also taught that the essence of Change (the absolute ultimate) is *ch'i*. A parallel view exists between Change as *ch'i* and God as Spirit. The chiological approach also finds the other sources of theology from Taoism, Confucianism, and even Shamanism in East Asia. The pneumatological immanence of God especially in the Hebrew Bible is ratified in the Taoist's construal of *ch'i* that interpenetrates all entities as a vital energy. Furthermore, the pneumatological immanence is also seen in the five primary virtues of Confucianism, namely, *jen* (love or benevolence), *i* (righteousness), *li* (propriety or kindness), *hsin* (good faith or faithfulness), and *chih* (wisdom). With ease, one can uncover many affinities between the five Confucian virtues and the fruit of the Holy Spirit in Gal 5:22. Moreover, the gifts of the Holy Spirit such as healing and prophecy, listed in 1 Cor 12:8–10, are "formally" manifested in indigenous Shamanism in East Asia although these manifestations still lack the material and concrete aspects of the Spirit of Christ.

---

82. St. Augustine, *On the Trinity*, in *A Select Library of the Nicene and Post-Nicene Fathers* (Grand Rapids: Eerdmans, 1956) 3:89.

The Chiological Approach as Postcolonial

The Basic Shape of Postcolonialism

The fourth foundation that characterizes the chiological approach is postcolonial. Postcolonialism began around the 1950s and 1960s when many colonized nations fought for independence in the remaining British and French colonies. Since then, it has developed quickly to become a major area of intellectual and political debate. Generally speaking, the term *postcolonialism* is viewed as the multifaceted political, economic, cultural and philosophical responses to colonialism from its inception to the present day.[83] As a working definition, postcolonialism can be regarded as a process of liberating the natives from colonial imposition and domination that include the political, social, economic, intellectual, and cultural areas. Postcolonialism does not simply stop after decolonization,[84] but goes into a new phase wherein liberated subjects strive for new images, new ideas, new concepts, new thought forms, and new societies that ensure the value of their humanness and native cultures.

The prefix *post* still engenders many debates because many scholars still do not believe that the colonial period is over. Edward Said, one of the most conspicuous scholars on Postcolonialism, warned that it might be premature to speak of postcolonialism because colonialism still continues today and is simply replaced by new forms of colonialism, namely, neocolonialism.[85] Postcolonialism differs from "anti-colonialism" that underscores particular movements of resistance to colonialism. On the contrary, postcolonialism signifies the broader and multifaceted areas.

One has to first understand colonialism against which postcolonialism reacts. By colonialism, we mean the conquest and thereafter control of other countries. Naturally, it involves the subjugation of native peoples, their political leaders, and economy. The process of colonizing other nations usually involves propagating a colonial ideology that stresses cultural supremacy, e.g., white supremacy. Behind the politi-

---

83. Jane Hiddleston, *Understanding Postcolonialism* (Stocksfield: Acumen, 2009) 1.

84. See Pui-lan Kwok, *Postcolonial Imagination & Feminist Theology* (Louisville: Westminster John Knox: 2005) 30.

85. Edward Said, "In Conversation with Neeladri Bhattacharya, Suvir Kaul, and Ania Loomba," in *Relocating Postcolonialism*, ed. David Theo Goldberg and Ato Quayson (Oxford: Blackwell, 2002) 2.

cal and economic project of colonization, one detects the spreading of a discourse of hegemony and superiority that drives and espouses the colonial ruling. At an intellectual and literary level, colonization comes with the promulgation of a colonial ideology that justifies the colonizers' presence and conquest on the basis of bringing their "superior knowledge" and "civilization."[86]

Colonialism slightly differs from imperialism although both of them share a common ground. Imperialism entails a broader kind of cultural dominance, whereas colonialism often refers to a more concrete act of conquest. In other words, colonialism exemplifies a specific manifestation of imperialist ideology. Imperialism refers to a larger structure of economic or socio-political dominance that does not always result in the direct rule and subjugation of other countries. In this sense, imperialism could easily continue long after the end of colonial rule. Indeed, many critics have spoken against the economic dominance of global markets by the United States as a new form of imperialism. Imperialism is also associated with Western capitalism, which often has imposed its capitalist system on the other parts of the world. Colonial subjugation and settlement helped spread the Western capitalist system.[87] Even after departures of colonizers, colonial ideology continuously exerted its pressure and lingering effects on the ex-colonies because it takes a long time to disengage from the remnants of this colonial dominance that had settled and become involuntarily integral elements of the colonized nations.

Edward Said's Orientalism

In 1978, Edward Said published a groundbreaking volume entitled *Orientalism,* which became one of the most important works in the field of postcolonial studies. Said, a Palestinian, was born in Jerusalem in 1935. After being educated in Cairo in his younger years, he moved to the United States in order to continue his studies and to develop his career. In his intellectual life, he endeavored to combine literary criticism with politics and cultural philosophy. He had a broad audience of both academicians and the general public. One of the main arguments in *Orientalism* is that one finds a clear link between culture and politics

86. Hiddleston, *Understanding Postcolonialism,* 2.
87. Ibid.

when she or he analyzes colonial discourse that has the mechanics of conquest as well as economic exploitation. With careful eyes, one can also find that Orientalist discourse's attempts, to some degree, resulted in diffusing colonial power.[88]

The word *Orientalism* possesses three interrelated meanings. First, it refers to the academic studies of the Orient (Asia). In this regard, anyone who teaches, writes about, or researches the Orient belongs to this department, although this term has been outdated due to its association with nineteenth and early twentieth-century European colonialism. The second meaning signifies "a style of thought based upon an ontological and epistemological distinction between 'the Orient' and (most of the time) 'the Occident.'"[89] This binary distinction has been employed by many European Orientalists or colonialists, such as poets, novelists, philosophers, and imperial administrators, in order to underscore the difference between the West and East.[90] The third meaning of Orientalism refers to a set of European constraints and thoughts upon native Orientals that supports and justifies the European dominance and occupation as well as European superiority over Asian inferiority from the late 18th century.

Orientalism inculcates that the Orientals (Asians) are childlike, irrational, depraved (fallen), and different, while the Occidentals (Europeans) are mature, rational, virtuous and normal.[91] In chapter two of *Orientalism*, Said illustrates an attitude of British superiority with Arthur James Balfour's lecture, delivered in the House of Commons on June 13, 1910. According to this lecture, English colonizers "knew" Egypt better than Egyptians themselves, who did not have a capability to govern themselves according to the colonizers. Moreover, the English colonizers entered Egypt in order to civilize the primitive Egyptians and to save them from the wretchedness.[92] Balfour stated, "We are in Egypt not merely for the sake of the Egyptians, though we are there for their sake; we are there also for the sake of Europe at large."[93]

88. Ibid., 83–84.

89. Edward Said, *Orientalism* (New York: Pantheon, 1978) 2.

90. Ibid., 43.

91. Ibid., 40.

92. Ibid., 33–35.

93. This is a statement from Balfour's lecture in the House of Commons in 1910, quoted in Edward Said, *Orientalism,* 33.

Orientalism was much more than simply justification or rationalization "after" European colonizers successfully conquered many parts of Asia. Said writes, "To say simply that Orientalism was a rationalization of colonial rule is to ignore the extent to which colonial rule was justified in advance by Orientalism, rather than after the fact."[94] From 1815 to 1914, European colonial territories expanded from 35 percent to about 85 percent of the earth's surface. Beneath this rapid European colonial expansion, there was already this Orientalism—embedded in European colonizers' cultures—that provided the colonizers with an ideology, vocabulary, rhetoric, and attitude.[95] Orientalism was brought forth as an objective study whose process of construction and categorization has served to prop the colonial vision of conquest and subjugation.[96]

Orientalism that Said elaborates can be regarded as a "discourse" in Foucault's sense that is a wide network of texts, images, and preconceptions, shaped by power and in turn to serve the power, namely, European colonizers.[97] Discourses are not neutral realities; rather, they are constructed by the power structures in order to prop up the colonizer's hegemony and rule.[98] Foucault believed that "discourse" came to surface in the early 1600s, but disappeared in the late 1700s.[99] Moreover, one can easily detect Foucault's influence on Said's *Orientalism* throughout the book.

European supremacy of Orientalism also applies to Oriental religion, which is the base of almost any culture. For Said, a focal point is Islam, which symbolizes fanaticism, barbarism, and terrorism. By disproving the religions of the Orientals, the colonizers strived to devalue the entire culture of the Orientals. In doing so, the colonizers maintained European superiority and undermined the value of the Oriental

94. Said, *Orientalism*, 39.

95. Ibid., 41.

96. Hiddleston, *Understanding Postcolonialism*, 77.

97 Ibid., 85.

98. Cf. Paul Lakeland, *Postmodernity: Christian Identity in a Fragmented Age* (Minneapolis: Fortress, 1997) 12–18. Lakeland speaks of three reactions to the postmodern world: 1) radical postmodern, 2) nostalgic postmodern, and 3) late modern. Michel Foucault belongs to the first group who deny any objective theory of knowledge and universal and independent "reason." One's reason stays contextual and dependent on power relations and desire.

99. Michel Foucault, *The Order of Things: An Archaeology of the Human Sciences* (New York: Pantheon, 1970) 81, 235–36.

cultures. This attitude of the colonizers can be detected with respect to Mohammed. One obvious point of Orientalist discourse was to portray Mohammed as an imposter. Said writes, "Mohammed is always the imposter (familiar, because he pretends to be like the Jesus we know) and always the Oriental (alien, because although he is in some ways 'like' Jesus, he is after all not like him)."[100]

Postcolonialism and the Chiological Approach

ERADICATING NATIVE RELIGIONS

As we have seen in *Orientalism,* the European colonizers devalued the religions of native Asian peoples. Religion in general is deemed as the base of every culture. The Yale historical theologian George Lindbeck conceives religion as a cultural-linguistic framework or medium which shapes the entire life and thought.[101] In this regard, by overriding indigenous religions, the colonizers more or less disparaged the entire life and culture of native subjects.

The Orientalists promulgated the notion that religion of the West as a whole was superior and valid, whereas religion of the East as a whole was inferior and invalid. This assumption was clearly seen in their attitude towards Islam. One step further, this Orientalist conviction was also prevalent in the Far East. Most Westerners from the eighteenth century to the early part of the 20th century disproved, or even demonized, Confucianism, Taoism, Buddhism, and Shamanism in East Asia, although Matteo Ricci (1552–1610), an Italian Jesuit missionary to China, recognized the general, formal works of God in Chinese Confucianism. In disavowing Chinese Confucianism, in 1704, Pope Clement XI banned the use of the traditional Chinese equivalents for God—*T'ien* (Heaven) and *Shang-ti* (Sovereign on High)—because these words were rooted in Confucianism.[102] H. G. Underwood (1859–1916), who was one of the first Presbyterian missionaries to Korea, at first did not use the traditional Korean term *Hananim* (the equivalent for God) because of its origination from the *Sinkyo-Mudang* tradition (Korean form of Shamanism), which

---

100. Said, *Orientalism,* 72.

101. George Lindbeck, *The Nature of Doctrine: Religion and Theology in a Postliberal Age* (Philadelphia: Westminster, 1984) 33.

102. Paul Chung, *Constructing Irregular Theology: Bamboo and Minjung in East Asian Perspective* (Leiden: Brill, 2009) 107.

is the oldest form of Korean religion.[103] Many early Western missionaries disavow and demonized the practice of *Mudang* (female shamans).

The Western missionaries with Orientalism strived to underscore discontinuity between Christianity and indigenous East Asian religions by disapproving and demonizing the indigenous East Asian religions. Thus, instead of using the traditional Asian terms for God, they introduced "newly created names" of God, such as *T'ien-chu* (the Lord of Heaven). In other words, in order to devalue indigenous Asian cultures, colonizers started attacking the legitimacy of the indigenous religions, and in doing so the colonizers promulgated the inferiority of native Asian cultures.

The chiological approach, on the other hand, approves and underscores the continuity between Christianity and traditional East Asian religions. It teaches that 'one' God created all people, and all people are God's children who have not been neglected by this God, continuously demonstrating multifarious means of communication and caring of His children. As I stated above, the chiological approach affirms the continuity between Christianity and East Asian religions in terms of the *formal* dimension of the Holy Spirit, albeit there may be some discontinuity in terms of the material, categorical dimension of the Spirit. The Spirit of God has been present and active "formally" as *ch'i* (*ki* in Korean and Japanese) in East Asia, although the *material* aspect (the Spirit of Christ) of the Spirit has not been concretized in the traditional East Asian religions until the arrival of Christianity.

THE JAPANESE COLONIZERS

In the sixth century CE, Chinese Buddhism (Mahayana Buddhism) came to Japan mainly through Korea. In the face of this Buddhism named *Butsu-do* ("the way of Buddha"), Japanese realized that they needed to come up with the term that designated their traditional indigenous religion, so they named it *shin-to* (the way of gods), coming from the Chinese term *shen dao* (神道). It is also known as *kami-no-michi* in a more native Japanese vocabulary. At the initial stage of Buddhism in Japan, Buddhist monks regarded Shinto *kami* as different forms of Mahayana Buddhas and bodhisattvas who had been worshiped in Japan under Shinto names. Thus, the Buddhist introduction to Japan was relatively smoother com-

---

103. Jung Young Lee, *Korean Shamanistic Rituals* (New York: Mouton, 1981) 25.

pared to other religions. Blending Japanese Shintoism with Buddhism took place without severe hardships.[104]

Shinto was reestablished as a cultural counterpart that would keep the "Japanese spirit" when the Western colonizers in the late nineteenth century forced Japan to accept Western modernization. In 1868, Mutsuhito, who was known as the Emperor Meiji, came to the throne, and soon he stated the process of modernizing Japan. He assimilated the European and American governmental, military, and educational systems into Japan. Many Japanese historians believe that this was a turning point in Japanese history, known as the Meiji Restoration. At this juncture, it was forced to demarcate Shintoism from Buddhism. Shintoism reemerged as a national religion. As a result, Buddhists in Japan had to undergo persecution. By underscoring the divine origin of the emperor, many political leaders of Japan at that time connected Shintoism with a growing spirit of Japanese nationalism.[105]

In 1882, State Shinto officially became a national religion. Soon thereafter, thousands of Shinto shrines and priests received government financial support, and the Shinto priests became the official government employees, who in return propped up the imperial government and later supported the militaristic expansion. The Japanese government more and more pressured State Shinto to generate patriotism especially during the military buildup of the 1930s and the Second World War. The Japanese colonizers indoctrinated the divinity of their emperors as the descendants of *Amaterasu,* the spirit of the sun. This indoctrination was practiced daily in schools.[106]

Colonization involved not only military politics and economy but also religions. In East Asia, colonialism was not merely a European subjugation; Japanese, having learned from European colonizers, also attempted to colonize many parts of East Asia, and they became especially successful in the peninsula of Korea. Japanese annexed Korea into their empire in 1910. In order to domesticate and "Japanize" Korea, the Japanese colonizers not only demolished the Royal lineage of Korea but also enforced Shinto worship by divinizing their emperor. By realizing that complete colonization is not possible devoid of domesticating

104. Michael Molloy, *Experiencing the World's Religions: Traditions, Challenge, and Change,* 5th ed. (New York: McGraw-Hill, 2010) 264–67.

105. Ibid., 269.

106. Ibid., 270.

Korean religions, the Japanese colonizers became unduly forceful from July of 1937.[107] In this process, thousands of pious religious Koreans, including numerous Korean Christians were martyred. From the 1930s, Japanese started to eradicate Korean Christianity and to expel the Western Christian missionaries in Korea. From the second part of the 1930s, the Japanese colonizers became even more forceful with a thread of killing the people who did not participate in Shinto worship. As a result, many Korean religious leaders reluctantly worshiped the *kami* including the Japanese emperor at Shinto shrines.

Language (or Discourse) as Power

Indubitably, one of the main teachings of Michel Foucault is a close connection between knowledge and power. Power brings forth knowledge, and power and knowledge affect each other.[108] Foucault points out three fundamental mistakes of the West for the last three centuries. First, there is a body of objective knowledge that needs to be discovered. Second, Western societies believe that they, to some degree, possess this neutral knowledge that is not class-biased. Third, all humankind, regardless of one's social class and gender, will receive the benefits from this pursuit of knowledge.[109] Against this three-century-long Western assumption, Foucault avers that knowledge is inescapably connected to *power* due to its tie to *discourse*. Regarding this correlation between power and discourse in Foucault's view, Sheldon Wolin states, "Every discourse embodies a power drive, and every arrangement is repressive."[110]

In Foucault's world, everything in one's culture, such as words, beings, things, institutions, and relationships, is infused with power. Every social space is affected by power relationships; every aspect of a social world is dominated by power.[111] In this sense, every language and word to a certain extent is shaped and determined by the power relationships.

107. Seung-tae Kim, "Japan's Policy of Christianity and Japanization of Korean Church." This unpublished paper was presented at Symposium on Indigenization of Christianity in China and Korea on November 7, 2009, at Shanghai University, China.

108. Michel Foucault, *Discipline and Punish: The Birth of the Prison*, trans. Alan Sheridan (New York: Vintage Book, 1977), 27–28.

109. Sheldon Wolin, "On the Theory and Practice of Power," in *After Foucault: Humanistic Knowledge, Postmodern Challenge*, ed. Jonathan Arac (New Brunswick: Rutgers University Press, 1988) 186.

110. Ibid.

111. Ibid.

Biases of discourse or human language can be easily detected in many areas. For instance, the phrases such as the Near East (the Middle East) or the Far East (e.g., China, Korea, and Japan) is defined and categorized from the European perspective. The place is "Near" and "Far" on the basis of the distance from Europe. Another good example is the current debate over the appellation of the marginal sea between Japan and Korea. Japanese want to dub this "the Sea of Japan," while Koreans want to name this "the East Sea." Koreans argue that this sea was originally named "the East Sea" until the Japanese Occupation of Korea (early 20th century). On the other hand, Japanese claim that the original name of the sea was "the Sea of Japan" even from the early 19th century. Beneath this debate concerning the name of the marginal sea, there is a power struggle to have a control over this.

When European colonizers came to various parts of Asia, they imposed their languages (e.g., English and French), and their religions (e.g., Roman Catholic, Anglican, Presbyterian, and Methodist). At the same time, they condemned native religions and "inferior" native languages. In India, English colonizers even tried to change many names of geographical places with the words that are more congenial to their English words. As we have seen in Orientalism, the European colonizers undermined native religions, native vocabulary, native imagery, and native governing political systems in order to maintain Western superiority. As a result, many of the subalterns devalued their indigenous religions, languages, arts, various styles of dress, and philosophies. In other words, the European colonizers have directly or indirectly instilled Orientalism into the natives.

While Michel Foucault frequently speaks of knowledge as power, the chiological approach reiterates language as power. One of the first things after the military conquest of the Oriental lands was to impose European languages and religions with an ambition to obviate indigenous cultures. In the case of the Japanese colonizers in Korea, they even banned speaking in Korean in the later stage of their colonization. Often, native people who learned to speak the languages of the colonialists received better positions and jobs in the colonial government. Native people who refused to speak the colonialists' languages were frequently punished. On the surface, Orientalists and the colonialists appeared to promote dialogue with natives, but the European colonialists have imposed rules of a dialogue or rules of "a language game."[112] A dialogue can only take place in English only or French only—the languages of the colonizers. Imposing the European languages of power was a way to oppress the natives, and it was also to maintain the European superiority and dominance. Eventually many natives who could not speak English or Spanish felt inferior and inane due to their inability to communicate with others.

At the age of seventeen, my family immigrated into the United States, and then right away, I realized how language could become suppressive. Some students in my high school made fun of my "Konglish" accent and my inability to speak English. Although I was deemed a bright student who never failed any test in South Korea, I failed many exams during my first year in the United States. I felt shame, guilt, and incompetence that resulted in a mild form of depression.[113] I had to undergo the shock of a different "language game" from Korean to English. "The rules of a language" game changed. Thus, I had to learn American English in order to communicate with other Americans. I had to follow the grammatical rules of English. Moreover, I was pressured to accept a body of American cultural assumptions and social norms in order to fit in and survive in this new nation.

Some of my Korean friends who live in South Korea often share their struggles as scholars. One of them is the language barrier. Although they want to publish their theological articles in international journals, they are having a really hard time, writing in English and German. For this reason, they often become unenthusiastic and even give up publishing articles in international journals. Sometimes, I wonder about the reverse world: What if we are living in a world where major global publishers only accept writings in Korean, or Japanese? The people whose native language is English do not seem to understand the difficulty of learning English, German, and French. In this sense, European languages can serve as a part of European dominance. Many theologians often speak of a "paradigm shift," but I sometimes think of a "language shift."

112. See Ludwig Wittgenstein, *Philosophical Investigations,* trans. G. E. M. Anscombe, 3rd ed. (New York: Macmillan, 1953) 2–51, 112–44.

113. See Sang Hyun Lee, *From a Liminal Space: An Asian American Theology* (Philadelphia: Fortress, 2010) 1–34. Lee elaborates on Asian American experiences of being marginalized by dominant groups in America.

The chiological approach seeks, therefore, to "decolonize" Orientalism, and at the same time retrieve indigenous worldviews, vocabularies, discourses, theologies, and philosophies. By retrieving the word *ch'i* (*ki* in Korean and Japanese) and accepting some continuity between *ch'i* and the *formal* dimension of the Holy Spirit, the chiological approach ratifies the presence and activity of the Holy Spirit long before the arrival of Western Christian missionaries. By avowing a common ground between *Hananim* (the native Korean term for God) and the Christian Sovereign God, it affirms the fact that *one* God created all peoples and that this loving God has never neglected or forsaken God's own people even at the moment when humans became most rebellious and sordid. Instead, this God has continuously revealed His attributes in East Asian classics such as the *I Ching, Tao Te Ching*, and *Mencius*. Instead of continuously approaching God with the lens of Western colonialists and Orientalists, the chiological approach seeks to conceive God with "sound East Asian" worldviews, discourses, and philosophies. In doing so, the chiological approach will bring out "other" dimensions of God that will compliment Western theologies.

Conclusion

In this first chapter, I have expatiate upon the four foundational characteristics of the chiological approach: *ch'i*, synthesis, holism, and postcolonialism. First, the chiological approach conceives the essence of reality as *ch'i*, and the form of *ch'i* is *change*. *Ch'i* is not only the essence of all natural objects but also the essence of *Tao* and *I* (the ultimate reality or the Divine). In this regard, the chiological approach underscores the continuity and affinity of all beings including natural and divine beings. The chiological approach within a Christian horizon descries the immanence of God.

Second, the synthetic element of the chiological approach promotes a *trilogue* with three pivotal rudiments: 1) the experiences of the past (e.g., the Bible and Western Christian traditions), 2) the experiences of the present (e.g., personal and communal experiences and present culture), and 3) the experiences of other religions and wisdoms. Among these three rudiments, one can find a supra-cultural common ground. For example, the Johannine author (in John 4:24), Karl Barth, Wolfhart Pannenberg, the *I Ching*, and Taoism accede to the supra-cultural doctrine that the ultimate reality (e.g., God, the Divine, *Tao*, or *I*) is Spirit/*ch'i*.

The third foundation that characterizes the chiological approach is holistic. Theology and religion not only involves the cognitive (*Ji*) aspect but also emotuitional (*Jeong*) and actional (*Che*) elements. Moreover, this *Ji-Jeong-Che* view applies to both metaphysics and God. Jesus Christ primarily remains *Che* (the embodiment) of God the Father (the Creator)— *Ji*. The Holy Spirit stands as *Jeong*, the emotuition of God. Nevertheless, *ch'i* is the essence of all beings. The word *holistic* also alludes to the *loci theologici* (the sources of theology). While God disclosed Godself in the Bible and the Christian church, this God also has revealed Godself in "other" cultures and religions especially in terms of *sang* (K. 상, C. 象). Hence, holistic theology attends to these other Asian sources of God's revelation.

The fourth foundation that characterizes the chiological approach is postcolonial. Postcolonialism truly commenced around the 1950s when the colonized nations fought for independence. Postcolonialism is regarded as a process of liberating natives from colonial imposition and domination that includes political, social, economic, intellectual and cultural areas. The colonizers and Orientalists propagated the ideology that Western culture and religion was superior to those of Asians. Thus, the colonizers imposed their languages, dress styles, discourses, religions, and philosophies on indigenous Asian people. When possible, the chiological approach wants to occlude colonialism and Orientalism by retrieving or reinventing indigenous worldviews, vocabularies, discourses, theologies, and philosophies. Language and discourse do not stay neutral; usually, they tend to favor the powerful and dominating. With indigenous Asian terms and worldviews, the chiological approach helps promote the neglected and "other" dimensions of God that have been often despised by Western people.

2

The *I Ching* and *Ch'i (Qi)*

INDUBITABLY, THE MOST IMPORTANT SINGLE WORK IN THE HISTORY OF Chinese philosophy is the *I Ching* (易經), known as *the Book of Change* in English. This book has remained the main source of Chinese cosmology and the foundation of Chinese culture. The *I Ching* has penetrated every Chinese mind. Richard Wilhelm states, "Nearly all that is greatest and most significant in the three thousand years of Chinese cultural history has either taken its inspiration from this book [*I Ching*], or has exerted an influence on the interpretation of its text."[1] Furthermore, no one can underestimate its influence on other areas of East Asia such as Korea and Japan. Both Taoism and Confucianism at their inceptive stage extracted moral and cosmological teachings from this book. Many scholars believe that Confucius or his disciples authored the earlier commentaries of hexagrams, e.g., the *Commentary on the Judgment (tuan-chuan),* and the *Commentary on the Images (hsiang-chuan)*. Basically, the *I Ching* is the compilation of works of many authors. As the final product, the *I Ching* contains 64 hexagrams and the Ten Wings.[2]

In the Book of Change (*I Ching*), Change *(I)* refers to the ultimate reality or "the great ultimate," and this Change is manifested in being or substance. Because the essence of yin and yang is the great ultimate (or Change), Change precedes the substance of yin and yang.[3] The essence of the great ultimate is the alteration between yin and yang.

---

1. Richard Wilhelm, "Introduction," in *The I Ching or Book of Changes,* trans. Richard Wilhelm and Cary Baynes (Princeton: Princeton University Press, 1977) xlvii.

2. JeeLoo Liu, *An Introduction to Chinese Philosophy* (Malden: Blackwell, 2006) 26–29.

3. Jung Young Lee, *Embracing Change: Postmodern Interpretations of the I Ching from a Christian Perspective* (Scranton, PA: University Press of Scranton Press, 1994) 27.

The Chinese word *I* (易) is the combination of the sun (日) and the older ideogram of the moon (月). The sun exemplifies the yang; the moon exemplifies the yin. That is why the sun is known as *t'ai yang,* the Great Light, and the moon is known as *t'ai yin,* the Great Dark.[4] The Chinese word "yang" (陽) literally means the sunny side of a hill, while "yin" (陰) is the shady side of a hill. Furthermore, the symbol of yang includes the sun, south, light, day, fire, red, dryness, heat, spring-summer, and so forth. On the other hand, the symbol of yin includes the moon, north, darkness, night, water, black, cold, moistness, autumn-winter, and others. Regarding yin and yang, *Ta Chuan* writes:

> The terms yin, the dark, and yang, the light, denote respectively the shadowed and the light side of a mountain or a river. Yang represents the south side of the mountain, because this side receives the sunlight, but it connotes the north side of the river, because the light of the river is reflected to that side.[5]

The *I Ching* depicts the cosmos and the human world in constantly changing and moving ways. Every condition is in motion. At the bottom of the universe is the change. There are 64 hexagrams in the *I Ching*. Each hexagram depicts developments and movements from the bottom line to the top line. The first line (the bottom line) of each hexagram speaks of the beginning of a development, and the sixth line (the top line) explains the completion of a particular movement.

Three Stages of the *I Ching*

The First Stage: Eight Trigrams

The construction of the core of the *I Ching*, which was written by various authors, took place from 2000 BCE to 500 BCE. In the first stage of formation, there were only eight trigrams, and each trigram consisted of three lines.[6] These lines were either broken (soft) or solid (hard). The solid line exemplifies yang; the soft line signifies yin. The legendary ruler Fu Hsi (ca. 2000 BCE) is known as the person who constructed the earliest form of the *I Ching*.[7] Fu Hsi is regarded as the person who invented

4. *Ta Chuan* in *The I Ching,* trans. Richard Wilhelm and Cary Baynes (Princeton: Princeton University Press, 1977) 302.

5. Ibid., 297.

6. Alfred Huang, *The Complete I Ching* (Rochester: Inner Traditions, 1998) xx–xi.

7. Liu, *An Introduction to Chinese Philosophy*, 27.

	Ch'ien	K'un	Chên	K'an	Kên	Sun	Li	Tui	
									*Trigram
*Name	the Creative	the Receptive	the Arousing	the Abysmal	Keeping Still	the Gentle	the Clinging	the Joyous	*Name
*Image	Heaven	Earth	Thunder	Water	Mountain	Wind	Fire	Lake	*Image
*Quality	Strong	Devoted, yielding	Inciting movement	Dangerous	Resting	Penetrating	Light-giving	Joyful	*Quality
*Family	Father	Mother	1st Son	2nd Son	3rd Son	1st daughter	2nd daughter	3rd daughter	*Family

FIGURE 1: Elucidations of the Eight Trigrams

the linear symbols of *the Book of Change*.[8] The eight trigrams symbolize the eight natural elements: heaven, earth, water, fire, wind, thunder,
mountain, and lake. These eight natural elements are formed out of the
interplay between yin and yang. The eight elements are not mere repre-
sentations of the physical objects in our universe; they are the images of
all that happens in heaven and earth. Moreover in *Shuo-kua* (*Discussion
of the Trigrams*) the eight elements are associated with human sons and
daughters. Figure 1 (above) shows the elucidations of the eight trigrams.

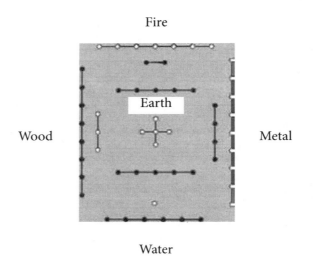

Fire

Wood   Earth   Metal

Water

FIGURE 2: The River Map

Accordance with Chinese tradition, Fu Hsi secured the River Map
(*Ho T'u*)[9] from the Yellow River in China. It is reasonable to believe that
Fu Hsi constructed the eight trigrams based on this River Map. This map
consists of black and white (light) circles. All the light circles represent
odd numbers: 1, 3, 5, 7, and 9, whereas the dark circles represent even
numbers: 2, 4, 6, 8, and 10. Moreover, the odd numbers refer to Heaven,
and the even numbers refer to Earth. Whereas yang is the primordial
symbol of Heaven, and yin is the symbol of Earth. In addition, the odd
numbers are known as yang numbers, and the even numbers are called

8. Richard Wilhelm, "Introduction," in *The I Ching* (Princeton: Princeton University
Press, 1977) lviii.

9. See Figure 2 for the River Map.

yin numbers. Not only numbers are divided into the two groups (yin and yang), but all the things that exist in this universe are divided into the two groups.[10]

The Second Stage: 64 Hexagrams

The second stage of *I Ching* took place when the eight trigrams were doubled and became 64 hexagrams with six lines. According to many Chinese scholars, King Wen of the Chou Dynasty (ca. 1150 BCE) was responsible for the creation of 64 hexagrams. Although King Wen was simply the head of the western state that suffered from a severe oppression from the house of Shang (Yin) and never became a king, his son Wu, the first ruler of the Chou dynasty (1150–249 BCE) gave him the title of king posthumously by his son Wu.[11] At this point *I Ching* was much more than a book of divination; it was becoming a philosophy of life.[12]

The Third Stage: The Ten Wings

The third development of the *I Ching* was attributed to Confucius and his disciples, who authored further commentaries that are known as the Ten Wings (*Shih I* 十翼). The Commentary on the Judgment (*tuan-ch-uan*) rectified the mystical elements of the ancient texts into philosophical expositions of various life situations. Another pivotal addition was Commentary on the Images (*hsiang-chuan).* In general, Commentary on the Judgment and Commentary on the Images were attributed either to Confucius or his immediate followers.[13] Other commentaries of the Ten Wings such as *Ta Chuan* (also known as *Hsi Tz'u Chuan*) attached to the *I Ching* as late as the Han Dynasty (206 BCE–220 CE).

How to Read the Trigrams and Hexagrams

According to Richard Wilhelm, the *I Ching* at its beginning was the book that contained a collection of linear signs to be used as oracles. In ancient China, a single unbroken line (–) meant "yes," and a broken line (--)

---

10. Jung Young Lee, *Embracing Change: Postmodern Interpretations of the I Ching from a Christian Perspective* (Scranton: University Press of Scranton Press, 1994) 35.

11. Wilhelm, "Introduction," lix.

12. Liu, *An Introduction to Chinese Philosophy*, 27.

13. J. Y. Ibid., 28.

meant "no." However, the single lines became two lines (=) because there was a need for differentiation.[14]

Each duogram has its own meaning. The two divided lines designate the "old yin," whose number is 6. The "young yin," whose number is 8, is symbolized with a divided line at the bottom and the undivided line at the top. On the basis of the River Map, the number 6, consisting of 6 dark circles, refers to water, whereas the number 8—which consists of 8 dark circles—designates wood. The "old yang" is represented by two undivided lines, which refers to metal. The number 9 indicates the old yang. On the other hand, the "young yang" is represented by an undivided line below and a divided line above, and this young yang refers to fire, whose number is 7.[15] The odd numbers are assigned to the yang force, and the even numbers are assigned to the yin force.

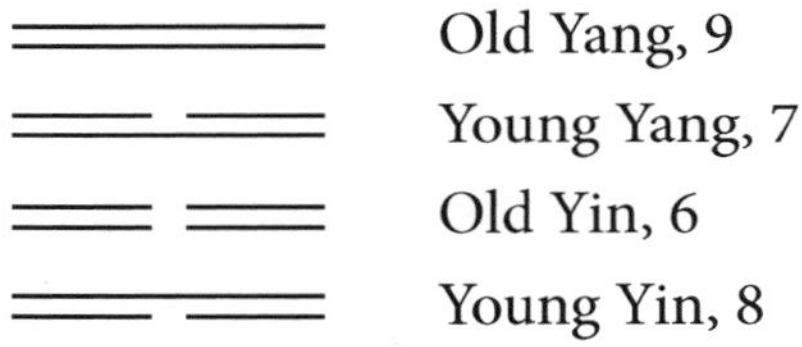

Old Yang, 9

Young Yang, 7

Old Yin, 6

Young Yin, 8

FIGURE 3: Duogram

The third line (≡) was added in order to differentiate a thing further, and as a result, it produced the eight trigrams. The purpose of each trigram was not to depict a state of non-moving being; rather, it was to depict a state of continual transition. In other words, each trigram tried to portray a tendency in movement.[16]

The eight trigrams eventually came to carry manifold meanings. Not only they represented certain processes in nature, but they also represented family members. For example, Ch'ien (Qian) represented a father, and K'un represented a mother.

The original purpose of the trigrams was to ascertain destiny. Because divine beings do not bestow unmediated expression on humans, ancient Chinese had to come up with some mediums through which

14. Wilhelm, "Introduction," xlix–l.

15. J. Y. Lee, *Embracing Change*, 36.

16. Wilhelm, "Introduction," xlix–l.

they received oracles.[17] It is likely that ancient Chinese diviners tried to read the oracles from the pattern of the cracks of tortoise shells. They believed that a tortoise had the most mysterious and oracular powers partly due to the reason that it could live longer than any other living beings. The Book of Songs (*Shih Ching*) supports this view. But for a practical reason, the shell oracle reading was later replaced by the yarrow-stalk oracle reading.[18]

How should one read each line of the hexagrams? The bottom line of a trigram depicts the condition of earth; the middle line describes the condition of humanity; the top line explicates the condition of heaven. In other words, humanity is regarded as *subject*; earth is viewed as *object*; heaven is understood as *content*. When the three lines (trigrams) became the six lines (hexagrams), the two bottom lines represented the conditions of earth. The third and fourth lines symbolized the conditions of humanity. The top two lines refer to the conditions of heaven.[19] All three agents of heaven, humanity, and earth consist of yin and yang forces. Heaven is the alteration between dark and light; humanity is the alteration love and rectitude (righteousness); earth is the combination of the yielding and the firm.[20]

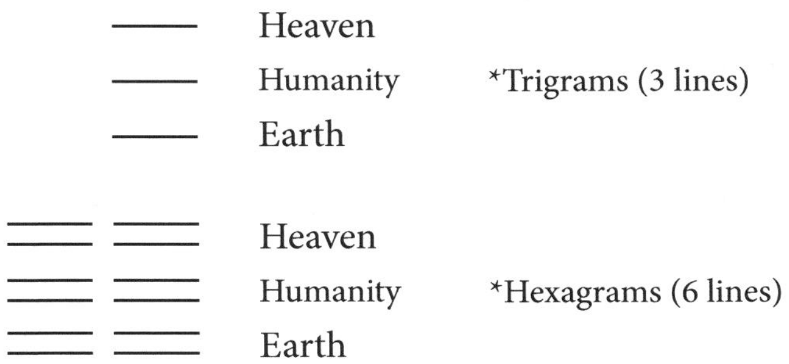

FIGURE 4

To procure a greater multiplicity, the eight trigrams were combined with other eight trigrams. As a result, they became hexagrams consisting of six lines, whereby a total of sixty four images were created. Each line is

17. *Shuo Kua* in *The I Ching,* 262–63.

18. J. Y. Lee, *Embracing Change,* 31–32.

19. *Shuo Kua,* in *The I Ching,* 264–65.

20. Ibid., 264.

capable of change. For instance, a divided line (--) can change into an undivided line (—). When a line changes, a meaning of a hexagram also changes.

For an example, let us look at the hexagram *Kun*, which represents earth and mother. Among many seasons, it refers to late autumn, when all the forces of life are resting.[21]

When the lowest line changes, a new hexagram is created, namely, *Fu,* which means "return." This hexagram alludes to the month of the winter solstice. Fu (24) is a combination of the two trigrams: 1) *K'un* (Earth) above, and 2) *Chen* (Thunder) below.[22] As a result, *"Fu"* represents "thunder." Moreover, it symbolizes the return of light.

This is how one read each line of a hexagram. The number 9 designates the positive lines that move, whereas the number 6 designates the negative lines that move. Non-moving positive lines are designated by the number 7, and non-moving negative lines are represented by the number 8. Thus, numbers 7 and 8 serve structural purposes devoid of intrinsic meanings, and they are disregarded in interpreting the oracle.[23] Thus, the above hexagram *Fu* can be read in this way:

> 9 at the beginning
> 6 in the second place
> 6 in the third place
> 6 in the fourth place
> 6 in the fifth place
> 6 at the top

21. Wilhelm, "Introduction," li.
22. J. Y. Lee, *Embracing Change,* 24.
23. Wilhelm, "Introduction," lii.

The Contents of the *I Ching*

Most English translations of the *I Ching* are composed of two parts: 1) the main text, and 2) the appendices (the supplementary texts that are known as the Ten Wings).

The main text contains the sixty-four hexagrams, and it is divided into two main sections: 1) the first thirty hexagrams (上經), and 2) the second thirty-four hexagrams (下經). The former section mainly deals with cosmic phenomena, and the latter depicts human affairs. They complement each other. Each hexagram comprises lines (divided or undivided). *The divided line (--) represents the yin force whereas the undivided line (—) symbolizes the yang force.*[24]

Each hexagram has its own name, which is the most concise definition of it. The name discloses its symbolic function.

Next, you will see the brief text of each hexagram, which is called the *"Judgment" (T'uan)*. One can compare the Judgment on the hexagram with a decision of a trial judge, who proclaims a judgment on a particular case. Often the Judgment contains the three parts: 1) a diagnosis of a current situation, 2) a prediction of possible future, and 3) a prescription for action. Even though the Judgment includes brief statements, it is the most important text of the hexagram.[25]

Followed by the Judgment, one will normally see the Symbol (or Image) of the hexagram. *Originally, the Symbol did not belong to the main text. It belonged to the third and fourth wings of the appendixes;* however, many English translators put the Symbol in the main text of their works because it remains the most helpful commentary in understanding the 'structural' aspects of the hexagram. Jung Young Lee thinks that the Symbol resembles parables and metaphors of Jesus' teachings whereas the Judgment bears a resemblance to the *kerygma* of the New Testament.[26]

The judgment on the line exemplifies the final division of the *I Ching*. The word "judgment" is spelled with a lower case "j" in contrast to the "Judgment" on the hexagram with an upper case "J." The judgment on the line interprets a meaning of each line while the Judgment on the hexagram the overarching meaning of each hexagram. In other words, the Judgment on the hexagram elucidates the whole, whereas the judg-

---

24. J. Y. Lee, *Embracing Change*, 20.

25. Ibid., 22.

26. Ibid., 23.

ment on the line speaks of each line. Moreover, the judgment on the line starts with the lowest line of each hexagram and ends with the top line, and it provides the process of evolvement from the beginning and the end of the hexagram.[27]

The supplementary texts are known as the Ten Wings (*Shih I* 十翼), which consist of ten commentaries.

The first two wings are known as the Commentary on the Judgment *(T'uan Chuan)*. They elaborate on the Judgment on the hexagram (in the main text) further.

The third and fourth wings are called the Commentary on the Symbol (*Hsiang Chuan*). Many English translations put the Commentary on the Symbol in the main text in order to understand the hexagram better.

The fifth and sixth wings are known as the Great Commentary (*Ta Chuan*), and it is also known as the Commentary on the Appended Judgments (*Hsi Tz'u Chuan*). It is the most comprehensive and scholarly works on the main text, and it also elucidates the basic philosophy of the *I Ching*.[28]

The seventh wing is known as the Commentary on the Text *(Wen Yan)*. It only contains elucidations of the first and second hexagrams.

The Discussion of the Trigrams (*Shuo Kua*) is the eighth wing. It speaks of the symbolic correlation of yin and yang and the philosophical background of the trigrams, but it remains very brief.

The Sequence of the Hexagrams (*Hsu Kua*) is the ninth wing. It tries to explicate the order of the hexagrams. For example, it attempts to explain why the *I Ching* begins with *Ch'ien* and *K'un* instead of other hexagrams.[29]

The tenth wing consists of the Miscellaneous Notes on the Hexagrams (*Tsa Kua*). This bestows a brief note on each hexagram. For instance, the note on the first hexagram states, "Heaven is firm."

27. Ibid.
28. Ibid., 26.
29. Ibid., 27–28.

The Trinitarian Principle in the *I Ching*

The Trinitarian Principle 1 in Tao, Yin, and Yang

The Yin-yang worldview in the *I Ching* teaches the trinitarian principle. Although many people have thought that the yin-yang cosmology endorsed dualism, a thorough investigation points to the trinitarian approach. With respect to this point, *Ta Chuan* states, "In the last analysis, *this cannot be called dualism.* The two principles are united by a relation based on homogeneity; they do not combat but complement each other."[30]

There are at least two kinds of dualism. The first one is the Western, *conflicting* dualism, which espouses two "stuffs" at the most fundamental level. René Descartes (1596–1650) taught this conflicting dualism. This Cartesian dualism inculcated that the essence of mind was to think. He used the Latin phrase *res cogitans* for mind, which literally meant "thinking thing." On the other hand, the essence of body was "to be extended," so he used the Latin phrase *res extensa,* meaning "extended things."[31] Descartes argued for *conflicting* dualism, so he wrote in *Meditations on First Philosophy*, "And this leads us to recognize that the natures of mind and body are not only different, but in some way *opposite*."[32]

The second one is *complementary* dualism (duality) that is portrayed in the Diagram of the Great Ultimate *(t'ai chi t'u)*.[33] In this diagram, although yin and yang are opposite, they are united in the Great Ultimate or Change *(I)*.[34] Existentially, they are opposite, but essentially they are united as one.[35] This complementary dualism, which I call "duality," eventually leads to the trinitarian principle in the Diagram of the Great Ultimate. I label this duality, not dualism, insofar as yin cannot be separated from yang, and vice versa. Furthermore, when yin grows and reaches its sublimity, it starts becoming yang. Also, when young yang

---

30. *Ta Chuan,* 281–82.

31. William James Earle, *Introduction to Philosophy* (New York: McGraw-Hill, 1992) 105.

32. René Descartes, *Meditations on First Philosophy,* trans. John Cottingham (Cambridge: Cambridge University Press, 1986) 10.

33. *Ta Chuan,* 299.

34. Tao and *I* (change) are interchangeable in the *I Ching*. For this, see J. Y. Lee, *Embracing Change,* 54.

35. Jung Young Lee, *The Trinity in Asian Perspective* (Nashville: Abingdon, 1996) 27.

grows and reaches its pinnacle, it thereafter becomes yin. The two are not separable.

Also, one should not forget that in the *I Ching*, the ultimate metaphysical reality is *I* (Change), and this dynamic act of Change is the metaphysical reality of the yin-yang symbol. In other words, *change* is the most fundamental "stuff" from which other things emerge. Logically speaking, Change precedes being; Change creates *ontos* (being). In this sense, Change takes priority over ontology. Furthermore, the reality of Change is not a *static substance;* rather, it is a dynamic movement. This opposes the fundamental premise of Greek philosophy, namely, 'substantial' ontology. In the *I Ching*, being is a product of the Change.

In the *I Ching*, Tao (or *I*) was seen as the source or origin of other beings, and yin and yang are the two constituents of Tao (or *I*), then one can draw out a trinitarian principle that is very similar to Barth's intra-trinitarian relation of origin. Barth insists, "The Son and the Spirit are of one essence with the Father, in this unity of divine essence the Son is from the Father and the Spirit is from the Father and the Son, while the Father is from Himself alone."[36] In the analogous way, Tao (or *I*) is the origin or source from which other beings emanate. Ultimately, Tao (or *I*) is "one" unity; however, there are also three, namely, Tao (or *I*), yin and yang. In this sense, the trinitarian principle can be detected in the *I Ching*.[37]

The Trinitarian Principle 2 in the Diagram of the Great Ultimate

One can also uncover another trinitarian principle in Chou Tun-yi's Diagram of the Great Ultimate. Chou Tun-yi (or Chou Lien-ch'i, 1017-1073), a Neo-Confucian scholar, learned from religious Taoism and reinvented the Diagram of the Great Ultimate. His view on the Non-

36. Karl Barth, *Church Dogmatics*, trans. G. W. Bromiley (Edinburgh: T. & T. Clark, 1936) I/1:293.

37. According to Paul Chung, the trinitarian principle is also found in philosophical Taoism. Tao remains the one source, to which all beings will return eventually. *Te* and *Ch'i*, which are the two elements of Tao, originate from Tao, as the Son and the Holy Spirit come from the Father in the traditional relation of origin in Barth's Theology. Tao is "one," and it becomes "three" when it generates *Te* and *Ch'i* (*Tao, Te, Ch'i*). See Paul Chung, *Constructing Irregular Theology: Bamboo and Minjung in East Asian Perspective* (Leiden: Brill, 2009) 85–86.

ultimate was also influenced by Taoism and Buddhism. He elaborates on the Diagram as follows:

> The Ultimateless (*Wu-chi* 無 極)![38] And also the Great Ultimate (*T'ai-chi* 太極)! The Great Ultimate through movement generates the yang. When its activity reaches its limit, it becomes tranquil. Through tranquility the Great Ultimate generates the yin. When tranquility reaches its limit, activity begins again. Thus movement and tranquility alternate and become the root of each other, giving rise to the distinction of yin and yang, and these two modes are thus established.
>
> By the transformation of yang and its union with yin, the five agents of water, fire, wood, metal, and earth arise. When these five material-forces *(ch'i)* are distributed in harmonious order, the four seasons run their course.
>
> The five agents constitute one system of yin and yang, and yin and yang constitute *one* Great Ultimate. The Great Ultimate is fundamentally the Non-ultimate. The five agents arise, each with its specific nature.
>
> When the reality of the Non-ultimate and the essence of yin and yang and the five agents come into mysterious union, integration ensues.[39]

If one carefully looks at the Diagram of the Great Ultimate, she/he will conclude that it does not endorse dualism; rather, it points out trichotomistic monism inasmuch as the Great Ultimate (*T'ai-chi*) is *one* with unity. However, this oneness is constituted by the three (trinitarian) principles in the Diagram of the Great Ultimate. There are yin, yang, and "the inner connecting principle" which refers to the "dots" in both yin and yang. In other words, there are three elements in the Diagram: 1) yin, 2) yang, 3) "inness" (or dots) in yin and yang. (See Figure 5.) Like the Holy Spirit in the Augustinian concept which affords the fellowship between the Father and the Son, this inness connects yin and yang so that a mutual relation can take place. Therefore, one, two, and three are inherent in the Diagram of the Great Ultimate. In this sense, the trinitarian principle is clearly present in the Great Ultimate.

---

38. The Chinese word *Wu-chi* has many English translations such as the Ultimateless and Non-ultimate.

39. Chou Tun-yi, *T'ai-chi-t'u shuo,* quoted in Wm. Theodore De Bary, Wing-tsit Chan, and Burton Watson, comps. *Sources of Chinese Tradition* (New York: Columbia University Press, 1960) 1:458. Italics are mine.

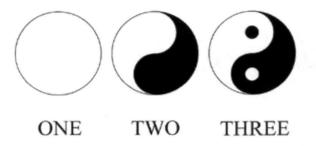

ONE   TWO   THREE

FIGURE 5

The trinitarian principle can also be detected in chapter 42 of *Tao Te Ching* that states: "The Tao gives birth to one. One gives birth to two. Two gives birth to three. The three gives birth to all." The Tao here represents the Absolute Itself that is the unnamable and the unsymbolizable, like the name of the God in the Hebrew Bible. When Moses asked the name of God in Exod 3:13, God replied, "I am who I am" or "I will be who I will be." This is the tetragrammaton YHWH that signifies the unnamable, mysterious side of God. Often, this side of God is known as transcendence. This unnamable Tao gives birth to 'one'. Here, 'one' connotes our understanding (or human idea) of the divine as the absolute. Two is the product of one. It is most likely the two refers to the yin-yang symbol. Three is the product of the two. It is important to know that there is no four after three.[40] Instead, the three gives birth to all other entities. In this regard, the number *three* is the symbol of completion. In this existential word, all three (one, two, and three) are the manifestations of the Tao. In a similar manner, one can easily regard the Creation as the works of the Christian trinity, namely, the Father, Son, and Holy Spirit.

The Trinitarian Principle 3 in the Structure of the Trigram and Hexagram

The trinitarian principle has been also detected in the structure of trigrams and hexagrams. "One" hexagram is constituted by "three" elements. In the trigrams, the bottom line describes earth; the middle line depicts humanity; the top line portrays heaven. In the hexagrams, the

---

40. J. Y. Lee, *Trinity*, 62.

two bottom lines symbolize the conditions of earth; the third and fourth lines describe the conditions of humanity; the top two lines speak of the conditions of heaven. Concerning each line of the hexagram, *Ta Chuan* explains, "The six lines of each hexagram are divided among the three primal powers, heaven, earth, and man. The two lower places are those of the earth, the two middle places belong to man, and the two upper ones to heaven."[41]

The trinitarian principle embedded in the hexagrams is labeled "cosmo-anthropological" *(Cheon-Ji-In)* approach. Jung Young Lee underscores differences between Western cosmology and East-Asian cosmology. He argues that the West more or less has utilized an anthropocentric approach while East Asia has employed a cosmo-anthropological approach. In East Asia, one cannot demarcate anthropology from cosmology. In fact, anthropology is a part of cosmology. A person is deemed as a microcosm of the cosmos. Cosmo-anthropology highlights *oneness* of the cosmos and humanity. Thus, in order to understand the nature of a person, one first has to investigate the make-up of the universe. Since the cosmos operates with a yin-yang relationship, a person, as a microcosm of the cosmos, also operates with the yin-yang relationship. However, even this yin-yang symbolism in essence is trinitarian because of "inness."[42]

Ch'i in the Three Layers of the *I Ching*

The *I Ching* has many layers although many people tend to highlight only on the divinatory element of the book. It has at least three layers: 1) the symbolism, 2) the divinatory judgments, and 3) the philosophical commentaries.[43] The symbolism offers an inductive-empirical metaphysics that represents major interrelated events and phenomena of the cosmos in a dynamic system of symbols. The divinatory judgments afford an evaluative metaphysics that prescribes the correct guidance of practical decisions and actions. The third layer (the philosophical commentaries) offers an explanatory metaphysics arising from the first two. The explanatory commentaries were derived from profound observations and

41. *Ta Chuan*, 289.

42. J. Y. Lee, *Trinity*, 18.

43. Chung-Ying Cheng, "*Li* and Ch'i in the I Ching: A Reconsideration of Being and Non-being in Chinese Philosophy," *Journal of Chinese Philosophy* 14 (1987) 1.

experiences of life.[44] The third layer clarified some equivocal areas, which were elucidated further by various scholars.

The Symbolism in the I Ching

In terms of the symbolism, *I* (Change) as a unity and a source of creativity refers to *T'ai-chi* or *tao*. *I* as a multitude and process refers to the works of yin and yang and numerous forms of ten thousand things. Hence, Chou Tun-yi states, "The five powers [*ch'i* of fire, water, wood, metal, and earth] are *one* yin-yang; yin-yang are *one* T'ai-chi; and *T'ai-chi* is originally *Wu-chi*."[45] Here, the *wu-chi* speaks of the constancy and simplicity of the *tai-chi*.

In the *I Ching*, *li* and *ch'i* are the two sides of the change (*I*). *Ch'i* represents the substance of the dynamic quality, namely, change (*pien*), transformation (*hua*), and movement (*tung*), whereas *li* portrays the pattern, form (*hsing*), and order of the substance. The two aspects of the same unity (namely, *I*) are represented by the two sets of the dynamic (*ch'i*) and formal qualities (*li*). The two substances of *li* and *ch'i* remains one, and they are not separable. Between *li* and *ch'i*, it is clear that *ch'i* or *ch'i-hua* is closer to the essence of Change (*I*). Again, *ch'i* cannot be separated from *li* insofar as *li* as forms are inherent qualities of *ch'i* that are to be brought out in the process of change. To be sure, one should preserve the inseparability and unity of the two in the symbolism. Simplistically speaking, *I* is *ch'i*, and *hsing* (form) is *li*.[46]

The eight trigrams stand for the chief forms and patterns of the natural world that are detected via experience and observations, and these forms and patterns remain interrelated. (See Figure 1.) The eight trigrams also depict principles and qualities of the natural processes and structures, namely, 1) *ch'ien* (strong), 2) *kun* (soft), 3) *chen* (movement), 4) *kan* (falling in), 5) *ken* (stopping), 6) *sun* (entering), 7) *li* (traveling in pair), and 8) *tui* (joy). Additionally, the eight trigrams also allotted to various seasons and directions. For example, in the Inner-World

---

44. Ibid., 8.

45. Chou Tun-yi, *T'ai-chi-t'u shuo,* quoted in Wm. Theodore De Bary, Wing-tsit Chan, and Burton Watson, comps. *Sources of Chinese Tradition* (New York: Columbia University Press, 1960) 1:458. It also contains the author's own translation.

46. Chung-Ying Cheng, "*Li* and Ch'i in the I Ching: A Reconsideration of Being and Non-being in Chinese Philosophy," *Journal of Chinese Philosophy* 14 (1987) 11–12.

Arrangement, *Li* is allotted to the south and summer.[47] The qualities of the trigrams are derived from the experiences of nature, and they are again interrelated. Furthermore, the world of human and the world of nature are mutually related.[48]

With respect to the relationship between *ch'i* and *li*, it is clear that the order and patterns of the natural phenomena consist of *ch'i*. "*Ch'i* is the natural process of change while *li* is the end product of the natural process of change."[49] Moreover, *li* cannot exist apart from *ch'i*, and *li* is the most primitive form of t'ai-chi. *Li* by itself cannot become a creative agent because it exemplifies *the internal structure* of the *ch'i* process.[50]

The Divine Judgments

In view of the divination judgments, the 64 hexagrams (卦, *kua*) help a person to evaluate a given life situation, predict a possible future, and prescribe a proper action because the life situation engenders a problem for people.[51] Here, *li* is a deep understanding of the problematic life situation as well as an insight which provides the proper ways to eschew chaos and invite a propitious order. Still, *li* cannot be separated from *ch'i*, and *li* is generated from *ch'i*. The problematic life situation can turn into a non-problematic situation by allowing "change" to a particular context.

What kind of method did the ancient Chinese use for divination? It appears that the earliest method was done by means of the tortoise shell.[52] It was heated with fire by a diviner, who read the cracks of the tortoise shell.[53] It seems that they believed the tortoise to be the most mysterious thing because it has a longer lifespan than any other living being. The tortoise was the symbol of immortality. In the Book of Songs (*Shih*

47 *Shuo Kua* in *The* I Ching (The Wilhelm/Baynes translation) 268–70.

48. Ibid., 12.

49. Cheng, "*Li* and Ch'i in the I Ching," 12.

50. Ibid., 12.

51. Dae-won Suh, *Juyeokkangeui* (Seoul, Korea: *Eulyumunwhasa*, 2009) 33–34.

52. For the most convenient and contemporary method of divination, see Brian Walker, *The* I Ching *or Book of Changes* (New York: St. Martin's Griffin, 1992) 1–2. By using three coins, a person can find out his or her *kua*. One also needs to pay a special attention to the changing lines with a value of 6 (old yin) or 9 (old yang). See Figure 3 for the meaning of these numbers.

53. Yu-lan Fung, *A History of Chinese Philosophy,* trans. Derk Bodde (Princeton: Princeton University Press, 1952) 1:379–80.

Ching), there is a piece of writing (II, 2:18) that stems from the twenty-third century BC. It already mentioned a divination by means of reading the tortoise shell. Later, this method of the tortoise-shell reading was replaced by reading the stalks of a divine plant because reading oracles from the cracks of the tortoise stayed hard and complicated.[54]

What does it mean when a certain *kua* (卦) is given to the divining individual? If the sixth *kua*, *Sung* (訟), is given to the individual, the diviner will look into the Judgment of the *kua*, which states as follows:

> Conflict. Trust is obstructed. The middle path (中) brings good fortune, but the end of the road (終) brings misfortune. You will gain by seeing the great person, but will lose if you try to cross the big river.[55]

The first sentence of the Judgment depicts the current situation: "Trust is obstructed." The second sentence prognosticates the future (fortune or misfortune). The final sentence prescribes what kind of action the individual one needs to take, namely, seeing the great person (大人) and not crossing "the big river."[56]

In relation to the actual judgment of evaluation in divination, one can say that *li* refers to the natural forces which the situation proposes. On the other hand, *ch'i* is what brings forth the situation, and the forms and values. *Ch'i* is the operation of change, transformation, and movement, so it is the underlying creative power of a situation that sustains or rectifies the situation. Moreover, *ch'i* bestows free will upon humanity.[57] In other words, "*li* is an inherent quality of ch'i and gradually takes shape in the evolution of natural or human situations . . . Ch'i, on the other hand, can be said to be the situational matrix from which *li* emerges."[58]

The I Ching *Read as the Philosophical Commentaries*

The third layer of the *I Ching* is the philosophical commentaries, which finally comes to elucidate the relationship between *ch'i* and *li*. The *Hsi Tz'u Chuan* and *Shuo Kua* afford a coherent metaphysics of change (*pien*), transformation (*hua*), and movement (*tung*). Indubitably, in the

---

54. J. Y. Lee, *Embracing Change*, 32.

55. This is the author's direct translation from the Judgment in Chinese.

56. J. Y. Lee, *Embracing Change*, 22. Suh, *Juyeokkangeui*, 113–15.

57. Cheng, "*Li* and Ch'i in the I Ching," 13–15.

58. Ibid., 16.

Hsi Tz'u and *Shuo Kua*, the ultimate and original reality (or "the original substance of reality" in Neo-Confucian terminology) is identical with the creative force of the Change *(I)*, which presents itself in the ordering and structuring activities of yin and yang.[59]

Undoubtedly, yin and yang exemplify the two primary aspects (forms) of *ch'i*-creativity which find empirical bases. Yin-yang activities (e.g. opposite and complementary forms) can be found in the things of the world. With respect to the *ch'i*-creativity, the activities of *ch'i* remain one unitary whole inasmuch as "ch'i begins with a unity of formless creativity and ends with a unity of order and harmony."[60]

The *Hsi Tz'u* inculcates that the unity or alteration of yin and yang is the *Tao*.[61] One step further, the unity of yin and yang is also called *tai-chi*. Again, according to the *Hsi Tz'u*, the *ch'i* creativity includes the *li* activity of ordering the structure. In this sense, *li* is a part of the larger *ch'i*.

Chapter XI, section 5 clarifies the relationship between *I* and other crucial Chinese categories.[62] It says in Chinese: 易有太極 是生兩儀 兩儀生四象 四象生八卦. It can be translated as follows: "In *I* (the Change), there is the t'ai-chi (the Great Ultimate). This begets the two forces (yin and yang). The two forces beget the four images. The four images beget the eight trigrams."[63] One can infer from the above that *I* and *T'ai-chi* remain interchangeable terms in the *I Ching*. Moreover, the four images signify 1) old yang, 2) old yin, 3) young yang, and 4) young yin. The eight trigrams are 1) *Ch'ien*, 2) *K'un*, 3) *Chên*, 4) *K'an*, 5) *Kên*, 6) Sun, 7) *Li*, and 8) *Tui*.

The first paragraph of the *Shuo Kua* teaches that *li* exemplifies *the principles of change* found in yin and yang, and these principles are also found in the relationships of soft and hard in the natural world, and in human virtues such as love and righteousness. The paragraph does not suggest either its ontological status or independence devoid of *ch'i*.[64] Rather, *li* is an ordering activity of *ch'i* expressed in yin-yang.

That is why Chu Hsi's interpretation of the *I Ching* became problematic because his interpretation misled other people to believe that *li*

---

59. Ibid., 17.

60. Ibid., 17.

61. *The* I Ching (The Wilhelm/Baynes translation) 348.

62. Ibid., 318–19.

63. This is the author's translation.

64. *The* I Ching (The Wilhelm/Baynes translation) 262.

and *ch'i* are two separate things. Chu Hsi stated, "The alteration of one *yin* and one *yang* is called the *tao*. The alternating movement of *yin* and *yang* is *ch'i*. The principle of this was the so-called *tao*."[65] Here, Chu Hsi apparently demarcated the *ch'i* of yin-yang from the *li* of *Tao*, and spoke of the alteration of yin and yang as the *Tao* and hence was the *li*.

This Chu Hsi's dualistic understanding of *li* and chi is not warranted in the *I Ching*. *Li* does not have an independent metaphysical status in the *I Ching*. Instead, *li* remains simply as an attribute of *ch'i*. *Ch'i* is ontologically the source of *li*. One step further, the *Hsi Tz'u* indentifies the Great Ultimate (*T'ai-chi*) with *ch'i* instead of *li*. Hence, Chu Hsi's dualistic understanding does not find its solid ground in light of the I Ching. Ontologically speaking, *li remains the ordering and differentiating activities of the creative ch'i, whereas ch'i stands for the source and substance of creativity.*[66]

Conclusion

Many Western people still regard the *I Ching* as a book of divination and magical spells. On the contrary, the *I Ching* can be read in many different levels, such as symbolism, divination, and philosophical teachings. Especially, the Ten Wings (*Shih I*) are imbued with rich philosophical and even theological insights. Basically, in the *I Ching*, the essence of I (Change) is *ch'i*, which can be easily translated as "Spirit" in English. Like the word "Spirit" in English, the Chinese word "*ch'i*" denotes "power, force, energy, breath, vapor, and air." Interestingly, John 4:24 also speaks of the essence of God as Spirit, which can be translated as "*ch'i*" in Chinese.[67]

Furthermore, the *I Ching* also identifies *ch'i* with change, transformation, and movement and with the life creativity (*sheng-sheng*) and all the changing things in the world. On the other hand, one can equate *li* with all the 'specific' forms of change, transformation, and movement. *Li* is also the activity of *ch'i*, such as ordering, differentiation, balancing, harmonizing, unifying, classifying, relating, and organizing. *Li* is the

---

65. See Chu Hsi's *Chou I Pen I*, quoted in Chung-Ying Cheng, "*Li* and *Ch'i* in the I Ching," 35. Underlines are mine.

66. Cheng, 19–20.

67. In chapter 3 of this monograph, I will elucidate this similarity further.

activity of *ch'i*, which creates order and harmony in the world. From this perspective, Chang Tsai called *ch'i* the Great Harmony (*t'ai-ho*).

Ch'i refers to the endless source of change and activity, and it cannot be identified with any specific thing.[68] In this regard, *ch'i* itself stays indeterminate and indeterminable. For this reason, Chang Tsai called *ch'i* the Great Void (*T'ai-hsü*). Since *ch'i* is indeterminable, it is also without any form (*hsing*); it is the movement itself (*tung*). Because *ch'i* never has form, one can call it *Wu-chi* (ultimateless), beyond which nothing can be sought according to Chu Hsi. In the *I Ching* sense, this *Wu-chi* should not be construed as total emptiness, nothingness, or void.

---

68. See Grace Ji-sun Kim, "A Global Understanding of the Spirit," *Dialogue & Alliance* 21.2 (2007) 21–22. Kim accedes to the author's point that *ch'i* is the source of all existents, and the original *ch'i* remains formless.

3

The Historical Development of *Ch'i* (*Qi*) in East Asia

AS WE HAVE SEEN IN CHAPTER ONE, IN THE *I CHING* "CHANGE" IS THE ultimate reality beyond which nothing exist. Moreover, everything in this world goes through change including the human concept of *ch'i*. In this chapter, I have chosen six great philosophers in East Asia in order to explore their constructs of *ch'i*. In the *I Ching*, *ch'i* is the essence of *I* (change). This idea of *ch'i* was developed further by Mencius, who regarded *ch'i* as the psychophysical energy that united moral, physical, and spiritual entities. The next person in line was Chou Tun-yi, considered as the first major Sung scholar who undertook the task of redefining Confucian cosmology and metaphysics. In his Diagram of the Supreme (Great) Ultimate, he equated the Supreme Ultimate (*T'ai-chi*) with the Ultimateless (*Wu-chi*). For Chou, the Supreme Ultimate consisted of *li*, not *ch'i*. The third Asian Philosopher that I chose was Chang Tsai, who argued that the Great Void (*T'ai-hsü*) was constituted by *ch'i*. In fact, the Great Void was the original substance of *ch'i*. Chu Hsi is the fourth scholar we will look at in this chapter. He was known as the complicated dualist who more or less demarcated *li* from *ch'i*. For Chu Hsi, *T'ai-chi* and Tao consisted of *li*, and *li* was ontologically prior to *ch'i*. The fifth is Yi Yulgok, the Great Korean Neo-Confucian scholar, who is best-known for his theory in elucidating *li* and *ch'i*: Not One, Not Two. Yi argued that *li* and *ch'i* cannot be separated or mixed; they can only be distinguished. The sixth is Kaibara Ekken, one of the premier Neo-Confucian scholars in Japan, and he promulgated a monism of *ch'i* in Japan. As I reflect on these thinkers and their various constructs of *ch'i*, the central question is this: How does one relate *li* to *ch'i*?

Mencius (371–289 BCE)

The Fourth Century View of Ch'i

In order to grasp Mencius' teaching on *ch'i*, it is necessary to have some idea about the prevalent cosmology during the fourth century BCE. Most Chinese people during this time assumed that the universe was made up of *ch'i*, which had various consistencies. The grosser and heavier *ch'i* eventually became the earth, whereas the refined and lighter *ch'i* rose to develop into the sky. Humanity, being halfway between the two, is a balanced mixture of the two kinds of *ch'i*. While the body of a human is made up of the grosser *ch'i*, one's heart consists of the refined *ch'i*. One's blood lies somewhere in between insofar as it is neither as solid as the body nor as refined as the heart (or breath). Nevertheless, the blood resembles more of the refined *ch'i* than the grosser *ch'i* due to the reason that it is not static and circulates in the body. It is mainly due to the refined *ch'i* that a person is alive and his faculties are working properly. Since the refined *ch'i* sits in one's heart, one has to have a regimen for the heart in order to have a healthy and long life.[1]

During the fourth century BCE there were at least two schools of thought on *ch'i*. The first school inculcated that the original fund of *ch'i* cannot be refilled, so a person dies when he or she uses up this limited amount of *ch'i*. The second school taught the notion that one's *ch'i* can be replenished although a person is born with a fixed fund of *ch'i*. The *ch'i* located outside one's body can enter through various apertures in one's body. As a result, more *ch'i* is added to one's inborn *ch'i*. A person has to have a clean and unclouded heart in order to acquire this *ch'i* from the outside (the external *ch'i*) and to make this *ch'i* stay in one's heart. Mental activities as well as excessive uses of one's thought and senses tend to use up a certain amount of *ch'i*. Hence, the motto of the first school is this: keep your apertures shut. When a person depletes one's entire fund of *ch'i*, he or she becomes defunct. On the other hand, the motto of the second school is this: keep your apertures open! In doing so, the external *ch'i* can enter into one's heart which results in the expansion of one's *ch'i*.

Mencius, being a part of the Chinese culture of the fourth century BCE, took over and tweaked his contemporary understanding of *ch'i*. For instance, Mencius seems to talk about the grosser *ch'i* and the refined *ch'i* when he elucidates the *ch'i* that fills the body and the *ch'i* that moves

1. D. C. Lau, "Introduction," in *Mencius* (London: Penguin Books, 2003) xxiv.

the heart. Yet, he seems to depart from his contemporary view when he speaks of affinities and continuity between the physical *ch'i* and the refined *ch'i*.[2]

The Earliest Appearance of the Word Ch'i

One of the earliest appearances of the word *ch'i* in the classical period can be found in the works of Mencius. He understood *ch'i* as "that which fills the body."[3] In this context, *ch'i* can be regarded as "vital force" or "vital power." *According to Mencius, ch'i can be directed by one's will.* Mencius once stated, "The will is commander over the ch'i while the ch'i is that which fills the body."[4] He teaches that a person should neither abuse nor block the flow of *ch'i*. If one truly cultivates one's *ch'i*, the space between Heaven and Earth will be filled with its power.[5]

The mind/heart (Chinese 心 *hsin*, Korean 심 *sim*) possesses four functions: 1) thinking (reflection), 2) feeling (having emotions and sentiments), 3) willing (*zhi:* that which makes resolution), and 4) the cultivation of *ch'i*. Moral failures take place due to the mind/heart that is not functioning properly. Furthermore, if one does not take care of the *ch'i* correctly, this energy can lead the mind/heart astray.[6] One's *hsin* has to direct and nourish his or her *ch'i*. It is clear that Mencius was not only familiar with his *ch'i*, but he was also good at cultivating his "flood-like" *ch'i* (*hao jan chih ch'i*).[7]

Mencius often speaks of *ch'i* as a "flood-like" entity and a "strong, moving power." It is hard to elucidate this flood-like *ch'i*. Nevertheless, one is called to develop this *ch'i*.[8] Concerning this point, he states:

> It is difficult to explain. This is a ch'i which is, in the highest degree, vast and unyielding. Nourish it with integrity and place no obstacle in its path and it will fill the space between Heaven and Earth. It is a ch'i which unites rightness and the Way. Deprive it of these and it will starve. It is born of accumulated rightness and

2. Ibid., xxv.

3. Mencius, Book II, Part A, Section II [Hereafter, 2:A2], trans. D. C. Lau (London: Penguin, 2003) 32.

4. Ibid.

5. Ibid., 33.

6. JeeLoo Liu, 76–77.

7. Mencius, 2:A2, 33.

8. JeeLoo Liu, *An Introduction to Chinese Philosophy,* 77.

cannot be appropriated by anyone through a sporadic show of rightness. Whenever one acts in a way that falls below the standard set in one's heart, it will starve.[9]

Ch'i *Needs to Be Nourished*

Indubitably, this psychophysical energy should be nourished inasmuch as it connects humans with other living beings. *Ch'i* in human beings is a special form of energy that can be cultivated in order to bring out moral and physical well-being. By meliorating the *ch'i* in humans and by connecting ourselves to this *ch'i* in nature, humans will be able to fully participate in the dynamic, transformative process of the universe. *Ch'i* remains the underlying unity of life, which unites moral and physical, as well as spiritual and material. This idea of Mencius is further elucidated by Chang Tsai, Chu Hsi, and Luo Ch'in-shun in China, as well as other Neo-Confucians such as Yi Yulgok in Korea and Kaibara Ekken in Japan.[10]

Ch'i can be also regarded as one's moral spirit. A person can utilize the *ch'i* so as to overcome undesirable temptations. Mencius teaches that one's moral *ch'i* manifests itself via his/her appearance and behavior. He writes, "That which a [superior person] follows as his nature, that is to say, [humanity], righteousness, [propriety], and wisdom, is rooted in his heart, and manifests itself in his face, giving it a sleek appearance. It also shows in his back and extends to his limbs, rendering their message intelligible without words."[11] The condition of this moral or inner *ch'i* can be traced through the pupils of one's eyes.

It is interesting to notice that Mencius regards *ch'i* as breath, which is also a primary meaning of the Hebrew word *ruach* (spirit) in the Old Testament. Mencius states, "Now stumbling and harrying affect the *ch'i* [*qi*], yet in fact palpations of the heart are produced.[12]

Chou Tun-yi or Zhou Dun-yi (CE 1017–1073)

Chou Tun-yi was a vital pioneer of Neo-Confucian thought during the Sung dynasty (C.E. 960–1279), who redefined Confucian cosmology and

9. Mencius, 2:A2, 33.

10. Tucker, 14.

11. Mencius, 7A:21, 149.

12. Mencius, 2A:2, 32.

metaphysics. In terms of his doctrine, he borrowed heavily from religious Taoism. According to the *Sung Shih* (History of the Sung Dynasty), he was a native of Ying-tao in Tao-chou (Hunan Province). His original personal name was Tun-shih, but he had to change this name because the second word of his personal name overlapped with the personal name of Emperor Ying-tsung, namely, Tsung-shih. In those days, it was disrespectful to use the words employed in the personal names of one's father and emperor. With the help of his uncle, Cheng Hsiang, who was a scholar of the Dragon Chart Pavilion (a repository for important government documents), he was able to become Assistant Prefect of Fen-ning (present northern Kiangsi). Towards the end of his life, he moved to Nan-k'ang-chüng, where he died at the age of fifty seven. Later, many scholars described him as a man of brilliant scholarship and exceedingly high character.

T'ai-chi T'u and His Contributions to Chinese Philosophy

His major contribution to Chinese philosophy was the *T'ai-chi T'u* (Diagram of the Supreme Ultimate) and the commentary on this Diagram.[13] Chou's other major contribution to Chinese Philosophy is the *T'ung-shu* (*Explanatory Text*) that is also known as the *Yi T'ung* (Explanation of the Changes). In this book, Chou was heavily borrowing from the *Book of Change*.

The Diagram itself and Chou's *Commentary on the Diagram* are known as *the T'ai-chi T'u-shuo* (hereafter referred to as the Commentary on the Diagram). This Commentary on the Diagram contains the quotations below:

> The Ultimateless (*Wu-chi* 無極)! And yet also the Supreme (Great Ultimate (*T'ai-chi* 太極)! The Supreme Ultimate through movement (*tung*) produces the *yang*. This movement, having reached its limit, is followed by quiescence (*ching*), and by this quiescence it produces the *yin*. When quiescence has reached its limit, there is a return to movement. Thus movement and quiescence, in alternation, become each the source of the other. The distinction between the *yin* and *yang* is determined, and their Two Forms (*liang yi*) stand revealed.

---

13. Fung Yu-lan, *A History of Chinese Philosophy,* vol. II, trans. Derk Bodde (Princeton: Princeton University Press, 1983) 434–35.

By the transformation of yang and its union with yin, the five agents of water, fire, wood, metal, and earth arise. When these five material-forces *(ch'i 氣)* are distributed in harmonious order, the four seasons run their course.

The five agents constitute one system of yin and yang, and yin and yang constitute *one* Great Ultimate. The Great Ultimate is fundamentally the Non-ultimate. The five agents arise, each with its specific nature.

When the reality of the Non-ultimate and the essence of yin and yang and the five agents come into mysterious union, integration ensues.

It is man alone who receives [the material forces] in their highest excellence, and therefore he is most intelligent. His corporeal form appears, and his spirit develops consciousness. The five moral principles of his nature (humanity, righteousness, decorum, wisdom, and good faith) are aroused by, and react to, the external world and engage in activity; good and evil are distinguished and human affairs take place.[14]

(See Figure 6 for the Diagram itself.)

According to Chou Tun-yi, the essential nature of the yin and yang as well as the five elements (fire, water, wood, metal, and earth) is *ch'i* (氣, 기). This understanding is repeatedly ratified in the Commentary on the Diagram of the Great Ultimate. The interaction of the yin *ch'i* and yang *ch'i* produces and reproduces a myriad of things, as well as keeps transforming and changing things without an end.[15]

Introducing Ch'i *and* Li *to Neo-Confucianism*

The term *ch'i* became one of the central words in Neo-Confucianism. This is equivalent to what Westerners would call "ether" or "matter." The other central key term is *li* (理, 리), often translated as "principle" (or "Principle"). In the *Explanatory Text*, Chou expatiates upon *li* as "a designation for the immaterial and metaphysical principle or principles that underlie, yet transcends, the physical universe."[16] *Li* is often used as a synonym for the Supreme Ultimate. Hence, when Chou speaks of the

14. Chou Tun-yi, *T'ai-chi-t'u shuo,* quoted in Wm. Theodore De Bary, Wing-tsit Chan, and Burton Watson, comps. *Sources of Chinese Tradition* (New York: Columbia University Press, 1960) 1:458. It also contains the author's own translation.

15. Fung Yu-lan, *A History of Chinese Philosophy,* vol. II, trans. Derk Bodde (Princeton: Princeton University Press, 1983) 437.

16. Ibid., 444.

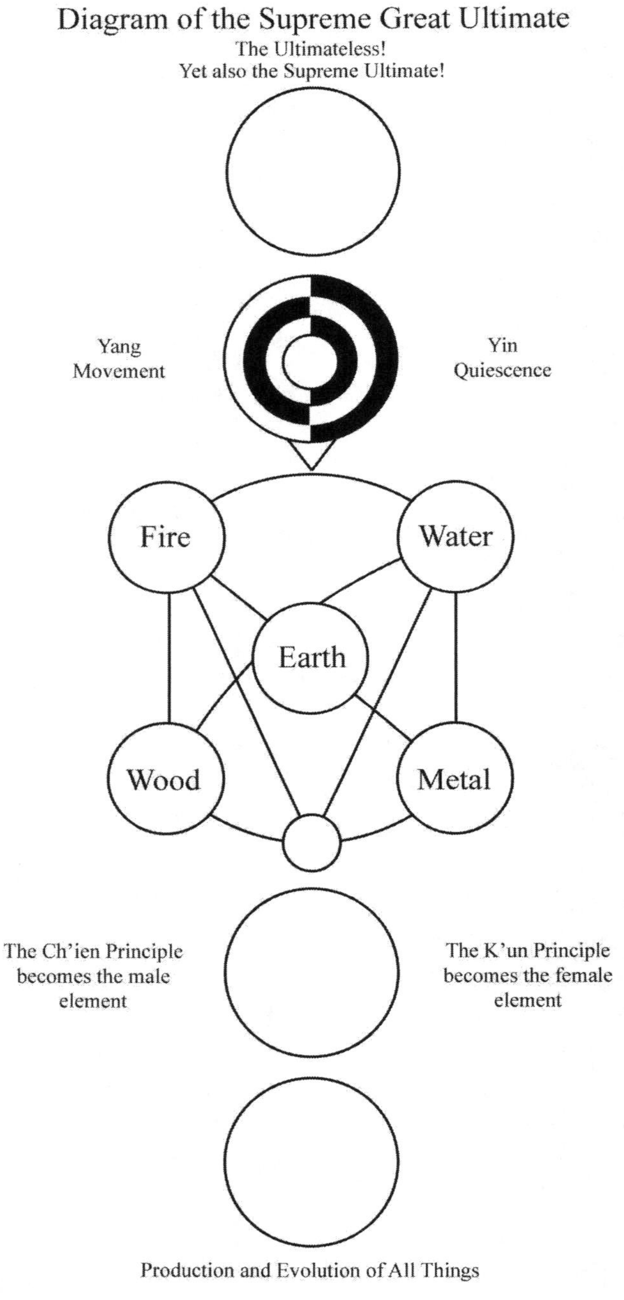

Diagram of the Supreme Great Ultimate

The Ultimateless!
Yet also the Supreme Ultimate!

Yang
Movement

Yin
Quiescence

Fire

Water

Earth

Wood

Metal

The Ch'ien Principle
becomes the male
element

The K'un Principle
becomes the female
element

Production and Evolution of All Things

FIGURE 6: The Great/Supreme Ultimate

Supreme Ultimate, it belongs to the sphere of *Li or Principle*; when he speaks of the yin and yang, it pertains to the sphere of *Ch'i or Matter*.[17]

Chou is credited for introducing the vital apposition between *li and ch'i* in later Neo-Confucianism. This apposition was fully elucidated by Chu Xi. In *Explanatory Text*, Chou inculcates that everything in the physical world comes from "oneness" (Principle) that is the Supreme Ultimate. But the Supreme Ultimate[18] is also actually present within all material things. Therefore, it is both transcendent and immanent.[19]

Regarding the human nature, Chou writes: "It is man alone, however, who receives all these in their highest excellence, and hence is the most intelligent (of all beings). His bodily form thereupon is produced, and his spirit develops consciousness. The five principles of his nature react (to external phenomena), so that the distinction between good and evil emerges and the myriad phenomena of conduct appears."[20] From the above quotation, one can infer that a person is filled with both the metaphysical *li* (Principle of the Supreme Ultimate) and the essence of the physical five elements (*ch'i*). Furthermore, the Principle of the Supreme Ultimate stays "unmixed and supremely good." Likewise, the human nature (*hsing*) is also fundamentally good.[21]

In chapter 7 of the *Explanatory Text*, Chou remarks, "In the nature, there are hardness and softness, (which may result in) goodness or evil. All (is right) when there is the mean (*chung* 中, 중)."[22] *Chung* (the mean) refers to harmony and proper proportion, which is the highest Way *(Tao)* of the world and goal of every sage. A human is filled with the yang principle (hardness) and the yin principle (softness). Instead of having the mean (*chung*), humans sometimes do not act in accordance with the mean and righteousness, which in turn results in evil. Evil is not an active, outside force; rather, evil is a deviation from the mean. For instance, the goodness of the due hardness (yang) is exemplified by righteousness

17. Ibid., 445.

18. *The Way *(Tao)* is another name for the Supreme Ultimate.

19. Ibid., 445.

20. Cho Tun-yi, *The Commentary on the Diagram,* quoted in Fung Yu-lan, *A History of Chinese Philosophy,* vol. 2, trans. Derk Bodde (Princeton: Princeton University Press, 1983), 445.

21. Ibid., 445–46.

22. Cho Tun-yi, *The Explanatory Text,* quoted in Fung Yu-lan, *A History of Chinese Philosophy,* vol. II, trans. Derk Bodde (Princeton: Princeton University Press, 1983) 446.

(yi 義, 의), straightforwardness (chih, 直, 직), decisiveness, strictness, firmness, determination, and steadfastness. On the other hand, examples of the evil in the extreme hardness (yang) are ruthlessness, intolerance, force, and violence. Likewise, the yin can be embodied both in goodness (e.g. compliance and docility) and evil (e.g. indecisiveness and under-handed sycophancy).[23] Therefore, one should stay away from the false bifurcation that yang represents good and yin represents evil. Both yang ch'i and yin ch'i come with potential goodness and evil.

Deriving the Diagram of the Supreme Ultimate

From where did Chou derive the Diagram of the Supreme Ultimate? It is likely that the Diagram was inspired by the *Book of Changes* and the *Taoist Cannon*. In the *Book of Changes* (Appendix III), there is the Supreme Ultimate that produced the Two Forms (yin and yang). These Two Forms brought forth the four emblems (*hsiang* 象, 상), and these four produced the eight trigrams, which serve to determine good and bad fortunes of human life. In a similar way, Chou describes the Supreme Ultimate that generates yin and yang (the Two Forms); however, Chou speaks of *the Five Elements* instead of the four emblems and the eight trigrams of the *Book of Changes*.[24] From religious Taoism, Chou derived the Five Emblems.

Chou's Diagram of the Supreme Ultimate is also influenced by the Taoist Canon. There are many similarities between Chou's Diagram and the *Diagram of the Truly First and Mysterious Classic of the Transcendent Great Cave* in religious Taoism. Like Chou's Diagram, the *Diagram of the Truly First* put the empty circle at the top; below that, it puts a circle with several concentric parts, consisting of interlocking black and white bands. And then, the Five Elements (fire, wood, water, metal, and earth) are located. It appears that Chou was very familiar with both religious Taoism and the *Book of Changes*.[25]

Chang Tsai or Zhang Zai (CE 1020–1077)

Chang Tsai was born in CE 1020 at *Ta-liang* (modern *Keifeng*, in *Honan*). He was a contemporary of Chou Tun-yi and Shao Yung. His greatest

23. Fung, *History,* II:447.

24. Fung, *History,* II:438.

25. Ibid., 442.

contribution to Chinese Philosophy was his explication on *ch'i*. In his youth, he was engrossed in military affairs but later devoted himself to literary pursuits. Eventually, his talents were recognized by Fan Chung-yen (989–1052), who held an important position in the court. Fan encouraged Chang to read the *Doctrine of the Mean,* but Chang did not find it satisfactory. He turned his attention to the writings of Buddhists and Taoists, yet he was not impressed with these writings. Finally through his nephews, Ch'eng Hao and Ch'eng I, Chang was introduced into Neo-Confucianism, with which he found the most satisfaction. At this point, he was also exposed to the Neo-Confucian writings of Chou Tun-yi. Thereafter, he vigorously studied orthodox antiquity. As a result, he became one of the most renowned scholars of his era. He was known as Master *Heng-ch'ü* by the people of his time.[26]

He died in 1077 and left three pivotal books: 1) *Cheng Meng (Correct Discipline for Beginners),* 2) *Ching-hsüeh Li-k'u (Assembled Principles of Classical Learning),* and *Yi Shuo (Comments on the Book of Changes).*[27]

The Great Void and Non-Existence

Chang Tsai taught that *ch'i* is synonymous with the Great Void (C. *T'ai-hsü* 太虛, K. 태허), which is similar to Chou Tun-yi's concept of the Supreme Ultimate. The term *T'ai-hsü* came from Taoism and often appeared in Buddhist writings; however, Chang's connotation of the term remained quite different from those of Taoism and Buddhism. In opposition to the Buddhist's understanding of the term that underscored the illusory quality of reality, Chang taught that the Great Void was not made of non-being or nothingness. Chang also stood against the Taoist's understanding that non-being (*Wu-chi* 無極) is the source of being. Furthermore, Chang insisted that the Great Void did not produce *ch'i*; rather, the Great Void consisted of *ch'i*. In other words, *ch'i* was not distinct from the Great Void.[28] Nor was *ch'i* finite whereas the Great Void was infinite. Regarding this point, Chang stated, "The Ether's [ch'i] condensation from and dispersion into the Great Void is like ice's freezing from and melting into water. Once we realize that the Great Void is the

---

26. Fung Yu-lan, *History*, II:477.

27. Siu-chi Huang, "Chang Tsai's Concept of Ch'i," *Philosophy East and West* 18, no. 4 (1968) 247.

28. Ibid., 252–53.

same as the Ether [ch'i], there is no non-existence (*wu*)."[29] In this sense, Chang identified the Great Void with *ch'i*.

Chang Tsai insisted that there is no non-existence: "If we realize that the Supreme Vacuity [the Great Void] is identical with material-force [ch'i], we know that there is no such thing as nothing [non-being]."[30] When the ether (*ch'i*) condenses, it produces its visibility. When *ch'i* disperses, it becomes invisible. This does not mean that the ether becomes 'non-existent.' It simply becomes invisible temporarily. Hence, Chang believed that it is an obsolete argument whether there is being or non-being. Rather, the question should be the question of being visible or invisible. Regarding this point, Chang elucidated, "When the Ether [*ch'i*] condenses, its visibility becomes apparent so that there are then the shapes (of individual things). But when it does not condense, its visibility is no longer apparent so that there are then no shapes. At the time of its condensation, can one say otherwise than that is but temporary? But at the time of its dispersion, can one hastily say that it is the non-existent? Hence the sage, as he gazes aloft or looks below, only says that he understands the cause of visibility and invisibility."[31] Therefore, Chang argued that one should not identify the Great Void with non-being (*Wu-chi*). The Great Void is not a vacuum; rather, it is a primordial, shapeless, and undifferentiated substance of *ch'i*.

The Great Void (T'ai-hsü 太虛, 태허) *is the original substance (Pen-t'i* 本體, 본체) *of ch'i.* When *ch'i* (material force) disperses, it returns to the Great Void. Chang wrote, "The Supreme Vacuity [the Great Void] has no physical form. It is the original substance of material-force [ch'i]. . . . The Supreme Vacuity [The Great Void] of necessity consists of material-force [ch'i]. Material-force of necessity integrates to become the myriad things. Things of necessity disintegrate and return to the Supreme Vacuity [the Great Void]."[32] Through the condensation of *ch'i*, the ten thousand things come to exist and become visible. On the other

29. Chang Tsai, *Cheng Meng (Correct Discipline for Beginners),* quoted in Fung Yu-lan, *A History of Chinese Philosophy,* II:480.

30. Chang Tsai, *Correct Discipline for Beginners,* quoted in *Sources of Chinese Tradition: From Earliest Times to 1600,* vol. 1, comp. WM. Theodore DE Bary and Irene Bloom (New York: Columbia University Press, 1999) 687.

31. Chang Tsai, *Cheng Meng,* II:481.

32. Chang Tsai, *Correct Discipline for Beginners,* quoted in *Sources of Chinese Tradition: From Earliest Times to 1600,* vol. 1, comp. WM. Theodore DE Bary and Irene Bloom (New York: Columbia University Press, 1999) 685.

hand, through the dispersion of *ch'i*, the ten thousand things return to the Great Void.

Ch'i *as a Constant Change*

As the vital force, *ch'i* is a constant, forever change like "wandering air." *Ch'i* represents the everlasting movement that constantly condenses and disperses. The basic element of *ch'i* remains ever changing and ever moving. Moreover, it is vital, active and dynamic insofar as the two modes (yin and yang) of *ch'i* continuously interact and complement each other. As a constant movement, *ch'i* ascends, descends, soars, and moves about.[33]

Chang Tsai taught a monism of *ch'i*. He writes, "When it is understood the Vacuity, Emptiness, is nothing but material-force [ch'i], then something and nothing, the hidden and the manifest, spirit and external transformation, and human nature and destiny, *are all one and not a duality*."[34] Therefore, Chang concluded that everything in this universe can be construed in terms of the twofold activity of *ch'i*.

Against Buddhism and Taoism

By using the metaphysical concept of *ch'i*, Chang attacked the Buddhist's notion that the universe stays illusory: "On the grandiose side, they [Buddhists] err in equating a particle of dust or mustard seed with all within the six directions. On the small side, they conceal [the truth] by treating the human world as dream and illusion."[35] Based on his empirical data, Chang argued that the phenomenal world is real and that the objective world also exists. Moreover, he refutes the Buddhist notion that all the things perceived are not real and become nothing in the end. Although he accedes to Buddhists that nothing perceived stays permanently and things are in flux, he opposes the doctrine that "nothingness" is the ultimate end of all things in the universe.[36]

33. Siu-chi Huang, "Chang Tsai's Concept of Ch'i," *Philosophy East and West* 18, no. 4 (1968) 249.

34. Chang Tsai, *Correct Discipline for Beginners,* quoted in *Sources of Chinese Tradition: From Earliest Times to 1600,* vol. 1, comp. WM. Theodore DE Bary and Irene Bloom (New York: Columbia University Press, 1999) 685. *Italics* are mine.

35. Chang Tsai, *Chang-tzu Ch'üan-shu (Complete Works of Chang Tsai),* quoted in Siu-chi Huang, "Chang Tsai's Concept of Ch'i," *Philosophy East and West* 18.4 (1968) 255.

36. Siu-chi Huang, "Chang Tsai's Concept of Ch'i," *Philosophy East and West* 18.4 (1968) 256.

Ch'i as an eternal movement represents the metaphysical reality. In other simple words, *ch'i* stays forever, although visible things (constituted by *ch'i*) in the world undergo the change of structure and shape. The existence of *ch'i* and visible things are real; things in this phenomenal world do not become nothing in the end. Nor is our objective world an illusion.

Chang Tsai refuted the well-known Taoist's presupposition that *non-being* is the source of being. Chapter 40 of *Tao Te Ching* writes, "*All things [in the world] are born of being. Being is born of non-being*" (C. 有生於無, K. 유생어무). "All things in the world" speak of individual beings with particular shapes and forms, and "being" refers to "existence per se." According to Lao Tzǔ, there is a clear progression from 1) Non-being (C. *wu* 無, K. *mu* 무) to 2) Being, and 3) beings in the world. Tao as the source of Being per se is identical with pure Non-being.[37] In opposition to this Taoist's doctrine, Chang argued that Non-being is not the source of Being or beings; rather, the source of Being should be another "Being" (C. *yu* 有, K. yu 유). In other words, the origin of Being is not Non-being. Chang discarded the Taoist's demarcation between the Great Void and *ch'i*. Instead, he inculcates the unity between the Great Void and *ch'i*. Both of them share the same essence, but they are different in terms of the process of change such as water and ice. To put it more simplistically, the myriad beings (or things) of this world find their origin in *ch'i*, which is synonymous with the Great Void.

Chu Hsi or Zhu Xi (CE 1130–1200)

In 1130, Chu Hsi was born to a literary family in Yu-hsi, where his father was serving as a district magistrate. From his childhood, he was known as a genius. Chu's precocious nature was ratified when he passed the government examination at age nineteen. As a result, Chu spent most of his life in a succession of official posts, during which he also instructed a considerable number of disciples. Toward the end of his life (1197–99), he suffered from an undeserved charge of a court intrigue. In 1200, he died of dysentery.[38]

The greatness of Chu Hsi was his creation of a coherent system based on all the ideas of his predecessors such as Cho Tun-yi, Shao Yung, Chang Tsai, and the Ch'eng brothers.[39] Ideologically, Chu is linked with

37. JeeLoo Liu, *Introduction,* 134.

38. Fung Yu-lan, *History,* vol. 2, 533–34.

39. Wm. Theodore DE Bary and Irene Bloom, comps., *Sources of Chinese Tradition:*

Ch'eng Yi, who established the Rationalistic school (*Li Hsüeh*). Chu Hsi more or less built his philosophy upon the foundation of Ch'eng Yi. In general, Chu is also credited for fully developing the Rationalistic school.[40] As a result, Chu Hsi's school of thought was known as the "Ch'eng-Zhu school, and the doctrine of Principle *(li)* represented the most salient feature of his teaching. Other pivotal topics which he elucidated further are the Supreme *Ultimate (T'ai-chi)*, material force *(ch'i)*, human nature *(hsing)* and the mind-and-heart *(hsin).*[41]

Li *(Principle) and* Ch'i: *"Above Shapes" and "Within Shapes"*

As a complicated dualist, Chu Hsi postulated that *li* remains ontologically prior to *ch'i.*[42] Moreover, before there were Heaven and Earth, there was *li.* Chu remarked, "There is Principle *(li)* before there can be the Ether *(ch'i).* But it is only when there is the Ether, that Principle has a place in which to rest. . . . If we are to pin down the word Principle, neither 'existence' *(yu)* nor 'non-existence' *(wu)* may be attributed to it. For before Heaven and Earth 'existed,' it *(li)* already was as it is."[43] In another place, when Chu was forced to answer regarding the priority of Principle, Chu said, "Nevertheless, if one must push into the question of their origins, one is forced to admit that Principle *[li]* has priority."[44]

Principle *(li)* belongs to the metaphysical world that is "above shapes" *(hsing erh shang* 形而上), whereas Ether *(ch'i)* pertains to the concrete world that is "within shapes" *(hsing erh hsia* 形而下). In this sense, *li* resembles what Greek philosophy called "form," whereas *ch'i* is similar to "matter." Concerning the difference between *li* and *ch'i,* Chu writes: "Within the universe there are *li* and *ch'i. Li* constitutes the Tao that is 'above shapes'; it is the source from which things are produced.

From Earliest Times to 1600, vol. 1 (New York: Columbia University Press, 1999) 697.

    40. Fung Yu-lan, *History,* vol. 2, 533.

    41. Wm. Theodore DE Bary and Irene Bloom, comps., *Sources of Chinese Tradition* (New York: Columbia University Press, 1999) 698

    42. Julia Ching, *The Religious Thought of Chu Hsi* (Oxford: Oxford University Press, 2000) 41.

    43. Chu Hsi, *Chu Wen-kung Wen-chi (Collected Writings of Chu Hsi),* quoted in Fung Yu-lan, *A History of Chinese Philosophy,* vol. 2, trans. Derk Bodde (Princeton: Princeton University Press, 1983) 539.

    44. *Chu-tzu Yu-lei (Classified Conversations of Chu Hsi),* quoted in Fung Yu-lan, *A History of Chinese Philosophy,* vol. 2, trans. Derk Bodde (Princeton: Princeton University Press, 1983) 540.

Ch'i (the Ether) constitutes the 'instruments' (ch'i 器) that are 'within shapes'; it is the (material) means whereby things are produced. Hence men or things, at the moment of their production, must receive this li in order that they may have a nature (hsing) of their own; they must receive this ch'i in order that they may have form [shape]."[45]

The world of "above shapes" transcends time and space, so beings in this transcendental world "subsist." On the contrary, the world of "within shapes" remains immanent in this visible world, in which beings in this world "exist." The world of Principle is synonymous with the Supreme Ultimate (T'ai-chi).[46] More specifically, the Supreme Ultimate consists of the Principles or li of all things in the universe. The Supreme Ultimate is another name for all the good things in the universe: "The Supreme Ultimate is simply an utterly excellent and supremely good norma- tive Principle. . . . What master Chou (Chou Tun-yi) calls the Supreme Ultimate is an appellation for all that is good in Heaven and Earth, and among men and things."[47]

Before the time of Chu Hsi, there was a major debate concerning the relationship between li and ch'i, especially among the Ch'eng broth- ers. Ch'eng Yi (1033–1108), the founder of the Rationalistic school devel- oped a distinct demarcation between li and ch'i. This demarcation looked a lot like Plato's teaching on form and matter. Like Plato's form, Ch'eng Yi's concept of li (Principle) subsisted eternally independent of the vis- ible world of shapes. In opposition to his brother Ch'eng Yi, Ch'eng Hao (1032–1085), who established the Idealistic school in the Neo-Confucian movement, taught that li (Principle) was nothing more than the natural tendency in any tangible object. Thus, li does not subsist apart from a particular, concrete object. The followers of Ch'eng Hao later insisted that there was no distinction between "what is above shape" and "what is within shape."[48]

---

45. Chu Hsi, *Chu Wen-kung Wen-chi (Collected Writings of Chu Hsi)*, quoted in Fung Yu-lan, *A History of Chinese Philosophy*, vol. 2, trans. Derk Bodde (Princeton: Princeton University Press, 1983) 542.

46. Mary Evelyn Tucker, *The Philosophy of Ch'i*, 44. Whereas Chang Tsai identified *T'ai-chi* with *ch'i*, Chu Hsi identified *T'ai-chi* with *li*.

47. *Chu-tzu Yu-lei (Classified Conversations of Chu Hsi)*, quoted in Fung Yu-lan, *A History of Chinese Philosophy*, vol. 2, trans. Derk Bodde (Princeton: Princeton University Press, 1983) 537.

48. Fung Yu-lan, *History*, vol. 2, 507–11.

Li *and* Ch'i *in an Existent*

According to Chu Hsi, *when Ether brings forth a being or thing, Principle is also present there.* In this sense, the total demarcation of the Principle from the Ether is not possible according to Chu Hsi. The world of Principle is "pure, empty, and shapeless," but it lacks volition and creative power. On the contrary, the concrete world of Ether (*ch'i*) has shape and body, as well as the power to create a being or thing. Nonetheless, in order to create a being, the Ether also necessitates the Principle. In other words, in order to produce a thing in the concrete world, both Principle and Ether are required. The relationship between the Ether and Principle is like a blueprint (Principle) and physical materials (Ether) in building a house. Such things like bricks, tiles, wood, and stone exemplify the Ether, while an architectural plan for the house exemplifies *li* or Principle. Here, Chu differs, in my opinion, from Plato in that Principle *(li)* is also present in the things of the concrete world, whereas Plato tends to underscore the gap between "form" in the intelligible world and "visible" things in the visible world.[49] From this, one can conclude that Plato remains a hard dualist, and Chu Hsi is a moderate dualist inasmuch as Chu does not totally demarcate the world of Principle from the world of Ether.

For Chu Hsi, Principle *(li)* can also reside in a concrete world. Principle can be found in both the invisible and visible worlds. As a matter of fact, a concrete object cannot exist without both Principle and Ether. Some examples of Principle include humanness, rightness, ritual decorum, and wisdom, while the examples of *ch'i* include metal, wood, water, fire, and earth.[50]

Yi Yulgok (CE 1536–1584)

Brief Sketch of Yulgok's life

On December 26, 1536, Yi Yulgok was born in Pukp'yŏng Village in Kang-wŏn Province. His family name was Yi, and his first name was I. Later, the pen name *Yulgok* was bestowed upon him, who became one of

---

49. Plato, *Republic,* quoted in *From Plato to Derrida,* ed. Forrest Baird and Walter Kaufmann (Upper Saddle River: Prentice Hall, 2000) 129–41.

50. Chu Hsi, "Principle and Material-Force," quoted in Wm. Theodore DE Bary and Irene Bloom, comps., *Sources of Chinese Tradition: From Earliest Times to 1600,* vol. 1 (New York: Columbia University Press, 1999) 698.

the greatest East Asian scholars.[51] Unfortunately, he passed away at the early age of 49.

Yulgok was born into a distinguished family. His father, Yi Wŏn-su, had served as an inspector at the office of Government Supervision, and thereafter he became Senior Assistant to the Prime Minister. Moreover, his mother, Madame Sin Saimdang, gained great praise and admiration from both of her contemporaries and later generations. She was well-versed in Chinese classics, poetry, calligraphy, and painting.[52] During this time, it was very rare to see a woman with such multiple talents.

In his childhood, people called Yulgok a prodigy. By the age seven, he mastered the Four Books and the Three Classics. At age 13, he became a *chinsa,* a title given to a scholar who passed the civil service examination in the literary department. As a result, he received many praises from the people whom he associated with. In the mean time, Yulgok also loved to read the Taoist classics and Buddhist scriptures. Yi's deep knowledge on Taoism and Buddhism later surprised many of his contemporaries.[53]

During his life time, the Yi dynasty was undergoing social and political unsettlements, as well as a gradual economic bankruptcy of the government due to the disorder in land ownership and the excessive exploitations by government workers. Under these circumstances, many scholars tried to seclude themselves in order to search for truth away from political turmoil. Yulgok warned against this recluse lifestyle of the scholars and proactively called for social reform even as a scholar. Truly, he remained both a great scholar and statesman with a far-reaching vision.

The Four-Seven Debate

The Four-Seven debate, one of the most conspicuous Neo-Confucian debates, took place during the Yi Chosŏn dynasty. Yi Yulgok was at the epicenter of this crucial debate.

---

51. An Pyŏng-ju, "Yi I (Yulgok) and His Thought" in *Main Currents of Korean Thought,* ed. The Korean National Commission for UNESCO (Seoul: The Si-sa-yong-o-sa Publisher, 1983) 94.

52. Ibid., 95.

53. Ibid., 96.

The first round of the debate occurred mainly between T'oegye and Kobong, starting in 1553, and the second round took place between Yulgok and U-gye, starting in 1572.[54]

This debate revolved around Chu Hsi's famous statement: "The Four Beginnings are manifestations of *li*; the Seven Emotions are manifestations of ch'i."[55] For some reason, Chu Hsi did not clearly elucidate this ambiguous statement further, so there have been numerous interpretations surrounding this statement. But for many, this statement suggested the ontological separateness between *li* and *ch'i*, as well as between the Four Beginnings (Korean 사단 *sadan,* C. 四端, *ssu-tuan*) and the Seven Emotions (Korean 칠정 *ch'ilchŏng,* C. 七情, *ch'i-ch'ing*). T'oegye construed Chu Hsi's statement dualistically in the dichotomous system of *li* and *ch'i*, whereas Yulgok interpreted the statement more non-dualistically in opposition to T'oegye.

The term "Four Beginnings" originates from a famous passage in the *Book of Mencius*:

> From this it can be seen that whoever is devoid of the heart [K. *sim*, C. *hsin*] of *compassion* is not human, whoever is devoid of the heart of *shame* is not human, whoever is devoid of the heart of *courtesy and modesty* is not human, and whoever is devoid of the heart of *right and wrong* is not human. The heart of compassion is the germ of *benevolence*; the heart of shame, of dutifulness [*righteousness*]; the heart of courtesy and modesty, of observance of the rites [*propriety*]; the heart of right and wrong, of *wisdom*. Man [All humanity] has these four germs [Four Beginnings] just as he has four limbs. For a man [person] possessing these four germs to deny his own potentialities is for him to cripple himself.[56]

In this passage, Mencius introduces the Four Beginnings, namely, 1) compassion, 2) shame, 3) courtesy and modesty, and 4) right and wrong. These Four Beginnings can be cultivated into the four major Confucian virtues (benevolence, righteousness, propriety, and wisdom). In other words, the heart of compassion can be cultivated into benevolence, and the heart of shame can be cultivated into righteousness. The

54. Michael C. Kalton, *The Four-Seven Debate* (Albany: SUNY, 1994) xxviii–xxxii.

55. Chu Hsi, *Chu Tzu yü-lei* (Classified Conversations of Master Chu Hsi) 53:20a, quoted in Ed Chung, Korean Neo-Confucianism, 44.

56. *Mencius*, IIA:6, in D. C. Lau, trans., *Mencius* (London: Penguin, 2003) 38. Italics are mine.

above passage evinces that the Four Beginnings of virtue are originally and naturally rooted in each human mind-and-heart (K. 심 *sim*, C. 心 *hsin*). In this sense, *self-cultivation* is a key foundation in understanding Confucianism. Mencius further states the result of cultivating one's Four Beginnings: "If a man [person] is able to develop all these four germs [beginnings] that he possesses, it will be like a fire starting up or a spring coming through. When these are fully developed, he can tend the whole realm within the Four Seas, but if he fails to develop them, he will not be able even to serve his parents."[57]

The concept of the Four Beginnings also stands on the assumption of Mencius' doctrine which inculcates the *original goodness of human nature* (*sŏng/hsing*). This creates an optimistic view on human nature, so through self-cultivation, a person can improve oneself. Moreover, evil is not innate in one's original nature. Evil is engendered by not expressing the natural goodness of human nature inherent in the mind-and-heart, and by failing to control bad outside influences.[58]

The Book of the Rites discusses the term *Seven Emotions* (*ch'ilchŏng/ch'i-ch'ing*) that are pleasure, anger, sorrow, fear, love, hatred, and desire. These exemplify the basic human feelings which are not procured through learning from the outside.[59] The Seven Emotions as basic human feelings refer to physical and mental states, and they can be aroused by the external things. The key in dealing with the Seven Emotions is to have equilibrium and harmony. Problems arise when there are excessiveness and disharmony.[60]

The kernel of the Four-Seven debate was this: what is the relationship between the Four Beginnings and the Seven Emotions in connection with *li* and *ch'i*. The Ch'eng-Chu school underscored the dualistic nature of the two, while Lo and many Ming Neo-Confucian scholars highlighted the "unity" of *li* and *ch'i*, as well as the connection between the Four and the Seven. T'oegye tended to be more dualistic, where as Yulgok appeared to be more non-dualistic because he strongly held to the inseparability of *li* a nd *ch'i*.

---

57. Ibid., 38–39.

58. Edward Chung, *Korean Neo-Confucianism*, 38.

59. James Legge, trans., *The Chinese Classics*, vol. 1 (Hong Kong: Hong Kong University Press, 1970, reprint) 379.

60. Edward Chung, *Korean Neo-Confucianism*, 39.

The Relationship between Li *and* Ch'i: *Cannot Be Separated or Mixed but Distinguished*

In Yi Yulgok's horizon, *li* and *ch'i* can be neither separated nor mixed, but Yi wants to preserve the "mysterious unity" between the two. In addition, *li* and *ch'i* can only be "distinguished" ontologically and conceptually. Regarding the inseparability of *li* and *ch'i*, Yi writes:

> Why is it said that i [*li*] and ki [*ch'i*] are not one? I and ki are inseparable from each other; however, in their mysterious unity, i is i in itself, and ki is ki in itself. Since i and ki are not intermingled as such, they are not one. Why is it said that they are not two? Although i itself is i and ki itself is ki, they are still merged one into the other in perfect harmony, thereby having no space, no priority and posteriority, and no separation and union between them. Since i and ki are not seen as two as such, they are not two. For this reason, movement and tranquility have no beginning, and yin and yang have no starting point. Since i has no starting point, ki also has no starting point. In general, i is nothing but one. Fundamentally, *in i there is no difference between the correct and the turbid, the pure and the impure.* But *the ki that is ridden by i* ascends and descends, flies and flutters, and becomes blended and irregular everywhere. It never stops its breath, while producing the myriad things of Heaven and Earth that become correct or partial, penetrated or blocked, clear or turbid, pure or impure, and so on.[61]

In accordance with Yi Yulgok, there are two aspects of *li* (*i* 이 in Korean). The first aspect is "the original essence of *li*" that is also known as "*li* in itself." Note that the original *li* exemplifies oneness. The second aspect refers to "the moving *li*" because it rides on *ch'i*. The moving *li* brings forth its various particularizations in concrete phenomena. In other words, the two aspects involve the ontological and phenomenal sides. The ontological, original *li* (K. 본연지이, C. 本然之理) is one that is also undifferentiated and purely good, yet *the moving li* riding on *ch'i* generates the myriad things in the concrete world.[62] Yi writes, "The original essence of *i* [*li*] is one; however, when it flows and circulates, its

---

61. Yi Yulgok, *Yulgok chŏnsŏ* (Complete Works of Yi Yulgok), vol. 1, 197, quoted in Edward Y. J. Chung, *The Korean Neo-Confucianism of Yi T'oegye and Yi Yulgok* (Albany: State University of New York Press, 1995) 111. Italics are mine.

62. Edward Y. J. Chung, *The Korean Neo-Confucianism of Yi T'oegye and Yi Yulgok* (Albany: State University of New York Press, 1995) 110.

particularizations are diverse. It is wrong to seek for the original *i* only while neglecting the *i* that flows and circulates."[63]

Both humans and other creatures have the same principle (*li*), but humans and other creatures possess varying degrees of grade and purity in terms of *ch'i*. The Principle (*li*) in Heaven and Earth, and humans and other creatures is the same one. It is the *ch'i* which brings forth particularity and uniqueness. Moreover, because of the varying degrees and grades of *ch'i*, human nature remains different from those of other creatures. *Ch'i* brings forth various particularizations because it is limited and particular.[64] To put it in more simplistic way, humans and other creatures are diverse mainly due to *ch'i*, not due to *li*.

Yi Yulgok accedes to Lo Ch'in-shun's view that *li* and *ch'i* are inseparable in concrete things. The Ming Chinese Neo-Confucian Lo Ch'in-shun (1465–1547) endorsed oneness of *li* and *ch'i*. For Lo, *li* was simply an aspect of *ch'i*. Against Lo's view, Yi argues that Lo went too far by ignoring the distinction of *li* and *ch'i* in Chu Hsi's philosophy. Furthermore, in Yi's mind, although there is the 'mysterious unity' among *li* and *ch'i*, they cannot be mixed into one.[65] In this sense, the two stay ontologically distinct. Yi wants to ensure this distinction repeatedly in his view.

Yi Yulgok wanted to cling to the orthodox *li*-chi dualism of the Cheng-Chu school and to oppose chi-monism of Lo and many Ming Neo-Confucian scholars. Furthermore, Yi Yulgok also unequivocally refuted Yi T'oegye's theory that both *li* and *ch'i* can emanate.[66] Against T'oegye's view, Yulgok inculcated that only *ch'i* could emanate and *li* could only ride on *ch'i*. It is clear that Yulgok accepted Lo's inseparability of *li* and *ch'i*, but he opposed Lo's chi-monism.

Unlike both Lo and Ekken, Yi Yulgok's concept of *Tai-chi* (the Supreme Ultimate) consists of *li*. Yi's view is very similar to the view of Chu Hsi. The whole of each principle (*li*) in all things is the One Supreme

63. Yi Yulgok, *Yulgok chŏnsŏ* (Complete Works of Yi Yulgok), vol. 1, 194, quoted in Edward Y. J. Chung, *The Korean Neo-Confucianism of Yi T'oegye and Yi Yulgok* (Albany: State University of New York Press, 1995), 110.

64. Edward Y. J. Chung, *The Korean Neo-Confucianism of Yi T'oegye and Yi Yulgok* (Albany: State University of New York Press, 1995) 112.

65. Ibid., 113.

66. An Pyŏng-ju, "Yi I (Yulgok) and His Thought" in *Main Currents of Korean Thought,* ed. The Korean National Commission for UNESCO (Seoul: The Si-sa-yong-o-sa Publisher, 1983) 107.

Ultimate. Again Yi states, "Although Heaven, Earth, human beings, and things each have principle, the principle of Heaven and Earth is, in fact, the same as the principle of the myriad things, and the principle of the myriad things is, in fact, the same as our principle. This is so called *One Great Ultimate* in its whole self."[67]

Difference between Li and Ch'i: Li without Beginning and Ch'i with Beginning

For Yulgok, *li* does not have both beginning and ending, but *ch'i* has both beginning and ending. *Li* by itself cannot act, but it can act and move when it rides on *ch'i* (the moving *ch'i*). The original, ontological *li* does not have any shape (K. 무형 *muhyŏng*, C. 無形 *wuhsing*) whereas *ch'i* comes with shape (K. 유형 *yuhyŏng*, C. *yuhsing* 有形). Often times, *ch'i* becomes a vessel of *li*. Moreover, *ch'i* emanates, but what makes *ch'i* emanate is *li*. In this sense, the cause of *ch'i's* emanation is *li*, although *li* cannot emanate by itself. In contrast to this Yulgok's view, T'oegye taught that both *li* and *ch'i* proceed into form or shape (emanate).[68] Yulgok writes, "That which is in movement and tranquility is *ki* [*ch'i*]; that which makes it move and become tranquil is *i* [*li*]."[69]

Yulgok also employs *the water-container analogy* in order to describe the relation between the two. Water symbolizes *li*, whereas its container symbolizes *ch'i*. From this perspective, "*i* [*li*] exists in *ki* [*ch'i*],"[70] just as water exists in its container. For this reason, for *li* to emanate into the tangible world, it should dwell or ride on *ch'i*, and of course, *ch'i* must also carry *li*.

67. Yi Yulgok, *Yulgok chŏnsŏ* (Complete Works of Yi Yulgok), vol. 1, 197, quoted in Edward Y. J. Chung, *The Korean Neo-Confucianism of Yi T'oegye and Yi Yulgok* (Albany: State University of New York Press, 1995) 112. Italics are mine.

68. An Pyŏng-ju, "Yi I (Yulgok) and His Thought" in *Main Currents of Korean Thought,* ed. The Korean National Commission for UNESCO (Seoul: The Si-sa-yong-o-sa Publisher, 1983) 106–7.

69. Yi Yulgok, *Yulgok chŏnsŏ* (Complete Works of Yi Yulgok), vol. 1, 308, quoted in Edward Y. J. Chung, *The Korean Neo-Confucianism of Yi T'oegye and Yi Yulgok* (Albany: State University of New York Press, 1995) 113.

70. Ibid., 114.

Kaibara Ekken (CE 1630–1714)

Neo-Confucianism passed from China to Korea and then to Japan. Kaibara Ekken (1630–1714), one of the leading Neo-Confucian scholars, was born in 1630 during the Tokugawa era (1600–1863). Ekken's birthplace was Fukuoka in northern Kyushu, and he grew up in a lower-ranking samurai family. The local provincial government (*han*) sent him to Kyoto for further education. As a consequence, he was hired by the provincial lord (*daimyo*) as a government adviser. This employment helped his scholarly life tremendously because he was relatively free from financial burden. Another huge factor that helped his scholarship was the peaceful time provided by the unification of the country under the Tokukawa era. Moreover, he received invaluable assistance and support from his wife.[71]

Ekken spent 7 years in Kyoto, the intellectual capital of his time. There, he studied various subjects and met many leading Confucian scholars of Japan, such as Kinoshita Jun'an (1621–1698), Yamazaki Ansai (1618–1682), and Ito Jinsai (1627–1705). Throughout his life time, Ekken maintained contact with these scholars in Kyoto. On various occasions, he also traveled to Edo (Tokyo), the political capital, where he met Hayashi Gaho (1618–1680), a great Confucian scholar and government advisor.[72]

From time to time, Ekken visited the port city of Nagasaki in Kyushu in order to purchase Chinese and Western books. At age twenty-one, in Nagasaki he procured the pivotal work of Chu Hsi, *Reflections on Things at Hand (Jinsilu)*. Several years after his procurement of the book, Ekken wrote the first Japanese commentary on Chu's work. Ekken's work was entitled *Notes on Reflections on Things at Hand (Kinshiroku biko)*, which marked a key moment of Neo-Confucianism in Japan. Ekken's *Notes on Reflections* signaled his life-time appreciation for Chu Hsi's Neo-Confucian synthesis.[73]

Ekken's life-time preoccupation with Chu caused him to introduce Neo-Confucian ideology and ethics into the Japanese culture in the 17th century. Although Ekken possessed a lifelong appreciation for Chu's work, his later work *Record of Great Doubts (Taigiroku)* illustrated both

71. Mary Evelyn Tucker, *The Philosophy of Ch'i* (New York: Columbia University Press, 2007) 1.

72. Ibid., 2.

73. Ibid.

his affirmation and dissent.[74] Ekken was a monist of *ch'i*, whereas Chu Hsi was known as a complicated dualist of *li* and *ch'i*.

Ekken Identified the Supreme Ultimate (T'ai-chi) with Ch'i

Ekken identifies the Supreme Ultimate (*T'ai-chi* 太極) with *ch'i*. As we have seen before, Chu Hsi identified the Supreme Ultimate with *li* (Principle), and Chu spoke of the two worlds. For Chu Hsi, the world of "above shape" (or "above form") was constitutive of *li*, whereas the world of "within shape" (or "below form") was constitutive of *ch'i*. *Li* was also synonymous with the Tao. Against this dualistic view of Chu's universe, Ekken calls for a single, unified universe. All things such as spirit and matter are unified in *ch'i*. Ekken argues that yin and yang do not have any physical substance, so they cannot belong to what is "below form." In fact, they belong to what is "above form." To put it in another way, Ekken opposes the bifurcation of *li* and *ch'i*. Regarding the bifurcation, Ekken remarks:

> The Cheng Brothers explained that yin and yang also were below form, and Zhu Xi's Original Meaning of the Classic of Changes followed this interpretation. There is constancy and transformation in the operations of yin and yang. Constancy refers to what is genuine and correct in the operation; this is deemed the Way. Transformation refers to mishaps and biases in the operations; we cannot regard it as the Way. *The Cheng brothers and Zhu Xi considered yin and yang to be below form, but this is dividing yin and yang and the Way into two. They also separated principle and material force.* They explained it by contrasting the Way as principle and yin as concrete things. . . . Yin and yang have no [physical] substance, so we can't call them concrete things. This is the second point of disagreement.[75]

Ekken's unified universe became possible due to his concept of *ch'i*. For him, *T'ai-chi is ch'i in a state of chaos* ("primal chi") before its separation into yin and yang. Moreover, yin and yang do not belong to "what is below form (or shape)"; rather, they belong to "what is above form" (C. *hsing erh shang* 形而上). Yin and yang via alteration bring forth the myriad things of the concrete world. Regarding the relation between

74. Ibid., 3.

75. Kaibara Ekken, *The Philosophy of Ch'i: The Record of Great Doubts*, trans. Mary Evelyn Tucker (New York: Columbia University Press, 2007) 124.

T'ai-chi and ch'i, Ekken states, "In my view, the Supreme Ultimate is the name applicable to the material force [ch'i] in the state of chaos existing before yin and yang separated and the myriad of things emerged."[76]

Defending the Metaphysical Nature of Ch'i

By defending the metaphysical nature of ch'i, Ekken gives a rebuff to the idea that Wu-chi (無極) is the origin of all existing things. (This idea was promulgated by Chou Tun-yi, and even Chu Hsi endorsed a close relationship between T'ai-chi and Wu-chi.) Ekken believes that this idea of Wu-chi is derived from Buddhism and Taoism, but not rooted in Confucianism: "To regard nothingness [Wu-chi] as the origin and fundamental spirit of all things is a Buddhist and Daoist idea. To regard existence as the origin and essence of all things is the teaching of the sages."[77] Here, Ekken alludes to chapter 40 of the Tao Te Ching which states, "All things are born of being. Being is born of non-being" (C. 有生於無). Against this Daoistic and Buddhistic idea of non-being as the origin, Ekken taught monism of ch'i as the metaphysical nature.

Ekken believed that the term Wu-chi originates from Taoism, not from Confucianism. More specifically, it is rooted in the teaching of Laozi that non-being precedes existence. The Confucian sages never endorsed this teaching. That is why Chou Tun-yi in his later years never used the term, although in his early years employed the term in the Commentary on the Diagram of the Supreme Ultimate. In the later years of his life, Chou recognized the Taoistic origin of Wu-chi, so he retracted his teaching on Wu-chi. With respect to this point, Ekken writes, "Even if Zhou [Chou] actually made the Diagram of the Supreme Ultimate in his early years, in his later years he never mentioned the nonfinite [Wu-chi], and after he progressed in learning, it is clear that he no longer considered his earlier position correct."[78] According to Ekken, Chu Hsi also made a mistake of using the term Wu-chi without being aware of the Taoistic origin of the term.

Ekken also opposed Chu Hsi's teaching that there was li before Heaven and Earth and that there was nothing except for li. Ekken could not believe that Chu Hsi, such an enlightened, wise person, could teach

76. Ibid., 127.

77. Ibid., 128. Italics are mine.

78. Ibid., 129.

that kind of false idea. For Ekken, Chu Hsi's teaching on *Wu-chi* and the precedence of non-being resembles more of the teaching of Laozi than the teaching of the Confucian sages.[79]

Still, there are many questions that remain open regarding the nature of *Wu-chi*. Does it refer to "nothingness" or "emptiness"? Or does it only appear empty and nothing because it consists of invisible or spiritual entities? Or does it appear empty because it is not yet reified or differentiated enough? Although Ekken construes *Wu-chi* as nothingness and emptiness, Chu Hsi's concept of *Wu-chi* cannot be equated with nothingness and emptiness. However, Ekken is right in that the teaching of *Wu-chi* as the origin of all exiting things can engender quietism and even escapism due to a faulty assumption that reality is nothing but illusion.

Conclusion

While chapter two analyzed the most foundational work in East Asian culture, chapter three has chosen some of the most influential sages and explicated their thoughts with a special attention to their concepts of *ch'i*. All the six sages construed the relation between *li* and *ch'i* in their own way. Dualists such as Chu Hsi and Yi T'oegye more or less tended to separate *li* and *ch'i*, whereas monists such as Chang Tsai and Kaibara Ekken spoke of the monism of *ch'i*. Chang Tsai avers that the Great Void (*T'ai-hsü*), a synonym of the Great Ultimate, is the original substance of *ch'i*. In an analogous way, Ekken tells of *ch'i* as the substance of the Great Ultimate (*T'ai-chi*). Yi Yulgok endeavors to synthesize the dualists and monists' view by endorsing the idea—*not one and not two*: One can neither mix the two into one nor separate the two.

If a person regards *T'ai-chi* (the Great Ultimate) as the Chinese counterpart to God (the Ultimate Reality) in Christianity, the Chinese debate regarding *li* and *ch'i* in relation to *T'ai-chi* becomes even more interesting. In the past, many Christians asked, "What is the essence of God?" Likewise, many Chinese sages have asked, "What is the essence (or substance) of *T'ai-chi* (or Tao)—their Ultimate Reality?" With respect to this inquiry, Chu Hsi and Yi Yulgok insisted that *T'ai-chi* consists of *li* (Principle), while Chang Tsai and Kaibara Ekken believed that *T'ai-chi* consists of *ch'i*. In accordance with Chu Hsi, some examples of *li* are

79. Ibid., 132.

benevolence (loving kindness), righteousness, propriety, and wisdom. A similar debate is taking place in Christianity to-date: "Is love (*li*) or Spirit (ch'i) the essence of God?" Although some might conclude both, I lean more towards the view that the essence of God or *T'ai-chi* is Spirit/*ch'i*.

4

Pneumatologies of Pannenberg and Barth
with a Chiological Response

Introduction

IN THIS CHAPTER I WILL EXPOUND THE PNEUMATOLOGIES OF WOLFHART
Pannenberg and Karl Barth. I will also offer a critique of their pneumatologies from a chiological perspective. Both Pannenberg and Barth
agree with the notion that the eternal essence of God is revealed in the
economy of salvation, and the essence of God is Spirit. Interestingly, the
I Ching also regards the essence of *I* (Change) and *Tao* as *ch'i*, which is
the Chinese counterpart to the English word *Spirit*. In view of the source
or "origin of the intratrinitarian relation" and creation, Barth deciphers
God the Father as the source, whereas Pannenberg underscores the trinitarian origin of creation. On the contrary, a chiological approach on the
basis of the *I Ching* will regard *ch'i* as the source of all creation. In terms
of the relationship between the immanent trinity and the economic
trinity, Pannenberg and Barth accede to the notion that the trinitarian
relation in revelation corresponds to the eternal identity of the trinitarian God with some qualification. In this sense, for both Pannenberg and
Barth, the eternal essence of God stays accessible to human beings. On
the contrary, the chiological approach based on the *I Ching* repudiates
the accessibility of the very essence of *ch'i* itself and Tao to humans because the essence of *ch'i* and Tao (whose equivalent term in English is
"God") remains inscrutable.

A Brief Biographical Sketch of Pannenberg and Barth

No other theologians in the twentieth century have been more influential than Karl Barth and Wolfhart Pannenberg. Pope Pius XII once described Barth as the greatest theologian since Thomas Aquinas. Karl Barth was born in Basel, Switzerland, on May 10, 1886, and he died in 1968. Three years after the birth of Barth, the whole family moved to Bern because his father, Fritz, had accepted the position to teach at the University of Bern, where he taught church history and New Testament. Fritz Barth advocated a moderate form of conservative Protestantism that was known as "positive theology."[1]

In Bern, Karl Barth received most of his early education, and on the eve of his confirmation, he decided to become a theologian. Later in his life, Barth in different German universities studied under Adolf von Harnack, Adolf Schlatter, and Wilhelm Herrmann. Barth's commentary on Romans, *Der Römerbrief* (1922)[2] shocked so many scholars at that time that it became "a bombshell on the playground of the theologians."[3] Standing on the line of Athanasius, Augustine, and Calvin, Barth called back to the Bible and to its foundation in Jesus Christ, and he opposed any kind of natural theology. For Barth, there is a huge gap between God and humanity, and that gap can be bridged by God alone. This gap has been connected by revelation in Jesus Christ. In 1932, Barth started to write his masterpiece, *Church Dogmatics,* albeit it was never completed. These thirteen volumes became as important as Aquinas' *Summa Theologica.* Thus, some people think that Karl Barth is the greatest theologian in human history.

Two generations later than Barth, in 1928, another great theologian by the name of Wolfhart Pannenberg was born in Stettin, Poland. He has taught at the University of Munich for the last forty years. He once was a great admirer of Karl Barth, studying under him for a term in Basel. However, he was dissatisfied by the lack of philosophical rigor

---

1. John Franke, *Barth for Armchair Theologians* (Louisville: Westminster John Knox, 2006) 1–2.

2. There are two different versions of *Der Römerbrief:* (1) the first edition in 1919, and (2) the second edition in 1922. Mainly through the second edition, Barth became known to the English-speaking world. For this insight, see Paul Chung, *Karl Barth: God's Word in Action* (Eugene: Cascade, 2008) 114–61.

3. Ed. Miller and Stanley Grenz, *Fortress Introduction to Contemporary Theologies* (Minneapolis: Fortress, 1998) 4.

in Barth's thought.[4] He was known for his eschatological approach in his theology. In his renowned book, *Jesus—God and Man,* Pannenberg viewed the resurrection of Jesus Christ as a historical fact. Also, due to this book, he became known for his "Christology from below." Unlike many other German theologians who understand "history" in many different ways including *Geschichte* and *Heilsgeschichte,* Pannenberg, generally speaking, holds the view that there is *a* history, and the Holy Spirit is immanent in this history.[5] More and more people have become his followers. As a result, his fame as a theologian has grown increasingly through the years.

Even though analyzing the profound pneumatologies of Pannenberg and Barth, especially Pannenberg's, has been a laborious task, I truly enjoyed writing this chapter. I have always had a great interest in this field of pneumatology since my college years. To grasp the pneumatologies of these two theologians, I felt it necessary to begin with the trinity. Without the right understandings of the trinity, the right understandings of the Holy Spirit seemed unimaginable. Accordingly, I was obligated to write a little about the trinity in order to write about pneumatology. The reverse statement stays also true. For both Barth and Pannenberg, the role of the Spirit occupies a pivotal place, so one needs to clarify the work of the Spirit in order to understand the trinity. Barth mainly understands the Spirit as well as the trinity in the context of revelation. It is the Spirit who enables us to hear the gospel in Jesus Christ. Without the Spirit's help, no one can decipher the Word of God, the objective side of revelation.

With respect to the *filioque* controversy and understanding of the 'three persons' in the triunity, Barth favors and defends the view of the Latin West. On the other hand, Pannenberg's view on these issues stay strangely more Eastern, and he often defends the single procession of the Holy Spirit and three different 'personhoods' in God, which resembles more of the Eastern view.

---

4. Wolfhart Pannenberg, "An Autobiographical Sketch," in *The Theology of Wolfhart Pannenberg,* ed. Carl E. Braaten (Minneapolis: Augsburg, 1988) 14.

5. Timothy Bradshaw, *Trinity and Ontology* (Edinburgh: Rutherford House, 1988) 163.

Wolfhart Pannenberg's Pneumatology

Pannenberg's Objection to the Traditional "Relation of Origin"

Pannenberg rejects the traditional theory of "relation of origin" which underlines the one way flow of deity. The Father is the fount of the source: The Father begets the Son; the Son is begotten of the Father. The Father and the Son breathe forth the Spirit; the Spirit proceeds from the Father and the Son (the *filioque*). This traditional understanding of deity in the Latin West runs in only one way. Accordingly, it creates the picture that the Father is the main source of the trinity. According to this traditional picture, somehow the other two persons, the Son and the Holy Spirit, are undermined. Both the Son and Spirit are relying heavily on the Father, yet the Father, as the origin of the other two persons, dominates them. In other words, this traditional view of the West is in danger of becoming subordinationism.

> Tradition has it that the Father alone is without origin (*anarchos*) among the three persons of the Trinity, that he is the origin and fount of deity for the Son and Spirit. In the order of the trinitarian persons he thus comes first. He alone, then, is in every respect God of himself (*a seipso*). This view seems to rule out genuine mutuality in the relations of the trinitarian persons, since it has the order of origin running irreversibly from Father to Son and Spirit.[6]

To some degree, one can say that the Arians rightly saw the problem of the early church model of the trinity even though they did not succeed in resolving the puzzle. The main problematic tenet of the trinity of the early church was "relations of origin," which created the tendency of subordinationism. If the Son is begotten from the Father, the son's deity is based on the Father. In other words, the Son's origin is the Father. Pannenberg states, "Indeed, the Arians had postulated that the Father alone is ingenerate and that he alone is thus God in the fullest sense, the origin of all else but in no need of any origin himself."[7] Therefore, the Son is simply subordinate to the Father. In my opinion, the Arians at least clearly identified the precise problem of this early church's trinity. With reference to this problematic trinitarian understanding, Pannenberg

---

6. Wolfhart Pannenberg, *Systematic Theology*, trans. Geoffrey Bromiley (Grand Rapids: Eerdmans, 1991) 1:312.

7. Ibid., 279.

suggests that a mutual dependence among the trinitarian persons needs to be added to resolve this dilemma.

Without emphasis on the mutual dependence, no other understanding of the trinity can draw a satisfactory answer. A good example is Athanasius' attempt. In his letters to *Serapion*, Athanasius argues that the term 'Father' cannot be understood as it is understood among human beings. Writing the letters against the Tropici, a sect of Arianism, Athanasius insists that both the Son and the Spirit are not creatures. The Tropici bring two main charges against Athanasius: First, the Spirit is a creature. Second, the Spirit is only different from the angels in degree, not in nature. Against these attacks, Athanasius claims over and over in his letters that God is not like a human person. Therefore, the terms "Father" and "Son" in the Triad should not be understood as they are used to describe filial relations. God does not have a genealogy: God as the Father, Jesus as the Son, and the Holy Spirit as the grandson. God cannot be treated like a human person. Furthermore, Athanasius insists this terminology is only employed to reveal Godself to human beings. Therefore, God's true essence does not have these relations.[8]

This understanding of Athanasius was good enough to defend the deity of the Son and the Spirit, but it did not explain how the three hypostases in the Godhead interact with each other. One step further, by separating the immanent trinity from the economic trinity, he insisted that the real essence of God was completely unknowable.

Walter Kasper also follows this traditional view of the relation of origin which sees only the one-way flow of giving without receiving. In contrast to Pannenberg's stance, Kasper's understanding of the trinity has no mutual dependency on one another. Kasper writes:

> In the Father, love exists as pure source that pours itself out; in the Son it exists as a pure passing-on, as pure mediation; in the Spirit it exists as the joy of pure receiving. These three modes in which the one being of God, the one love, subsists, are in some sense necessary because love cannot be otherwise conceived.[9]

---

8. See Athanasius, *The Letters of Saint Athanasius* trans. C. R. B. Shapland (London: Epworth, 1951). Generally, it has been accepted that four different letters were written by St. Athanasius regarding the deity of the Holy Spirit.

9. Walter Kasper, *The God of Jesus Christ*, trans. Matthew J. O'Connell (New York: Crossroad, 1984) 309.

This understanding of Kasper is heading towards the direction which Pannenberg attacks as a reappearing form of the early subordinationism. In order to avoid this form of subordinationism, one somehow has to underscore that even the Father needs an obedient response from the Son and Spirit. Without that mutual dependence, Kasper's model of the trinity also falls into the pitfall of subordinationism.

Seeing the problems of this traditional view, which saw only one-way flow of deity, Pannenberg emphasizes the importance of the 'reciprocity' in understanding the intra-trinitarian relations.

> In the handing over of lordship from the Father to the Son, and its handing back from the Son to the Father, we see a mutuality in their relationship that we do not see in the begetting. By handing over lordship to the Son the Father makes his kingship dependent on whether the Son glorifies him and fulfils his lordship by fulfilling his mission.[10]

The Father does not just beget the Son, and the Son, without its own freedom, does not just execute God's commands. The Father hands over all things to the Son, so that "his kingdom and his own deity are now dependent upon the Son."[11] However, in obedience, the Son hands back lordship to the Father. According to Pannenberg, the Son's obedience is most clearly shown by his death on the cross, and the Son's deity is reaffirmed by the resurrection done by the Father through the Holy Spirit. Thus, there is a mutual dependency between the Father and the Son, and mutuality of relations exists between them. Thus, the intra-trinitarian relations are reciprocal.

In my opinion, one has to give some credit to Pannenberg's innovative concept of mutual dependence in the understanding of the intra-trinitarian relations. Unlike the traditional understandings of "relations of origin," Pannenberg alleges that somehow the Son and Spirit must be active over against the Father. The Son is not just begotten, but he is also active in obeying and glorifying the Father. The Spirit is not just breathed in a passive sense, but it also glorifies the Son and the Father.[12] The Father is not simply the origin of the other two trinitarian persons; instead, in the intra-trinitarian relation, all three persons' deities rely on another

---

10. Ibid., 313.

11. Ibid.

12. Carl Braaten, ed., *The Theology of Wolfhart Pannenberg* (Minneapolis: Augsburg, 1988) 200.

person's active participation. Therefore, the Father's full deity is at stake without the active obedience of the Son. By the same token, the Son's deity is at stake without the Spirit's glorification of the Son.[13] The Father is not only an active person in these relations, but the other two hypostases stay also active as an independent person.

Furthermore, the Father can only find his selfhood in his relation to the Son and the Spirit. The Father cannot be the Father without the Son. Likewise, the Son cannot be the Son without the Father. The Father and the Son cannot have an intimate fellowship without the Spirit of love, who also unites the Father and the Son. Likewise, the Spirit of love cannot possess its distinctiveness and selfhood without the Father and the Son. Thus, each hypostasis finds its distinctiveness and selfhood in these relations. Even the distinctiveness of each hypostasis can only exist in his relation to the other hypostases.

> Each of the three persons is ec-statically related to one or both of the others and has its personal distinctiveness or selfhood in this relation. The Father is the Father in relation to the Son, in the generation and sending of the Son. The Son is the Son only in obedience. . . . The Spirit exists hypostatically as Spirit only as he glorifies the Father in the Son and the Son as sent by the Father.[14]

The Roles of the Spirit

> The raising of Jesus from the dead was one of the primary works of the Holy Spirit.
> The event of the crucifixion of Jesus does not merely bring the deity of the Father as well as the Son into question. It refers both to the work of the Spirit, who as the creator of all life raises Jesus from the dead. In a pre-Pauline formula the resurrection is the work of the Spirit (Rom. 1:4; 1 Tim. 3:16b). . . . It may thus be said that primarily the Spirit figures as the one who raises up Jesus from the dead.[15]

For Pannenberg, not only is the life of Jesus restored by the Spirit, but all other creatures' lives also come from the Spirit, who is the creative origin of all life.

---

13. Pannenberg, *Systematic Theology*, 1:315.

14. Ibid., 428.

15. Ibid., 314–15.

Another important role of the Spirit according to Pannenberg is that the Spirit reveals the deity of Jesus by glorifying the Son. "He [the Spirit] will glorify me, for He will take of what is mine and declare it to you" (John 16:14). Pannenberg writes:

> This fact emerges even more clearly in the Johannine statements about the glorifying of the Son by the Spirit. As the Son glorifies the Father on earth, making manifest his deity (John 17:4), so the Spirit will glorify the Son (16:14). The prayer of Jesus to the Father that the Father will glorify him is thus answered by the sending and work of the Spirit.[16]

Furthermore, the Spirit completes the revelation in Jesus Christ. The Spirit manifests the messiahship of Jesus. Since no one can know the Son without the Spirit, Pannenberg concludes that no human can know the Father without the Spirit.[17] John 14:6 states, "I [Jesus] am the way and the truth and the life. No one comes to the Father except through me." Thus, ultimately no one can know the Father without the Spirit as one cannot know the Father without the Son. The Spirit discloses the revelation in Jesus Christ.

The Spirit, as the medium of fellowship, enables the believers to participate in the fellowship with God. The believers' fellowship with the Son is not thinkable without the medium of the fellowship, namely, the Holy Spirit. Therefore Pannenberg writes, "Only on this basis may the imparting of the Spirit to believers be seen as their incorporation into the fellowship of the Son with the Father."[18]

Barth also agrees with this point that the Holy Spirit is the condition of our fellowship with God. "The Holy Spirit is the bond of union between God and humanity in Jesus Christ and between Christ and humanity and these unions in turn reflect how God is in himself [Godself]."[19] As the bond and communion of divine life, the Holy Spirit also brings out the fellowship between God and humanity.

There is another distinct role of the Holy Spirit in Pannenberg's understanding of the intra-trinitarian relations: the Spirit as the love connecting the Father and the Son. This is the unique role of the Spirit.

---

16. Ibid., 315.

17. Ibid.

18. Ibid., 316.

19. John Thompson, *The Holy Spirit in the Theology of Karl Barth* (Allison Park, PA: Pickwick, 1991) 27.

Both the Father and the Son are sometimes construed as the object of the other person's love, but the Spirit has never been described as the object of the love of the Father or the Son. Instead the Holy Spirit is the love uniting the Father and the Son together. Pannenberg writes, "We can understand this if the Spirit is the love by which the Father and the Son are mutually related even if as a hypostasis he stands over against both as the Spirit of love who unites them in their distinction."[20]

For Pannenberg, the Spirit is also the medium and condition of the fellowship of the Father and the Son, so the Spirit has a place in the eternal fellowship.[21] Thus, theoretically, without the Spirit, the eternal fellowship does not take place. In this regard, Pannenberg agrees even with St. Augustine who described the Spirit as the bond of union between the Father and the Son, yet Pannenberg disagrees with Augustine's view of the *filioque* and his understanding of intra-trinitarian relations in the vocabulary of "relations of origin." Nevertheless, both Pannenberg and Augustine agreed with the fact that the Spirit was the medium of the fellowship.

It seems that Kasper also senses that it has to be the Spirit if there is one hypostasis who is able to do this connecting job. No biblical tradition understands that the Father or the Son does this connecting work. Thus, one naturally looks at the third hypostasis, the Holy Spirit. Even though Kasper knew that it had to be the Holy Spirit who unites the Father and the Son, he does not go any further than that. Kasper does not explain how the Spirit works in connecting the Father and the Son. Thus, in my opinion, Kasper never fully develops the role of the Holy Spirit in his trinitarian understanding. But Kasper knew that it had to be the Spirit who unites the Father and the Son. Kasper writes:

> This unity of the faithful among themselves as well as with the Father and the Son is the work of the Spirit, according to John as well as the rest of the New Testament. The connection is clearly brought out in John 14:15–24.[22]

Kasper insists that more than one mode is necessary because love cannot be otherwise conceived.[23] Accordingly, it is understandable why

20. Ibid., 429.

21. Ibid., 316.

22. Kasper, *God of Jesus Christ*, 305.

23. Ibid., 309.

the role of the Son is significant. Kasper insists that "the Father as pure self-giving cannot exist without the Son who receives."[24] With the Son, the recipient of love exists. Then, why is the Holy Spirit as a third "mode" necessary? Kasper never comes out with any convincing reason for the necessity of the third person. In fact, in my opinion, this led Kasper to take the role of the Holy Spirit less significantly in comparison with the other two modes: the Father and the Son. Kasper remarks:

> Finally, in the Spirit the faithful receive the gift of the Father through the Son, so that they may share in this gift. *The Spirit is nothing by himself*; he is a pure receiving, pure donation and gift; as such he is pure fulfillment, eternal joy and blessedness, pure endless completion.[25]

This is such a weak view of the Holy Spirit; the Spirit simply just receives without any means of returning to God. Thus, the Spirit is simply relying on the giver, the Father, who is the origin of love. This view of Kasper creates the impression that the Father is superior to the Sprit since the Father as the origin simply gives. Accordingly, this creates an impression that the Father can exist without the Holy Spirit; on the other hand, the Holy Spirit cannot exist without its origin and source. Therefore the Spirit depends on the Father, but the Father does not depend on the Spirit. That is why Pannenberg stands against this one-way flow of relations, and he endorses the mutual dependency of three persons in the trinity.

For Pannenberg, "the Spirit is the love."[26] This Spirit and love, which is the only essence of God, constitute the common essence of deity; on the other hand, they come from the Holy Spirit. This is somewhat confusing, but basically, Pannenberg is saying that the Spirit is the common essence of the Godhead. However, the Spirit can be understood as an independent hypostasis over against the Son and the Father. Thus, Pannenberg states, "The essence of the Godhead is indeed Spirit."[27]

This Spirit is also a dynamic field:

> It is Spirit as a dynamic field, and as its manifestation in the coming forth of the Son shows itself to be the work of the Father, the

24. Ibid.
25. Ibid., 308.
26. Pannenberg, *Systematic Theology*, 1:429.
27. Ibid., 429.

dynamic of the Spirit radiates from the Father, but in such a way that the Son receives it as gift, and it fills him and radiates back from him to the Father.[28]

By utilizing the field theory of modern physics (especially Michael Faraday), Pannenberg uniquely depicts the Holy Spirit as a force field.[29] Faraday construes bodies as forms of forces that are not qualities of body; rather, these forms of forces are independent realities. Moreover, he regarded these forces as fields which occupy space.[30]

Pannenberg sees a parallel between the field theory and the biblical definition of *ruach* and *pneuma*. Actually, the idea of the force field goes back to Stoicism before Socratic philosophy. During this period, Anaximenes inculcated that "air" was the *archē* and that all things came to exist by means of compressions of air.[31] According to Max Jammer, the stoic view of the divine *pneuma* exemplified a precursor of the modern field concept. Stoics taught that the *pneuma* consists of the very fine stuff that interpenetrated all things. This view influenced both Philo and early Christians. Fewer contacts were made between Stoic philosophy and theology of the later church fathers, especially after Origen who robustly criticized the material nature of the *pneuma* in the Stoic doctrine. At the end, Pannenberg sees a convergence between the field theory of modern physics and the Christian doctrine of the dynamic work of the Holy Spirit.[32]

It is this Spirit, as a dynamic field and love that unites the Father and the Son. When this Spirit is understood over against the other hypostases, one can understand this Spirit of love as a hypostasis. At any rate, it is this Spirit which unites the Father and the Son, and it is also the medium of the fellowship. Thus, the Spirit as the love creates the unity in the Trinity.

---

28. Ibid.

29. For a good summary of Pannenberg's view of the Spirit as the force field, see Veli-Matti Kärkkäinen, *Pneumatology: The Holy Spirit in Ecumenical, International, and Contextual Perspective* (Grand Rapids: Baker Academic, 2002) 119–20.

30. Pannenberg, *Systematic Theology,* 2:80.

31. See chapter 3 of this book below. Most Chinese in the fourth century believed that the universe is made up with *ch'i*, which can also be translated as "air." Through the condensation and rarefaction of *ch'i*, all creatures came to exist. The Japanese philosopher Kaibara Ekken underscores the material aspect of *ch'i*.

32. Ibid., 2:81–82.

The Filioque Controversy

One can say that the schism between the Latin West and the Greek East was caused by two main doctrinal reasons; of course, there were some cultural and political differences which encouraged the schism. The two main doctrinal issues were 1) the papal claims, and 2) the *filioque*. The conflict that existed between the East and the West became uncontrollable when the pope insisted an exclusive jurisdiction over territories beyond the traditional purview of the Roman See. Before the schism, the Greek granted the Roman bishop a primary place of honor, but they never acknowledged the pope's universal supremacy or the infallibility of the pope. Up until now, for the Greek Orthodox Church, the Catholic Church's authority does not lie in the pope's hand; rather, the ultimate authority of the church comes from the ecumenical councils.[33]

The second doctrinal issue which separated the East from the West has to do with the *filioque* controversy. The Creed of Nicea and Constantinople states, "I believe . . . in the Holy Spirit, the Lord, the Giver of Life, *who proceeds from the Father*, who with the Father and the Son together is worshipped and together glorified." However, the Latin West added one more phrase, "and from the Son" (in Latin, *filioque*). Accordingly, the West confessed the creed with the *filioque*, "who proceeds from the Father and the Son." We still do not know exactly why the Latin West added the *filioque*. At any rate, this *filioque* became a great dispute between the East and the West, and Photius from the East claimed that "the *filioque* was the very crown of evils, the product of a poorly educated West."[34] In the beginning of the eleventh century, Pope Leo IX sent Cardinal Humbert and two other legates to Constantinople, but Humbert did not like the patriarch of Constantinople, Cerularius. By losing his patience, Humbert laid the Bull of Excommunication against Cerularius. Humbert accused the Greeks for omitting the *filioque* from their creed. In return, Cerularious anathematized Humbert.[35] Since then, the East and West were never able to reconcile with each other. Therefore, the *filioque* controversy was one of the main doctrinal reasons which demarcated the Greek East from the Latin West.

---

33. Stanley M. Burgess, *The Holy Spirit: Eastern Christian Traditions* (Peabody: Hendrickson, 1984) 12–13.

34. Ibid., 13.

35. Ibid., 13–14.

Still many Eastern theologians insist that the addition of the *filioque* was uncanonical. They insist that the Holy Spirit proceeds from the Father through the Son; on the other hand, in the past, the West insisted that the Spirit proceeded from both the Father and the Son. The West added the *filioque* clause to the third article of the Creed of 381.

St. Augustine, who represented the theology of the West with regard to the *filioque*, also affirmed the *filioque*. He contended that the Spirit proceeded from both the Father and the Son because the Spirit was the Spirit *of* both the Father and the Son.

> I had taught them by testimonies of the Holy Scriptures that the Holy Spirit proceeds from both [the Father and the Son], I continue: "If, then, the Holy Spirit proceeds both from the Father and from the Son, why did the Son say, 'He proceedeth from the Father?'" Why, think you except as He is wont to refer to Him, that also is that which He saith, "My doctrine is not mine own, but His that sent me?" If, therefore, it is His doctrine that is here understood, which yet He said was not His own, but His that sent Him how much more is it there to be understood that the Holy Spirit proceeds also from Himself, where He so says, He proceedeth from the Father, as not to say, He proceedeth not from me? . . . and hence the Holy Spirit has from the Father Himself, that He should proceed from the Son also, as He proceeds from the Father.[36]

If Augustine were the spokesperson of the Latin Western tradition, Photius was the spokesperson of the Greek Eastern tradition with respect to the *filioque*. No one spent more time and energy in defending the single procession of the Spirit from the Eastern Christian tradition than Photius did. Known as the "Great Eastern Christian champion of the doctrine of the single procession of the Spirit,"[37] Photius received a solid education as a boy. Because of this great education, he was appointed to be a professor of philosophy at the "University of Constantinople." Partly due to his brother's connection with the emperor, he became the patriarch of Constantinople.[38]

In his letter of 883 CE to the metropolitan of Aqueilias and his well-known treatise, *On the Mystagogy of the Holy Spirit*, he defends the

---

36. St. Augustine, *On the Trinity*, xv.27.48, quoted in Stanly M. Burgess's, *The Spirit & the Church: Antiquity*, 183.

37. Burgess, *Holy Spirit: Eastern Christian Traditions*, 48.

38. Ibid., 48–49.

single procession of the Spirit. He shows a couple of grounds on which he builds his argument against the *filioque*. First, he avers that the word "of" cannot be replaced by the word "from." In many places in the Bible, the Spirit is described as the Spirit *of* Christ; however, Photius insists this does not mean that the Spirit proceeds from the Son.[39] Actually, this argument is geared toward St. Augustine who drew his doctrine by equating "of" with "from."

The second point Photius makes in defending the single procession of the Spirit lies in the fact that most church Fathers including the Western Christians affirmed the single procession. For instance, Pope Leo the Great, Pope Gregory the dialogist (590–604) and Pope Zacharias (741–52) affirmed the single procession. On the other hand, not many church Fathers such as Ambrose, Augustine, and Jerome alleged the use of the *filioque* in the creed. Photius insists that St. Augustine said this impious thing in reaction to heresies. Otherwise, he would never have said such an impious thing. Therefore, Photius thinks that the *filioque* needs to be removed from the creed.

Still some Western theologians try to hold the *filioque* clause. Barth tried to defend the *filioque* by opposing the Orthodox position.[40] Kasper also sympathizes with the use of the *filioque* clause in the creed, the view of the West.[41] On the other hand, Jürgen Moltmann, heavily influenced by Eastern thought, has been extremely critical about the *filioque* and prefers to omit the *filioque* from the Creed.[42]

Barth defends the *filioque* against the Eastern rejection of the double procession of the Spirit. He writes:

> For us the Eastern rejection of the *Filioque* is already suspect from the formal standpoint because it is patently a speculation which interprets individual verses of the Bible in isolation, because it bears no relation to the reality of God in revelation and forth.[43]

---

39 Ibid., 51.

40 Karl Barth, *Church Dogmatics,* trans. G. W. Bromiley (Edinburgh: T. & T. Clark, 1936) I/1:477–82.

41 Pannenberg, *Systematic Theology*, 1:318. See the footnotes.

42 Jürgen Moltmann, "Theological Proposals towards the Resolution of the *Filioque* Controversy, in Lukas Vischer, ed., *Spirit of God, Spirit of Christ: Ecumenical Reflections on the Filioque Controversy* (London: SPCK, 1981) 164ff.

43. Barth, *Church Dogmatics,* I/1:480.

This response from Barth is understandable because in the past the East used to quote John 15:26 to reject the *filioque*. Barth evinces a couple of reasons why he holds the *filioque*. First, in the scripture, the Spirit is described as the Spirit *of* both the Father and the Son, thus Barth draws the conclusion that the Spirit proceeds from both the Father and the Son. He makes the same jump which St. Augustine made to defend the *filioque*. Barth writes:

> Even supporters of the Eastern view do not contest the fact that in the *opus ad extra*, and therefore in revelation (and then retrospectively in creation), the Holy Spirit is to be understood as the Spirit of both the Father and the Son.[44]

Since the Spirit is the Spirit of the Father and the Son, the Spirit proceeds from both the Father and the Son. Barth uses this logic to prove his point, but I think this argument is very weak because the word "of" is totally different from the phrase "proceed from." In the Bible, the Spirit is also the Spirit of "many other things" such as "the Spirit of love." Therefore, Barth's argument is not convincing.

The second argument for defending the *filioque* is that it is better to phrase the Spirit proceeds from the Father and the Son because the Son has all that the Father is and has. Barth states, "This Son of this Father is and has all that His Father is and has."[45] Thus, to some degree, the East and the West are saying the same thing with different phrases. However, the *filioque* clause was necessary according to Barth to fight against other heretics like the Macedonians who denied the deity of the Spirit. Barth postulates that no matter how one phrases it, we know that the Spirit is from one essence. *Ex Patre Filioque* does not refer to two different origins.

> With this explanation and proof, however, we have already said the final thing that has always been said, and must necessarily be said, in explanation of the Western view, namely, that the ex *Patre Filioque* denotes, not a twofold, but rather a common origin of the Spirit from the Father and the Son.[46]

I think Barth's argument hints at subordinationism, even though Barth concedes that he does not know exactly what the word "procession"

44. Ibid., 479.
45. Ibid., 484.
46. Ibid., 486.

means because it is a mystery. According to him, human beings cannot define God; instead, we can only define creatures. In this regard, no human can fully exhaust the mystery of the trinity. Still, Barth falls into the pitfall of subordinationism because he insists that the Spirit proceeds from one essence or origin. Therefore, Barth's second argument is also very problematic.

Thirdly, Barth claims that the Eastern rejection of the *filioque* undermines the fellowship and the unity of the trinity. According to Barth, "procession from the Father and the Son" exhibits the mutual fellowship within the trinity. If one discards the *filioque* clause, there are only two "modes" of being, but the Son is missing. Thus, this confession of the Nicene Creed also affirms the fellowship within the trinity. Furthermore, this *filioque* affirms the important role of the Spirit who unites the Father and the Son. On the other hand, if one rejects the *filioque* from the Creed, one cannot confirm this significant role of the Holy Spirit. The Spirit as love unites the Father and the Son; indirectly the *filioque* clause is reaffirming the unity of the Trinity.

> Finally and above all, the Spirit on this view [the view of the Eastern Orthodoxy] loses His mediating position between the Father and Son, and the Father and the Son lose their mutual connection in the Spirit.[47]

Pannenberg's Rejection of the Filioque

In answering Barth, Pannenberg will say the same words which he said against the early church Fathers, that is, "You understand the immanent trinity as relations of origin." These relations of origin can be found easily in Barth's writings:

> Thus the one Godness of the Father and Son is, or the Father and the Son in their one Godness are, the origin of the Spirit.[48]

> The Son is the first in God and the Spirit is the second in God, that is as God is the Father of the Son, and, as Father, begets the Son, He also brings forth the Spirit and therefore the negation of isolation, the law and the reality of love.[49]

---

47. Ibid., 482.

48. Ibid., 487.

49. Ibid., 483.

Again, Pannenberg will ask Barth, "If the origin of the Spirit is this 'Godness' and the origin of the Son is the Father, where is the origin of the Father?" Thus, Pannenberg concludes that this argument for the *filioque* is inappropriate and missing the mark. Pannenberg rejects the *filioque* clause not because John 15:26 states that the Spirit proceeds from the Father. Often this verse was adduced by the Eastern Orthodox Church to criticize the *filioque* that the West added to the Nicene Creed. The main reason for disagreeing with the *filioque* lies in the fact that the Son himself received the Spirit while Jesus was baptized. Then how can the Spirit proceed from the Son? According to Pannenberg, the Spirit proceeds from the Father and is received by the Son. It was not just the human nature of Jesus who received the Spirit when Jesus was baptized by John the Baptist; the person Jesus received the Spirit. This does not deny the fact that the Son gives the Spirit to his people. The Father sends the Spirit at the request of the Son. Believers share the sonship of Jesus by receiving the Spirit.[50] Therefore, Pannenberg thinks that it is better to withdraw the *filioque* clause from the Nicene Creed.

With reference to the *filioque*, Pannenberg inculcates that the West, including St. Augustine, made a great mistake. They saw the fellowship within the trinity in the vocabulary of "relation of origin." This defect is also common to the traditional theology in the East. The East also saw the relationship among the Father, Son, and Spirit as the relation of origin.[51] Therefore, both sides made a big mistake in this battle by starting with a wrong framework of their trinitarian theology, namely, the intra-trinitarian relations as the relation of origin.

Karl Barth's Pneumatology

Barth's Elucidation of the Trinity in Revelation

It is important to notice that Barth discusses the doctrine of the trinity under the umbrella of the revelation of God. In other words, Barth mainly explicates the trinity in the context of revelation. Thus, the right understanding of the trinity necessitates the right understanding of revelation. In Barth's theology, "revelation" means "God's coming, acting and speaking as the triune Lord, making himself known in Jesus Christ

50. Pannenberg, *Systematic Theology*, 1:317–18.
51. Ibid., 318.

as the fulfillment of Israel's history by the power of the Holy Spirit."[52] One of the main reasons why Barth locates the doctrine of the trinity in the section of revelation is that revelation itself is triune.[53]

What is the root of the doctrine of the trinity? Barth answers that the trinity is rooted in revelation taken from the Scriptures. Accordingly, it is rooted in the biblical revelation. Of course, nowhere in the Bible is it explicitly stated that God is triune, but one can draw out the concept of the trinity from the Bible. Once more, Barth emphasizes the importance of exegeses, but we cannot trust the exegesis of any person; rather, this has to be the church's exegesis. In biblical revelation, God reveals Godself in three different modes of being (*Seinsweisen*): 1) the Father, 2) the Son, and 3) the Spirit. In metaphysical terms, this revelation is also threefold: 1) the subject, 2) the object, and 3) the content of revelation. Some people argue that Barth's use of revelation originates from German idealism. It is likely that Barth, who received his theological education in Germany, was influenced by German idealism.

For Barth, God is the self-revealing God. God wants to reveal Godself; because of that characteristic of God, one can know the self-disclosing God. Barth states, "Revelation in the Bible means the self-unveiling, imparted to men, of the God who by nature cannot be unveiled to men."[54] A person can only know God when God reveals Godself.

The sinful human beings can never reach God, so human beings alone can never apprehend God unless God reveals Godself to us. Barth insists:

> If there really is, then it is in virtue of the acknowledgment which man cannot achieve and therefore cannot assert, but which comes by grace upon his work that is corrupt and dead through sin, for Christ's sake and not for the sake of his inner disposition.[55]

Human beings without the succor from God can do absolutely nothing to gain more knowledge about God. Human beings without God's succor can only come up with idols or false conceptions of deity. Hence,

---

52. Thompson, *Holy Spirit in the Theology of Karl Barth*, 53.

53. See Bruce McCormack, *Studies in the Theology of Karl Barth: Orthodox and Modern* (Grand Rapids: Baker Academic, 2008) 168. Here, McCormack ratifies my point.

54. Barth, *Church Dogmatics*, I/1:315.

55. Ibid., 220.

Barth strongly opposes natural theology because human reason is also corrupted.

Human beings are able to know God under two conditions: 1) the revelation in Jesus Christ, and 2) the illumination for the revelation by the Holy Spirit.[56] There are two dimensions of revelation: The first is the objective dimension, namely, God revealed Godself in Jesus Christ. The second is the illumination for this revelation by the Holy Spirit. Through the Holy Spirit in a person, one can appropriate and experience this revelation in one's life. So revelation comes from "above" and "below." Barth writes:

> It is God's reality in that God Himself becomes present to man not just externally [in Jesus Christ], not just from above, but also from within, from below, subjectively [by the Holy Spirit]. It is thus reality in that He does not merely come to man but encounters Himself from man. God's freedom to be present in this way to man, and therefore to bring about this encounter, is the Spirit of God, *the Holy Spirit* in God's revelation.[57]

For the sake of understanding Barth's definition of revelation, I can summarize in this way: Christian revelation has both objective and subjective dimensions. In Jesus Christ, the objective dimension of revelation has been accomplished, yet sin obscures this revelation in Jesus Christ. It is still up there in the air. It needs to be manifested to each human being. One needs to be open to this revelation in Jesus Christ. This manifestation to each person is the subjective dimension of revelation, and it is done by the Holy Spirit. Hence, one can say that due to the Holy Spirit in us, we can experience revelation. Again Barth writes:

> The Lord of the language is also the Lord of our listening to it. The Lord who gives the Word who gives faith, the Lord through those act the openness and readiness of man for the Word is true and real—is not another God, but the one God in this way—and that is the Holy Spirit.[58]

Philip Rosato also sees this subjective role of the Holy Spirit in us, and he writes, "The God who speaks His Word (the Father) and the God who is the Word spoken (the Son) must also be understood as the God

---

56. Thompson, *Holy Spirit in the Theology of Karl Barth*, 8–9.

57. Barth, *Church Dogmatics*, I/1:451.

58. Ibid., 48.

who makes the Word heard in man (the Holy Spirit)."[59] God leads a person to the point where he/she is open and ready to hear the Word. The God who speaks is the God who enables us to hear the Word. Regarding this subjective work of the Holy Spirit in us, both Thompson and Rosato agrees with each other.

In his famous and somewhat controversial book, *The Spirit as Lord*, Rosato avers that the Pneuma takes the central role in Barth's theology. Thus, Barth's theology is a pneuma-centric theology, and it should be interpreted pneuma-centrically. This is very different from most modern scholars' interpretations, which construe Barth's theology Christologically. John Thompson in his book, *The Holy Spirit in the Theology of Karl Barth*, insists that the Pneuma is important in Barth's theology, especially in revelation, but Barth's theology is not pneuma-centric. Thompson argues that Barth's theology is a Christocentric theology because we can know God only through revelation in Jesus Christ.

Unlike the early church Fathers, Barth prefers to use "mode of being" instead of "person" in explaining the distinctiveness of the trinity. He writes, "This distinction or order is the distinction or order of the three 'persons,' or as we prefer to say, the three 'modes (or ways) of being' in God."[60] The word *persona* lost its original meaning as "mask" in this modern world. Nowadays, we understand a "person" as an individual subject with a unique personality. Thus, this usage of the word "three persons" in the modern world is in danger of creating tritheism. For Barth, one God has only one personality, not three; however, if we use the word "person" as we understand it in the twentieth century, God in fact has three different personalities. With the use of the word "person" in our era, it is in the proximity of tritheism. Therefore, according to Barth we need a new terminology to understand the trinity correctly in this century without losing the definition which the early church Fathers employed,[61] so Barth uses this new phrase "mode of being" to explain the distinctiveness of God. This terminology can also be dangerous because its definition connotes modalism; one God appears in three different ways.

59. Philip J. Rosato, *The Spirit as Lord: The Pneumatology of Karl Barth* (Edinburgh: T. & T. Clark, 1981) 48.

60. Barth, *Church Dogmatics*, I/1:355.

61. Ibid., 355–58. In this extensive excursus, Barth explains how the word "person" has been used throughout human history.

> The statement that God is One in three ways of being, Father, Son and Holy Ghost, means, therefore, that the one God, i.e., the one Lord, the one personal God, is what He is not just in one mode but—we appeal in support simply to the result of our analysis of the biblical concept of revelation—in the mode of the Father, in the mode of the Son, and in the mode of the Holy Spirit.[62]

No one can fully grasp the trinity. For Barth, after all, the trinity is a mystery. John Thompson summarizes well in his statement, "Moreover, at one point he [Barth] can say that while the economic Trinity is intelligible to our conception, God in himself as Father, Son and Holy Spirit is beyond our understanding—essentially a mystery."[63] For Barth, maybe the economic trinity is intelligible to human conception with the help of the Spirit, but the *aseity* of God is unintelligible to human conception. Thus, it is a great mystery. Therefore, God is always God, and as human beings, we can never fully grasp the *aseity* of God. With this humble attitude, Barth approaches the trinitarian doctrine.

In my opinion, most human attempts to understand the trinity fall into either modalistic or tritheistic tendencies. It appears to me that Barth's paradigm falls into modalism. Barth does a wonderful job in explaining the unity of the trinity. This tendency is not just applied to Barth; over all, most Western theologians do well in explaining the unity of the trinity. On the other hand, they have many problems in explaining the "threeness" of the trinity. This is the undergirding problem of the Western understandings of the trinity. On the contrary, it seems that the Eastern Orthodox Church has the opposite problem, namely, it generally falls into tritheism. The Eastern Church has no problem in explaining the "threeness" of the trinity; on the other hand, by adopting a "tritheistic" model, Eastern theologians face a difficulty in explaining the "oneness" or unity of the trinity.

As a part of the mainline Western church tradition, Barth's model falls into a modalistic tendency. In order to avoid the danger of tritheism, Barth endorses a new terminology, "mode of being" instead of traditional usage of the word "person." By doing it, Barth was able to accomplish what he intended; on the other hand, now he is facing the danger of modalism. This terminology creates the impression that each hypostasis is simply a "mode" of one true God. In other words, there is this one real

---

62. Ibid., 359.

63. Thompson, *Holy Spirit in the Theology of Karl Barth*, 32.

God behind the scene, but this God has been expressed in three different modes. In metaphysical language, one can say that each hypostasis of the trinity is a form of a real substance.

The second example which shows Barth's modalistic understanding (more specifically "Sabellianism") can be found in his concept of "God's repetition in three different ways." Again, Barth writes:

> The name of Father, Son and Spirit means that God is the one God in threefold repetition, and this in such a way that the repetition itself is grounded in His Godhead, so that it implies no alteration in His Godhead, and yet in such a way also that He is the one God only in this *repetition*, so that His one Godhead stands or falls with the fact that He is God in this repetition, but for that very reason He is the one God in each repetition.[64]

Again, this gives me an understanding that one God repeats three times in three different modes.

Of course, Barth denies this accusation, but I do not see how he could avoid this modalistic tendency. God is three in one and one in three. He would therefore say it is a mystery. Of course, any Christian would say that. Still none of Barth's models can eschew this modalistic tendency.

Barth also belongs to the group who construes the intra-trinitarian relationship as the "relations of origin." Over and over, Barth emphasizes that there is only one divine essence of God. In this essence of God, the Son is from the Father; the Spirit is from the Father and the Son; the Father is from the Father Himself alone.[65] Each hypostasis relies on another hypostasis except for the Father. Thus, it creates an impression that the Father alone is superior and greater than the other two hypostases since they are from the Father. This view describes a one-way flow of deity. Immediately, Pannenberg would attack Barth by saying that this view is hierarchical and understands intra-trinitarian relations as "relations of origin." Then, Barth will reply "yes," but there are neither superiority and inferiority in the essence of God nor various quanta of deity. Also God is not a human being. That is why the trinity is a "great mystery." Still, Barth lacks coherency in his understanding and does not provide a satisfactory, alternative model.

---

64. Barth, *Church Dogmatics*, I/1:350.
65. Ibid., 393.

This hierarchical tendency in intra-trinitarian relations can also be found in his understanding of revelation which reflects the immanent trinity, the relationship in Godself. Barth often depicts the Father as the Revealer, the Son as the Revelation, and the Spirit as Revealedness. I think the terminology itself is problematic. The Revealer is active and does work. On the other hand, the Revelation is an "object," and Revealedness is simply describing passivity. Therefore, the Father as the Revealer, to some degree, is in control of the revelation process.

Again, Barth would deny the hierarchy among the intra-trinitarian relations, yet I do not see how he can escape this accusation logically, except for saying that the trinity is simply a mystery.

The Roles of the Holy Spirit with Respect to Divine Love and Relation

Barth understands the Holy Spirit as the common element or fellowship of the Father and the Son.[66] Because of the Holy Spirit, the union between the Father and the Son is formed. St. Augustine also understood the Spirit as the bond between the Father and the Son. Thus, one can say that Barth follows Augustine's view in this regard. This Holy Spirit is also active, and it unites the Father and the Son. The Spirit is also the love unites the Father and the Son. Barth writes, "In this eternal begetting of Himself and being begotten of Himself, He posits Himself a third time as the Holy Spirit, i.e., as the love which unites Him in Himself."[67] Barth again states, "Thus God—and to this degree He is God the Holy Spirit—is 'antecedently in Himself' the act of communion, the act of impartation, love, gift."[68]

According to Barth, it is significant to notice that the Pneuma itself is a neuter. Thus, as the common element of the father and the Son, *it* is neutral. This Spirit is reciprocal, and it does not favor either the Father or the Son. Also by being neutral, the Pneuma distinguishes itself from the other two hypostases.[69] Accordingly, the Spirit is not a "person" in the modern sense of the term. The Spirit should not be considered as the third "person." "In a particular way the Holy Spirit is what the Father

66. Ibid., 470.
67. Ibid., 483.
68. Ibid., 470.
69. Ibid., 469.

and the Son are."[70] It[71] is not a third subject, but it is truly qualified to be called "a third mode of being."

The Holy Spirit is also the giver of life. The Spirit with the Father is the subject of creation. To some degree, all human beings are lost and dead without their relationships with God. Barth writes, "The Spirit of God is God in His freedom to be present to the creature, and therefore to create this relation, and therefore to be the life of the creature."[72] Human beings are unable to recover this relationship without the giver of the life, the Spirit.

Based on his exegeses, Barth draws three important conclusions about the work of the Holy Spirit in the event of revelation. First, the Pneuma guarantees a person's participation in revelation. Because of this Spirit in us, one can say "yes" to God's revelation. Therefore, all this knowledge, faith and obedience is possible only in the Holy Spirit. Secondly, the Spirit guides and instructs a believer, who alone cannot instruct him/herself. It [the Spirit] is the teacher and leader of humanity. Even though this Spirit is in us, it never intrudes on human subjectivity. The Paraclete is not identical with a human being. The Spirit remains as the Lord in us. Even though the Spirit is in us, we as persons can never control it. Therefore, the Spirit remains as God in us, but we still remain as sinful human creatures. Barth states, "But this also means that the creature to whom the Holy Spirit is imparted in revelation by no means loses its nature and kind as a creature so as to become itself, as it were, the Holy Spirit. Even in receiving the Holy Ghost man remains man, the sinner sinner."[73] Thirdly, because of this Spirit, a human being can speak of the Christ and he/she can actualize God's revelation in his/her life.[74] Due to the Spirit in us, we can talk about God and revelation. The Spirit gives us a right to talk about God.

The Spirit is not just the love, the giver of life and the teacher of a believer, it is also the redeemer. As the Father is often described as the Creator and the Son as the Reconciler, the Holy Spirit is construed as

---

70. Ibid., 469.

71. I will use the pronoun "it" instead of "he" or "she" in describing the Holy Spirit in this chapter, since the Greek term *pneuma* is a neuter. By choosing that, I am aware of the fact that I lose some personal aspects of "person."

72. Barth, *Church Dogmatics*, I/1:450.

73. Ibid., 462.

74. Ibid., 453–54.

the Redeemer. This is a way that Barth distinguishes the works of the three "persons" or "modes of being." Barth accepts the traditional model of the Father as the fount or origin of the whole deity. Accordingly, in Barth's picture of the intra-trinitarian relationship, the Son comes from the Father. Accordingly, the Father is the source from which the Son receives his eternal existence. This understanding of God as the source applies not only to the immanent trinity in Godself, but it also applies to the other creatures including humanity.[75] Thus, the creation is primarily attributed to the Father. Therefore, He is God the Creator.

In Jesus Christ, we have the Reconciler; Jesus was the one who was incarnate. Of course, the other two hypostases also participated in this incarnation, but the other two were not incarnate. Through the incarnation, Jesus Christ reconciled humanity with God.[76]

The Holy Spirit is primarily the Redeemer. To some degree, this Spirit completes this salvation as a process. The Spirit brings us this reconciliation with God. The Holy Spirit as the true Redeemer sets us free from bondage. Due to the work of the Spirit in us, human beings are redeemed and liberated, and we become the children of God. Therefore, one has to confess that even our confession about Jesus Christ is the work of the Holy Spirit.[77] Therefore, the Spirit as the redeemer redeems us.

> That God the Holy Spirit is the Redeemer who sets us free is a statement of the knowledge and praise of God. In virtue of this statement we ourselves are the redeemed, the liberated, the children of God in faith, in the faith we confess with this statement, i.e., in the act of God of which this statement speaks.[78]

Comparing Karl Barth and Wolfhart Pannenberg

The Immanent and Economic Trinity

Both Barth and Pannenberg agree that the essence of God is accessible to human beings, albeit no human being will fully understand that until he/she reaches the final eschaton. In this sense, they both follow the mainline Western tradition. Most Eastern Orthodox theologians postulate

---

75. Thompson, *Holy Spirit in the Theology of Karl Barth*, 22.

76. Ibid., 22.

77. Karl Barth, *Church Dogmatics*, I/1:462.

78. Ibid., 462.

that one cannot know the essence because God in Godself is different from the God *ad extra*. They insist we cannot simply assume that the God who revealed Godself in Jesus Christ is the same as the eternal God in the immanent trinity. Schleiermacher was skeptical about human accessibility of the essence of God; he limited the being of God to human conception of God, thus isolated a person within the circle of his/her own being.[79] In the face of these views, Barth insists that the God in Godself "antecedently" is the God known to us "externally." Without this maxim, no one can know God. God really became Jesus, so by looking at Jesus, one can know God at least partially with the succor of the Spirit. In terms of Barth's understanding of the relationship between the immanent and economic trinity, John Thompson summarizes well as follows: "Barth has a central and definitive answer, namely, what God is in Godself is known from what he is and does in revelation. It has sometimes been put like this—the economic Trinity, that is, what God is in the economy of salvation in the world for us, he is as such in salvation. . . . The economic Trinity is the way to what is known as the immanent Trinity, how God is in himself."[80] Rosato also clearly sees the correspondence of the economic and the immanent trinity.

Barth repeatedly insists that the God in God's revelation is the God antecedently in Godself in terms of the content in the revelation. The reality of God which was disclosed in the revelation in Jesus Christ was the reality of God, materially speaking. Thus, the content of the economic trinity corresponds to the content of the immanent trinity; however, formally speaking, we cannot make this equation. For example, God is God; God is not a human person. God took the form of a human being in Jesus Christ, but that does not mean that God has two hands and two eyes as we do. Therefore, Barth admits that a huge gulf exists between humanity and God. Thus, in terms of its form, one cannot say that the economic trinity corresponds to the immanent trinity. Barth writes:

> The reality of God in His revelation cannot be bracketed by an "only," as though somewhere behind His revelation there stood another reality of God; the reality of God which encounters us in His revelation is His reality in all the depths of eternity. This is why we have to take it so seriously precisely in His revelation.[81]

79. Rosato, *Spirit as Lord*, 56.

80. Thompson, *Holy Spirit in the Theology of Karl Barth*, 21.

81. Barth, *Church Dogmatics*, I/1:393.

Pannenberg somewhat adopts Rahner's maxim that the economic trinity is the immanent trinity. He also agrees with Barth that the God who incarnated in history is the God in Godself; God did not disguise Godself in Jesus. Unlike Barth, Pannenberg's understanding of the relationship between the economic and immanent trinity is extremely sophisticated, but at least it can be said that for Pannenberg "the eternal self-identity of God cannot properly be conceived independently of the salvation-historical workings of the Son and of the Spirit."[82] It seems also that the eternal identity of God is affirmed or even shaped to some degree by the economy of salvation. In the incarnation, Jesus Christ had, theoretically but he did not, a real chance to rebel against God. In other words, Jesus as an independent hypostasis had some freedom or possibility to disobey God, especially when Jesus faced the crucifixion. For Pannenberg, there is an interaction between the immanent and economic trinity.

Relations of Origin

Pannenberg rejects the understanding of the intra-trinitarian relationship as "relations of origin," which endorses the view of the one-way flow of deity. The Father begets the Son, and the Holy Spirit proceeds from the Father, who is the fount and source of the other hypostases. Most Western theologians including Karl Barth fall into this group who understand the intra-trinitarian relationship in the context of "relations of origin." Barth states, "In this unity of divine essence the Son is from the Father and the Spirit is from the Father and the Son, while the Father is from Himself alone."[83] While standing on this traditional view of the intra-trinitarian relations, Barth is making two crucial mistakes. First, Barth failed to give a reasonable answer for the question of the origin of the Father. If the Son is from the Father and the Spirit is from both the Father and the Son, where does the Father come from? Barth simply says that the Father is from Himself! Then, one can ask Barth, "Why can't you just say that the Son is also from the Son Himself?" Barth would reply, "I know Jesus is the eternal Son based on the teachings in the scripture." Is biblical exegesis the key to understanding the Trinity? Corresponding to

---

82. Robert W. Jenson, "Jesus in the Trinity: Wolfhart Pannenberg's Christology and Doctrine of the Trinity," in *Theology of Wolfhart Pannenberg*, ed. Carl E. Braaten, 25.

83. Karl Barth, *Church Dogmatics*, I/1:393.

this question, Barth would say that ultimately the Trinity itself is a great mystery. Barth can avoid the question of the origin of the Father by giving different excuses, but in my opinion, Barth is standing on the wrong ground and trying to answer a wrong question.

This traditional framework also brings Barth the hierarchical understanding of the intra-trinitarian relations. The Father is the greatest since other two "modes of being" originate from the Father according to Barth's paradigm. Both the Son and the Spirit, to some degree, depend on the Father because they are "from" the Father, but the Father in the immanent trinity does not depend on the other two hypostases. With reference to this matter Pannenberg would say that we need to create an untraditional picture, which also underlines the Father's dependency on other "persons." Without this dimension of mutual dependency, no theologian can avoid the inequality among the divine persons. Of course, Barth disaccords with the notion that there is a hierarchy in the essence of God and that one hypostasis can be considered as a superior mode of being.

Against Barth in this regard, Pannenberg would say that Barth's construal of the intra-trinitarian relations is problematic since it starts with the assumption that there is a flow of deity. Again, Barth denies this accusation in his writings. But based on Barth's logic, I do not see how Barth would escape from this accusation. As long as Barth starts with this understanding of a one-way flow of the model, Barth will not solve the question of the origin as well as the question of a hierarchy in the immanent trinity.

Tritheism or Modalism

In explaining the trinity, usually a theologian is inclined to fall into either modalism or tritheism. Barth tends to be somewhat modalistic; on the other hand, Pannenberg tends to be tritheistic in his understanding of the trinity. Barth creates the picture that the God in essence has only one personality, and each person alone is simply a mode of this divine essence. Technically speaking, each hypostasis in the trinity does not have its own personality or personhood. Only this triune God as one has a personality. That is why Pannenberg attacks Barth's view of the trinity as simply a modified form of German idealism, "as the unfolding of a single divine subject."[84] For Barth, God is only one "person" if we define the term "person" in the modern sense. That is one main reason why Barth prefers to use the term "three modes of being" instead of three "persons." In his attempt, Barth tries to recover the original meaning of the term "person" by using this new terminology. The Latin term *persona* in relation to the trinity was first employed by Tertullian in the third century, referring to the notion of a "mask," as in theater. Later in the fourth century AD, the Greek term ὑποστασις (*hypostasis*) was used by the Cappadocian fathers in order to elucidate each divine person of the trinity. Barth is correct when he points out that the word "person" lost its original meaning in the fourth century, but his understanding of the trinity as only one subject in three different forms created even a greater, modalistic tendency. That is why many people today criticize Barth's trinity due to its modalistic tendency.

Pannenberg also criticizes Barth in this way, namely, Barth has no room for the plurality of persons in one God. Barth can only say that there are three different modes of being in the one divine subjectivity. Pannenberg summarizes Barth's writings about the trinity in this way:

> The subject of the revelation is only one. Barth could thus think of the doctrine of the Trinity as an exposition of the subjectivity of God in his revelation. This being so, there is no room for a plurality of persons in the one God but only for different modes of being in the one divine subjectivity.[85]

Unlike Barth, Pannenberg is leaning toward the opposite, namely, the tritheistic tendency. For Pannenberg, there are three "persons" in God in the modern sense. The fellowship of three "persons" constitutes the one divine essence.[86] Each person as the center of one's own action possesses a personality. Theoretically, in this view of Pannenberg, it is possible that the Son can stand against the Father, but the Son did not. Instead, the Son obeyed the Father out of his own choice. This understanding of Pannenberg is very innovative, and I also think that his innovative model is heading in the right direction. However, somehow he still has to be able to show the oneness of the trinity, which is not a simple task. Thus, the usual criticism for Pannenberg is that he is quite success-

---

84. Pannenberg, *Grundfragen,* 2:96–108, quoted in Carl E. Braaten *The Theology of Wolfhart Pannenberg,* 201.

85. Pannenberg, *Systematic Theology* 1:296.

86. Braaten, ed., *Theology of Wolfhart Pannenberg,* 200.

ful in describing the "threeness" of the trinity. Yet he fails to display the unity of the trinity; this tendency is often found in the Eastern Orthodox theologians.

To some degree, one can say, with regard to three hypostases, Barth represents the Western tradition; on the other hand, Pannenberg represents the Eastern tradition. Another good example of this can also be shown through the issue of the *filioque*. Again, as a part of the Latin Western tradition, Barth defends the *filioque*; on the other hand, sympathizing with the Eastern view, Pannenberg endorses the single procession.

Barth's and Pannenberg's Construal of the Spirit

Both Barth and Pannenberg have a very similar view on the Holy Spirit, even though Pannenberg has a broader definition of the Spirit. According to both Pannenberg and Barth, the Spirit is mainly the Spirit of *love*. As love, the Spirit unites the Father and the Son. In this sense, the Spirit as a person is active in the immanent trinity. Furthermore, the Spirit constitutes the divine essence of the Godhead. Pannenberg writes, "The essence of the Godhead is indeed Spirit."[87] Barth insists that the Spirit is the common element between the Father and the Son.

It is difficult to ascertain what the common element is between the Father and the Son in the immanent sense within Barth's thought, which leads me to conclude that Pannenberg has the broader definition of the Spirit. In my understanding of Pannenberg's theology, the Spirit embraces all of the Father and the Son. Both the Father and the Son move in this love field. Another example of Pannenberg's broader definition of the Spirit is manifested in terms of creation. For Pannenberg, it is the Spirit, as the creative dynamic, that brings forth the life of the creature. On the contrary, for Barth, this work of creation is primarily attributed to God the Father. Therefore, I conclude that Pannenberg has a broader definition of the Spirit.

The Filioque Controversy

With regard to the *filioque* controversy, a great difference exists between Barth and Pannenberg. Barth, standing on the Western tradition, de-

---

87 Wolfhart Pannenberg, *Systematic Theology*, 1:492.

fends the use of the *filioque* in the creed; on the other hand, Pannenberg opposes the use of the *filioque* in the creed.

It seems that Pannenberg's view on the *filioque* is more reasonable than Barth's view. Jesus the Son in fact received the Holy Spirit while he was on earth. It was not just the human Jesus who received the Holy Spirit while he was baptized by John; the whole person Jesus received the Spirit. In fact, John 15:26 states that the Spirit proceeds from the Father. Yes, as Barth insists, the Spirit was the Spirit *of the Christ*, but based on this phrase, one cannot and should not draw the conclusion that the Spirit *proceeds from* the Son also. I think it is better to phrase that the Spirit proceeds from the Father without the *Filioque*.[88] After all, Pannenberg insists, this kind of argument is in vain since this *filioque* controversy is based upon the assumption that the Father is the fount of deity.

Concluding Thoughts on Pannenberg and Barth

Indubitably, I am convinced that both Barth and Pannenberg are two great theologians in Christian history. Both of them are German-speaking theologians who received their important theological education in Germany. Even though they have somewhat similar backgrounds, Pannenberg has been more influenced by the Eastern Orthodox tradition. Unlike Barth, Pannenberg opposes the use of the *filioque* in the creed. In this regard, I am also convinced that the *filioque* should be withdrawn from the creed because it was added without the other half of Christianity. Barth, standing on the Augustinian tradition, alleges that the Spirit proceeds from both the Father and the Son because the Spirit is the Spirit of the Father and the Son; however, this argument did not persuade me at all because "of" is clearly different from "proceed from." Scripture clearly states that the Spirit proceeds from the Father (John 15:26), and Jesus also received the Spirit when he was baptized. However, for Pannenberg, all this argument is standing on a false ground, namely, the understanding of one-way flow of deity. As long as they keep this foundation, their discussion is useless because it creates the picture of subordinationism. Pannenberg's innovative idea is this: Somehow, not just the Son and the Spirit, but the Father's deity also depends on the oth-

---

88. Since I thoroughly discussed this controversy above, I simply stated my position in this section.

er two hypostases' action such as "glorification" and "obedience." Hence, Pannenberg insists that the mutual dependency in intra-relationship should be shown in this understanding of the relations in God.

Unlike most Western theologians including Barth, Pannenberg understands that each hypostasis has its own personality as a person in an almost modern sense. This has a tritheistic tendency like that of the Greek Orthodox theologians. Against this claim, Barth avers that there is only one subject in the trinity; however, Barth has a somewhat modalistic tendency.

Both Barth and Pannenberg agree that there is a way to know God partially, not fully. *For Barth, it is mainly through the biblical revelation in Jesus Christ; for Pannenberg it is through reflection on history.* Both of them also consent to the fact that only in the end, human beings are fully able to understand God as well as the trinity.

Interestingly enough, I think both Barth and Pannenberg have very similar understandings of the Holy Spirit. Both seem to emphasize the Spirit as the love who unites the Father and the Son. Yet, Pannenberg has a broader definition of the Holy Spirit. For Pannenberg, the Spirit as a love field encompasses the other two hypostases, but Barth does not go so far, despite admitting that the Spirit is the common element of the Father and the Son.

Chiological Response to Pannenberg and Barth

The Spirit or Ch'i *as the Essence of God, Tao, I, and the* Great Ultimate

In volume 1 of *Systematic Theology*, Pannenberg argues that the essence of God is Spirit. He states, "*The essence of God is indeed Spirit. It is as a dynamic field, and* as its manifestation in the coming forth of the Son shows itself to be the work of the Father, the dynamic of the Spirit radiates from the Father, but in such a way that the Son receives it as gift and it fills him and radiates back from him to the Father."[89] Moreover, *this Spirit is the love* that unites and mutually relates the Father with the Son.[90]

In Pannenberg's Pneumatology, the word "Spirit" has at least two meanings: First, the Spirit as a dynamic field exemplifies the very essence

---

89. Pannenberg, *Systematic Theology*, 1:429. Italics are mine.

90. Ibid., 429.

of the Godhead. Second, the Spirit as a hypostasis stands over against God the Father and God the Son.[91] In the first sense, the Spirit of love remains the divine essence.[92]

In the *I Ching*, the essence of *I* (change), *Tai-chi* (the Great Ultimate), and *Tao* (the Way or Divine) is known as *ch'i*. Even though there is no exact equivalent term for "*ch'i*" in English, various terms are rendered to depict this, such as "energy," "vital energy," "pure energy," "force," "material force," "spirit," "vapor," "breath," "air" and so forth.[93] With ease, one finds many similarities between the biblical understanding of the Spirit and the East Asian understanding of *ch'i*. In particular, there are many affinities between that of Pannenberg's and the East Asian's. One can easily notice that *ch'i* can be also translated as "force" and "spirit." In the East Asian context, the essence of *I*, the Great Ultimate (*T'ai-chi*), and Tao (that can be construed as God in English) is *ch'i*, which is the equivalent of the English word *spirit* and *force*.

Many Neo-Confucian scholars have debated the essence of *T'ai-chi* and *Tao*. The prominent Neo-Confucian Chu Hsi inculcated that *li* was the essence of Tai-chi and Tao. He even called for the ontological priority of *li* over *ch'i*. He understood yin and yang in the realm of concrete things. Most modern Asian scholars accused Chu Hsi of bifurcating *li* from *ch'i*. In contrast to Chu Hsi's bifurcation, Lo Ch'in-shun argues for the unitary basis of the reality, namely, *ch'i*.[94]

For Pannenberg, the Spirit is the Spirit of "love." The chiological approach would say that a moral and categorical embodiment of *ch'i* is love, although many followers of the *I Ching* and Neo-Confucians regard the *li* (principle) as the main form (or expression) of *ch'i*. The Great Korean Neo-Confucian Yi Yulgok (c. 1536–1584) inculcated the theory of *sa-dan-chil-jeong*. According to this theory, compassion, shame, courtesy and modesty (together), and right and wrong (together) are the four manifestations of *li* (principle), whereas pleasure, anger, sorrow, fear, love, hatred, and desire are the seven manifestations of *ch'i*.[95] In this

91. Ibid., 428–29.

92. See Veli-Matti Kärkkäinen, *The Doctrine of God: A Global Introduction: A Biblical, Historical, and Contemporary Survey* (Grand Rapids: Baker Academic, 2004) 151–52.

93. JeeLoo Liu, *An Introduction to Chinese Philosophy: From Ancient Philosophy to Chinese Buddhism* (Oxford: Blackwell, 2006) 6.

94. See chapter 2 for the detailed information on this.

95. Edward Y. J. Chung, *The Korean Neo-Confucianism of Yi T'oegye and Yi Yulgok* (Albany: State University of New York Press, 1995) 38–39.

sense, love is an expression of *ch'i*. Therefore, there is a lot of overlapping between Pannenberg's essence of God as the Spirit of love and the *I Ching's* grasp of the essence of *I* and Tao as *ch'i*, whose word can be decoded as "spirit" and "force." In this regard, Pannenberg's concept of the essence of God shares many affinities with the teachings of the *I Ching*.

In volume one of *Church Dogmatics*, Barth avers the essence of God is also the Spirit. Barth writes, "The event of revelation has clarity and reality on its subjective side because *the Holy Spirit*, the subjective element in this event, *is of the essence of God Himself*."[96] In another place, he remarks, "He [the Holy Spirit] is *the common element*, or, better, the fellowship, the act of communion, of the Father and the Son."[97] Moreover, Barth understands the Holy Spirit as *the act of God's love*.[98] In another place, Barth equates the love of God with the creative work of the Holy Spirit.[99] Barth also goes back to the biblical witness in the Johannine Literature, and he states, "To say 'love' in the Johannine sense is to say 'Spirit.'"[100] Being a biblical theologian, Barth's mind goes back to John 4:24: "God is spirit, and his worshipers must worship in spirit and truth." Another basis of Barth's equation is 1 John 4:8: "Whoever does not love does not know God, because God is love" (NIV). To put this in a more simple way, for Barth, the essence of God is constituted by the Spirit, and this Spirit is the Spirit of love.

Again, from a chiological perspective, that *God is Spirit* is best translated as "the Ultimate Reality (e.g., *I, Tao,* and *T'ai-chi*) is ch'i." Love is one main manifestation of *ch'i*. To this extent, Barth's view of the essence of God as Spirit is very compatible with the chiological notion that the essence of the Ultimate Reality is *ch'i*.

God the Father and Ch'i *as the Source of the Creation*

Barth writes, "The Son and the Spirit are of one essence with the Father. In this unity of divine essence the Son is from the Father and the Spirit is from the Father and the Son, while the Father is from Himself alone."[101]

---

96. Barth, *Church Dogmatics*, I/1: 466. Italics are mine.

97. Ibid., 470.

98. Ibid.

99. Barth, *Church Dogmatics*, IV/2:775.

100. Ibid.

101. Barth, *Church Dogmatics*, I/1:293.

Here, one can decipher Barth's elucidation of the intra-trinitarian relationship as a one-way flow of deity, which can be problematic. Another pivotal point that one can draw out from the above statement is Barth's construal of the Father as the source or fount of the other two persons of the Godhead. In addition, for Barth, the Father means "the Creator." In other words, Barth sees the Father as the source of the Son and the Spirit, as well as the source of all creatures.

Pannenberg rejects Barth's origin of relation in the trinity, which endorses the one-way-flow of deity. Barth's view falls into the traditional view: God the Son is begotten from the Father, and the Holy Spirit proceeds from the Father and the Son. God the Father is from the Father Himself. In other words, only the Father is without origin (*anarchos*).[102] On the contrary, Pannenberg endorses mutuality, reciprocity, and co-dependency with respect to the intra-trinitarian relationship. For instance, the Father handed over lordship to the Son, and the Son handed back the lordship to the Father. To this extent, there is a mutual dependency.[103]

Instead, Pannenberg promotes *the trinitarian origin of creation* and accuses Barth for almost exclusively ascribing creation to the Father.[104] Regarding God the Father, he states, "God is Father as Creator as the origin of creatures in their contingency by granting them existence, caring for them, and making possible their continual life and independence."[105] In terms of the Son, he remarks, "In the Son is the origin of all that differs from the Father, and therefore of the creatures' independence vis-à-vis the Father."[106] Moreover, the Spirit is also the origin of all life: "According to the biblical witnesses the Spirit was at work in creation (Gen 1:2), especially as the origin of life in the creatures (Gen 2:7; Ps 104:29f.)."[107]

From a Chiological perspective, it is the *ch'i* that is the source of all creation and the very essence of *I* (Change). In the *I Ching*, *ch'i* as *the creativity* represents the indeterminate and formless source of change and order. It brings forth all forms, things, and specific activities.[108] *T'ai-chi is also described as the undifferentiated original ch'i*. Moreover, Tao,

102. Pannenberg, *Systematic Theology*, 1:311.

103. Ibid., 1:312–313.

104. Ibid., 2:30.

105. Ibid., 2:21.

106. Ibid., 2:22.

107. Ibid., 2:32.

108. Chung-ying Cheng, *Li and Ch'i in the I Ching*, 22.

who is divine, spiritual, and unfathomable, designates the all-embracing entelechy that is the vital force (*ch'i*) directing growth and life.[109] In the *I Ching*, Tao is omnipresent and panentheistic insofar as all things exist in Tao and they also came to exist through it. Tao renews objects too.[110] From above, one can deduce a principle from the *I Ching* that *the Ultimate Reality consists of ch'i, from which all objects and things come out.* The Ultimate Reality (i.e., *Tai-chi, I,* or *Tao*) is composed of *ch'i.* Yin and yang are the two forms of this *ch'i.*[111]

While the *I Ching* regards *ch'i* as the source or origin of the world, *Tao Te Ching* views *Tao* as the origin of all existence.[112] In philosophical Taoism (*Daojia*), Paul Chung postulates that *Tao* remains formless and ineffable, yet from this one mystical *Tao, te (de)* and *ch'i (qi)* come out. As a result, *te* comes as realization and fulfillment of *Tao* in history and nature, and *ch'i* stands as a sustaining, guiding force of life.[113]

Barth avers that God the Father designates the source or origin of the other two persons (or modes) of the Godhead as well as all creatures. On the other hand, from an East Asian Chiological viewpoint, *ch'i is the source of all the objects and lives.* Furthermore, the whole universe is made of *ch'i* with various densities. For example, the grosser heavier *ch'i* became the earth, and the refined or lighter *ch'i* became the sky. The *ch'i* of humanity falls between the two kinds.

In sum, whereas Barth mainly views the God the Father as the source or origin of creation, Pannenberg underscores the trinitarian origin. In the *I Ching, ch'i* is the origin and source of all creatures.

The Immanent and Economic Trinity, and the Inscrutability of Tao and Ch'i

Pannenberg basically accepts Rahner's maxim that the economic trinity is the immanent trinity with some qualifications. God did not disguise Godself in Jesus Christ. God in salvation history reveals the eternal identity of God. One step further, it appears that the eternal identity of God is

109. *Ta Chuan,* in *The I Ching,* trans. Richard Wilhelm and Cary Baynes (Princeton: Princeton University Press, 1977) 323.

110. *Ta Chuan,* 299.

111. Chang Tsai also argues that *T'ai-chi* is constituted by *ch'i.*

112. In the *I Ching,* however, *Tao* and *I* are interchangeable terms.

113. Paul Chung, *Constructing Irregular Theology: Bamboo and Minjung in East Asian Perspective* (Leiden: Brill, 2009) 85–89.

ratified and even more or less shaped by the economy of salvation. Jesus on earth had genuine freedom to disobey God the Father when Jesus stood before the crucifixion. Regarding this point, Pannenberg writes, "The reality that is achieved in the eternal fellowship of the Trinity [the immanent trinity] and by the economy of its action in the world [the economic trinity] is one and the same."[114]

Barth agrees with Pannenberg in that the eternal essence of God stays accessible to humans. The immanent trinity corresponds with the economic trinity. Barth writes, "What He is in revelation He is antecedently in Himself. And what He is antecedently in Himself He is in revelation."[115] Barth, however, reserves some differences between the economic trinity and immanent trinity in terms of 'form' insofar as humans do not expect to see the God in eternity with two humanlike eyes and hands. Here, Pannenberg regards the economic trinity as "self-actualization" of God, and elucidates why his construal of self-actualization is better than Barth's view of the economic trinity as the "repetition" of the immanent trinity (i.e., God's inner trinitarian life). At any rate, both Pannenberg and Barth agree with the notion that humans have accessibility to the divine essence or the immanent trinity.

In the *Tao Te Ching*, the essence of Tao, or Tao itself, is not knowable. Tao itself refers to the absolute itself or Godself in Christianity. Tao is beyond human comprehension and grasp.[116] The eternal identity or essence of Tao is indescribable. Chapter 1 of the *Tao Te Ching* states, "The Eternal Tao cannot be described in human words. The Eternal Tao cannot be named."[117] In other words, the eternal essence of Tao remains the unnamable and unsymbolizable mystery.

Chapter 42 of the *Tao Te Ching* remarks, "The Eternal Tao gives birth to one. One gives birth to Two. Two gives birth to Three. Three gives birth to all things." Here, "one" signifies the absolute, the divine, or the human idea of God. "Two" seems to refer to yin and yang. "Three" symbolizes the "inness," namely, the yang element in yin and the yin element in yang as they interplay. One should notice that there is no "Four"

114. Pannenberg, *Systematic Theology*, 2:393.

115. Barth, *Church Dogmatics*, I/1:466.

116. See *Ta Chuan* in *The I Ching*, Trans. Richard Wilhelm and Cary Baynes (Princeton: Princeton University Press, 1977) 323. Here, Tao transcends the spatial world.

117. This is my translation.

after "Three." Three produces all things. In this regard, this chapter 42 speaks of the trinitarian (three) origin or foundation of our universe.

For both Pannenberg and Barth, the eternal identity (or the *aseity*) of God is accessible via the economic trinity. At the philosophical level of the *I Ching*, *I* (Change) as the Ultimate Reality is analogous to the Christian concept of God.[118] Moreover, Change and Tao stays almost identical. Ch'u Chai articulates, "In the *I Ching*, the word *I* is used interchangeably with the word *Tao*, since *Tao* is life, spontaneity, evolution, or, in one word, change itself."[119] Jung Young Lee avers that *I* (change) and *Tao* (Way) stand together as the two sides of one reality. He uses the analogy of "foreground and background." Tao is the background of Change *(I)*, and Change is the foreground of Tao. To this extent, both cannot be separated, and they can be used interchangeably.[120]

In terms of the chiological approach, *ch'i itself* as the formless creativity in the *I Ching* stays unknowable and cannot be pinned down, but when *ch'i* embodies itself in *li*, it becomes a knowable category. *Li*, which is the pattern and activity of *ch'i* in the concrete world, possess form. Thus, *ch'i* shows itself via *li*. In the *I Ching*, the eternal essence of *ch'i* and Tao (God in the Christian tradition) stays beyond our human comprehension. However, both trinitarian theologies of Pannenberg and Barth, the eternal identity (essence) of God is knowable through the economic trinity.

Overcoming Pannenberg's Tritheistic and Barth's Modalistic Tendencies with the Chiological Approach

Most theologians who attempt to decode the trinity fall into either modalistic or tritheistic tendencies. Barth's trinitarian view falls into the modalistic tendency, more specifically Sabellianism, teaching that the one true God appears in three different modes. In order to eschew the danger of tritheism, Barth comes up with the new term "mode of being" (*Seinsweise*) instead of the traditional word "person." But in doing so, Barth now stands in proximity to modalism.[121] The trinitarian terminol-

118. Jung Young Lee, *Embracing Change: Postmodern Interpretations of the I Ching from a Christian Perspective* (Scranton: University of Scranton Press, 1994) 41.

119. Ch'u Chai and Winberg Chai, eds., *I Ching: Book of Changes*, trans. James Legge (Secaucus: University Books, 1964) xl–xli.

120. J. Y. Lee, *Embracing Change*, 55.

121. Cf. Pannenberg, *Systematic Theology*, 2:296. Here, Pannenberg elucidates Barth's concept of "mode of being."

ogy which Barth employs is "three modes of one being (essence)."[122] By choosing "mode of being" instead of "person," Barth loses not only a "personal" dimension but also loses a "dynamic" dimension that is an integral part of a living being. Moreover, because of Barth's term "three modes of being" naturally engenders other theologians' suspicion and accusation that Barth's trinitarian concept stands near the modalistic tendency.

In the past, many Western theologians such as Augustine tended to underscore the unity or oneness of God, and they did an excellent job in explaining the essence or substance (*ousia* or *substantia*) of God. On the other hand, they had a difficult time in explaining the threeness of the trinity. Standing in this line of many Western theologians, Barth more or less continues to use that substantialist metaphysics which interprets the Ultimate Reality of God as *ousia* in Greek and *substantia* in Latin. Augustine also depicted God as a substance that is unchangeable, invisible, and eternal.[123] One step further, Thomas Aquinas indentified God with the fullness of being as pure act, which is devoid of becoming. Aquinas' God stays immutable and cannot go through change.[124] Change belongs to the realm of accident, not substance. Hence, Barth elucidates God in terms of substance or essence. In this regard, his God becomes more or less immutable.

If Barth's model of the trinity fell into the modalistic tendency, Pannenberg's model fell into the tritheistic camp. For Pannenberg, in God, there is not "one" subject, but "three." And these three subjects have dependent relation. One can only think of the identity of the trinity with the trinitarian relation. God the Father becomes the father only in relation to the Son's obedience. God the Son becomes the Son as he obeys the Father.[125] Moreover, the lordship of the Father is dependent on the obedience of the Son. In this sense, one can speak of Pannenberg's trinity as a unity of reciprocal self-dedication.[126]

122. Karl Barth, *Church Dogmatics,* I/1: 360.

123. St. Augustine, *On the Trinity,* in *A Select Library of the Nicene and Post-Nicene Fathers* (Grand Rapids: Eerdmans, 1956) 3:89.

124. Ted Peters, *God as Trinity: Relationality and Temporality in Divine Life* (Louisville: Westminster John Knox, 1993) 30–31.

125. Pannenberg, *Systematic Theology,* 1:313.

126. Wolfhart Pannenberg, *Jesus—God and Man,* 2nd ed. (Louisville: Westminster John Knox, 1977) 179–80.

There is, however, a big difference between the trinitarian relation and human relation. Each trinitarian person is totally dependent on its relation to the others, whereas a human person is not totally dependent on other persons in defining one's identity.[127] Regarding this point, Pannenberg writes, "The most important of these differences is that being a human is not so exclusively constituted by the relation to one or two other persons as it is in the trinitarian life of God."[128]

To some degree, Pannenberg still elucidates the trinity in terms of "essence" or "substance" although he is redefining in terms of the dependent relation. As long as God is understood in terms of substance and essence, it will be very hard to do away with the immutable and non-relational Western concept of God. For instance, Pannenberg views the reality of God as love and Spirit, but this love and Spirit constitute the "essence" of God: "As the one and only essence of God, it [love] has its existence in the Father, Son, and Holy Spirit."[129] In other words, Pannenberg's trinitarian terminology is ultimately grounded in the Greek *ousia* and Latin *substantia,* which in turn defined by Augustine as unchangeable, invisible, and eternal being. Although Pannenberg has attempted to break away from the Greek-Augustinian-Aquinas' substantial metaphysics, in the end it seems he is going back to that tradition. The God of this tradition remains immutable, non-dynamic, and unchanging.

One great advantage of the chiological approach[130] is that it tries to construe the Ultimate Reality[131] (e.g., God, *Tao,* and *I*) as "change" instead of the static substance. The chiological approach teaches that "change" antecedes "essence" or "substance." Change is prior to essence; in other words, before there is "essence," there has been the original "change." This idea is very different from the Western foundation—Augustine understood change as "accident." In the *I Ching,* Change is the Ultimate Reality, and nothing goes beyond that, and all things come from that. If we apply this chiological idea of Change to God, then the essence (*ousia*) of God

127. Peters, *God as Trinity,* 139.

128. Pannenberg, *Systematic Theology,* 1:431.

129. Ibid., 1:428.

130. For more information on the chiological approach, see chapter 1.

131. Many human symbols in different horizons are deployed in order to depict the Ultimate Reality: *Yahweh, Theos,* and God in the Christian horizon; *I* and *Tao* in the *I Ching* horizon; *T'ai-chi* and *Wu-chi* in the Neo-Confucian horizon.

(the Ultimate Reality) becomes "change," not "immutable substance." God is to be understood as the dynamic, moving, living "change." In contrast to the Ultimate Reality (i.e., God) of Augustine and Aquinas, the Ultimate Reality (i.e., *I* and *Tao*) of the *I Ching* remains constantly changing, moving, and living. Furthermore, this Ultimate Reality of the *I Ching* stays truly "relational" insofar as this Ultimate Reality is closely connected with humanity (*ren*) and earth (*di*). One step further, since the Ultimate Reality is "change," unity (undifferentiated state) and diversity (differentiated state) can coexist in the Reality. By using the chiological approach to theology, one will be able to retrieve the vitality, mutability, and relationality of God that have been undermined by Western theology for many years.

5

From Pneumatological to Chiological Approach to World Religions

The Cosmic Spirit and Ch'i

IN THE PAST, A CHRISTOLOGICAL PERSPECTIVE ON WORLD RELIGIONS brought forth division, dispute, and derogation of other faiths. In contrast, recent pneumatological perspectives help eschew unnecessary arguments and hostility between religions by underscoring the ubiquity of the cosmic Spirit.[1] In this chapter, I will first analyze pneumatologies of the two premier scholars today, namely, Jürgen Moltmann from Germany, and Stanley Samartha from India. Second, I will look at the implications of their works in the Asian context that is religiously plural. Third, by bringing an East Asian *chiological* perspective on world religion, I will point out that *ch'i* is the essence of all beings including God (or Tao) and that the *formal* dimension of the Holy Spirit has been present in East Asian religions despite the absence of the *material* dimension of the Spirit. Both Moltmann and Samartha support the idea that the Holy Spirit is present in people of other faiths. Moltmann particularly points out that Yahweh's *ruach* (Spirit) is present in every thing, and this understanding of the Spirit is very similar to the philosophical Taoism's view of *ch'i* (*qi* or *ki*), which is the power of life interpenetrating all entities including both animate and inanimate objects. Furthermore, both pneumatologies of Moltmann and Taoists underscore continuity between the Holy Spirit (the Primordial *ch'i*) and human spirit (substantial

---

1. See Veli-Matti Kärkkäinen, *An Introduction to the Theology of Religions: Biblical, Historical and Contemporary Perspectives* (Downers Grove: InterVarsity, 2003). This book provides an excellent overview of theology of religions. Kärkkäinen also introduces theologians who employ pneumatological approaches, such as Jacques Dupuis, Gavin D'Costa, and Amos Yong.

ch'i). At the end of the chapter, I argue that the *I Ching*, Confucianism, and Taoism ratify the *formal* activities of the Spirit.

Jürgen Moltmann

The Spirit of Father and the Spirit of Christ

In his groundbreaking book *The Spirit of Life*, Jürgen Moltmann avers that the Holy Spirit is both "the Spirit of the Father" and "the Spirit of Christ." The work of creation is generally assigned to the Father, so the Spirit of the Father refers to *the Spirit of creation*. This creative Spirit, Yahweh's *ruach*, animates and *gives life* to all God's creation.[2] As the divine energy of life, the creative Spirit interpenetrates all the living things according to the Hebrew Scriptures.[3] Moltmann writes, "There [in the Old Testament], God's Spirit is the life-force of created things, and the living space in which they can grow and develop their potentialities."[4] The creative Spirit not only stays inside the church, but also stays outside the church. Furthermore, this creative Spirit remains universal.[5]

On the other hand, "the Spirit of Christ" alludes to *the Spirit of redemption* since the work of redemption is generally ascribed to Christ. The redemptive Spirit works on salvation, which not only involves one's soul but also the resurrection of the body and the new creation of all things. Gnostics taught the false idea that salvation was simply to escape from the evil body, but in the biblical sense, God's whole creation, which consists of both material and immaterial things, is longing for salvation.[6]

God's creative Spirit and redemptive Spirit stay one and the same. In this sense, both one's experience in the Christian faith and experience of social love lead to the same Holy Spirit, who is also present in nature, plants, animals, and the ecosystem of the earth. In other words, both the creative and redemptive aspects of the Holy Spirit belong to the one, same Spirit.[7]

2. Jürgen Moltmann, *The Source of Life: The Holy Spirit and the Theology of Life*, trans. Margaret Kohl (Minneapolis: Fortress, 1997) 53.

3. Jürgen Moltmann, *The Spirit of Life: A Universal Affirmation*, trans. Margaret Kohl (Minneapolis: Press, 1992) 8.

4. Ibid., 84.

5. Ibid., 8.

6. Ibid., 9.

7. Ibid., 9–10.

I concur with Moltmann insofar as there are at least two aspects of the Holy Spirit, namely, creative and redemptive. Most Evangelical and Pentecostal churches in America as well as most churches in South Korea refute the cosmic, ubiquitous aspect of the Spirit and solely accept the redemptive work of the Spirit. In this regard, the Spirit is present only in the church. On the contrary, Moltmann argues that the Holy Spirit as the life-force (vitality) and the living space is present in all creatures.

Is God an Object of Human Experience?

"No" has been the answer of most modern European thinkers according to Moltmann inasmuch as their constitution of reason inculcated that God as an object could neither be known nor experienced.[8] Immanuel Kant insisted that God as an object was hidden and unknowable. In human objectivity, God does not exist. God cannot be perceived in objectivity, but God can only be experienced in subjectivity. Descartes endeavored to prove God's existence in human subject's certainty of herself, and Schleiermacher did in "immediate self-consciousness." God is experienced subjectively in one's self-consciousness as "transcendental" condition, which is categorized as "self-transcendence" by Karl Rahner and "ecstatic self-transcendence" by Wolfhart Pannenberg.[9]

Moltmann contends that the modern European concept of experience is too narrow to embrace real and potential experiences. The modern concept of experience solely deals with consciousness in active terms. Moreover, it has a homogeneous and uniform structure. Therefore, one needs to expand this modern European constitution of experience in order that experience of God is not limited to "self-consciousness" or the human subject's experience of self.[10]

God can be also experienced objectively in the experience of others, nature, and sociality, as the Wisdom of Solomon 1:7 states, "God's spirit fills the world and he who holds all things together knows every sound." The Wisdom 12:1 also says, "Thy immortal Spirit is in all things." One can experience God *in, with and beneath* everyday experiences of the world because God is in all things and all things are in God.[11] The notion

8. Ibid., 31.

9. Ibid., 31–32.

10. Ibid., 34.

11. Ibid.

that God is in all things find its further basis from several passages in the Hebrew Bible. Job 33:4 says, "The Spirit of God has made me and the breath of the Almighty gives me life." Psalm 104:29–30 (NRSV) remarks, "When you hide your face, they are dismayed; when you take away their breath, they die and return to their dust. When you send forth your spirit [breath], they are created; and you renew the face of the ground." On the basis of these verses in the Hebrew Scriptures, one can conclude that the Spirit not only dwells in human beings as their breath, but she is also present in all things. Therefore, a person can experience the Spirit of God both in the "spiritual" realm and in the realm of everyday, sensuous events.

Ruach and Spirit in Other Religions

It is very difficult to translate the Hebrew word *ruach* into English. Although the Greek *pneuma*, the Latin *spiritus*, and the German *Geist* are antithetical to matter and body, *ruach* should not be understood in this dualistic context. In the Hebrew Bible, *ruach* can be perceived as a storm or force in body and soul. Therefore, *ruach Yahweh* can be best understood as "the divine energetic force or presence." Furthermore, Yahweh's *ruach* has two sides, namely, transcendent and immanent. In terms of the immanent side, the *ruach* corresponds with *the power of life or power to live in all the living.* Ruach may be found in everything, and she keeps all things in being and in life.[12]

If one follows Moltmann's understanding of the Holy Spirit as the life-force or vitality of all created things, she or he cannot certainly deny the presence of the Spirit in other faiths. There is a life in other religions! Indubitably, people of other faiths have a robust desire for life and good living like Christians in the church. They are breathing because of the Spirit of life in them. These people of other faiths also longing for love, joy, peace, patience, kindness, generosity, faithfulness, gentleness, and self-control (Gal 5:22). Therefore, we cannot doubt the Spirit's presence in other faiths. Rather, we are to question the degree and purity of the Spirit within these faiths, and these criteria must apply to the Spirit in the church as well.

12. Ibid., 40–42.

Stanley J. Samartha (1920–2001)

Stanley Samartha, one of the premier theologians in Asia, was born in India in 1920. He was the son of a pastor of the Basel Evangelical Mission and grew up in the South of India. He received theological education both in India and abroad. At Union Theological Seminary in New York, he studied with Paul Tillich and Reinhold Niebuhr and completed his doctorate degree at Hartford Seminary. He also studied under Karl Barth in Basel, Switzerland before his return to India in 1952. In 1968, he joined the staff of the World Council of Churches as an Associate Secretary in the Department of Studies in Mission and Evangelism. In his life, he devoted his energy to ecumenical and interreligious dialogue. He passed away on July 22, 2001.[13]

The Two Obstacles for Interreligious Dialogue: Syncretism and Relativism

Before World War II, people of other religions were mostly treated as objects of Christian mission, but this situation has been drastically rectified after the war because more and more Christians have become acquainted with people of other faiths and ideological convictions. Christians today live in a religiously plural world. Often in this plural context, people raise the question concerning the presence of the Holy Spirit in other religions.[14]

There have been two main reasons which have stalled the debate about God's concern for people of other faiths. The first reason exemplifies syncretism that is defined as "an uncritical mixture of elements from other religions without center or integrating principle."[15] Despite such initial fear of syncretism during the 1970s and 1980s, no attempt within various interreligious dialogues was made to bring forth such a mixture of religions. Instead, interreligious dialogue usually pointed out difference. Hence, the fear of syncretism was proven to be unnecessary.[16]

13. Konrad Raiser, "Tribute to Dr. Stanley J. Samartha," The World Council of Churches; available from http://wcc-coe.org/wcc/what/interreligious/cd38-02.html.

14. Stanley Samartha, "The Holy Spirit and People of Other Faiths," *Ecumenical Review* 42 (2004) 250–52.

15. Ibid., 252.

16. Ibid.

The second reason stalling the debate deals with relativism, which accepts many absolutes so that truth is relative to each culture and religion. Many people feared that any recognition of the presence of God or the Spirit in other faiths would lead to the peril of relativism. During the past century, the study of religion in the West more or less has taught to perceive the other's thought and behavior in terms of what is absolute for him or her.[17] In order to become aware of one's "self-absolutization," one first needs to change his or her attitude toward other religions and cultures.

Samartha demarcates pluralism from relativism. The plurality of religions and cultures does not necessarily lead to relativism. Human theologies and concepts about God exemplify human *responses* to Truth that are conditioned and diluted by history, and they are fallible and tainted. Hence, although Truth can be absolute, the human statements about the Truth cannot be absolute.[18] Samartha insists on relativity of human concepts of God, not relativity of God.

Deeper Factors Precluding the Interreligious Debate on the Spirit

Samartha expatiates upon other sensitive and deeper factors that have precluded the discussion about the relation of the Holy Spirit to people belonging to other faiths. The first factor is the equivocality and vagueness of the Holy Spirit in the Trinitarian context. In order to have a dialogue with people of other faiths, Christians ought to have a better comprehension of the person of the Spirit. But the Christological or even Christomonistic orientation of Western theologies in the past did not provide much clarification regarding the person of the Spirit, and she[19] was treated as an addendum. Not much of theological reflection and clarification on the Spirit took place before the fourth century. Even the

---

17. Jean Jacques Waardenburg, *Classical Approaches to the Study of Religion: Aims, Methods and Theories of Research* (The Hague: Mouton, 1973) 75, quoted in Stanley Samartha, "Holy Spirit and People of Other Faiths," 253.

18. Samartha, "Other Faiths," 253.

19. The feminine pronoun *she* is used here because the Hebrew word *ruach* exemplifies a feminine noun, and also I want to underscore the feminine qualities of the Holy Spirit. For more information on this, see Donald Gelpi, *The Divine Mother: A Trinitarian Theology of the Holy Spirit* (New York: University Press of America, 1984) 11.

Nicea-Constantinople Creed of 381 did not unequivocally state the full divinity of the Spirit by not endorsing the *homoousios* of the Spirit.[20]

The second remains the question of *filioque*, namely, does the Spirit proceed from the Father alone or the Father and the Son? The Nicene Creed (325 CE) simply says, "And [we believe] in the Holy Spirit, and the Nicea-Constantinople Creed (381 CE) elaborates this further by stating, "I believe . . . in the Holy Spirit, the Lord, the Giver of Life, *who proceeds from the Father,* who with the Father and Son together is worshipped and together glorified."[21] The Latin Western Church added the *filioque* phrase (and the Son) later.[22] According to Samartha, this phrase has significant implication in terms of the presence and work of the Spirit in other faiths. The double procession of the Spirit, which accepts the *filioque,* may bring forth the limitation of the Spirit's activity because the Holy Spirit is available almost exclusively through the Christological channel. In contrast, the single procession of the Spirit in the Eastern Church allows a bigger space to the Spirit to breathe more freely through the whole creation, not limited to Christians in the church.[23]

The third factor which prevents the interreligious debate on the Spirit's presence has to do with the link between the outpouring of the Spirit in Acts 2 and the works of the Spirit before the Pentecost. The very fact that the Spirit spoke through various prophets of Israel in the Hebrew Bible might suggest some possibility of the Spirit's activity on prophets of other faiths.[24]

The fourth factor that averts further debate on the presence of the Spirit in other faiths is elicited by the relation between *baptism* and *gifts* of the Spirit. In the Acts of Apostles, especially chapter 10 and 19, the Holy Spirit was bestowed prior to the act of water baptism—for many Roman Catholics, this sacrament of (water) baptism brings a person into the church of Jesus Christ. Moreover, Samartha introduces a Hindu who receives many blessings from the Hindu divine *Sakti* (power or energy)

---

20. Samartha, "Other Faiths," 254.

21. Italics are mine.

22. For more information on the *filioque* controversy, see Barth, *Church Dogmatics,* I/1:479–87; Pannenberg, *Systematic Theology,* 1:317–19. Karl Barth defends the *filioque* phrase, whereas both Pannenberg and Moltmann refute the *filioque.*

23. Samartha, "Other Faiths," 255.

24. Ibid., 256.

by attending Christian Charismatic services.[25] Samartha illustrates the presence and activity of the Holy Spirit outside the Christian church.

Discerning the Works of the Holy Spirit

Samartha provides four criteria in response to the question, "How do we discern the marks or works of the Holy Spirit according to the Bible?" The first criterion is *freedom*. The work of the Holy Spirit is so spontaneous and unpredictable that no one can clearly tell where the Spirit is heading. Second, the Spirit as "wind" stays *boundless* in such a way that she often transcends one's theological system and conventional wisdom. Creating new relationships is the third criterion insofar as the Spirit engenders *reconciliation* between two hostile groups and religions. Samartha presents examples of religious reconciliation in this article. The fourth criterion deals with *new communities*. When the genuine Spirit works, it brings forth new and peaceful communities. The new communities are imbued with acts of compassion, service, humility, and sacrifice.[26]

Samartha postulates that the most obvious way of discerning the works of the Spirit outside Christianity is found in Gal 5:22–23 (NRSV), "By contrast, the fruit of the Spirit is love, joy, peace, patience, kindness, generosity, faithfulness, gentleness, and self-control. There is no law against such things." These fruits of the Holy Spirit remain genuine signs of the works of the Spirit so that they do not necessitate any further theological investigations.[27]

Besides *ethical dimensions,* Samartha speaks of *"inward" or "interior" dimensions* of the Spirit's presence. These are less visible and not readily recognizable qualities. A person can procure these by being rooted in the Spirit or abiding in the depths of God, which leads one to serenity, restfulness and inner peace. Inwardness or interiority underscores *being* in God, rather than *doing* something for God and other people. The Hindu and Buddhist traditions best emphasize this inwardness of the Spirit's presence.[28]

25. Ibid.

26. Ibid., 258–59. See also Stanley Samartha, "The Holy Spirit and People of Various Faiths, Cultures, and Ideologies," in *The Holy Spirit,* ed. Dow Kilpatrick (Nashville: Tidings, 1974) 33. Here, Samartha elaborates on two more criteria, namely, life and order.

27. Ibid., 261.

28. Ibid.

The major thrusts of Samartha's article are twofold: First, he concedes the presence of the Holy Spirit in people of other faiths. Second, the presence of the Spirit is somewhat discernable. In addition, according to the Hebrew Scriptures and New Testament, Christians are not called to *restrict* the presence and work of the Holy Spirit, but called to *discern* them. Therefore, Christians cannot monopolize the presence of the Holy Spirit.

The Holy Spirit and Ch'i (Ki) in Taoism
A Historical Development of Taoism

THE SHAMANIC ROOTS OF CHINESE RELIGION

No religion or philosophy is born devoid of its context. Several thousand years ago in ancient China, long before there was the idea of the Tao, tribal leaders made offerings to the sky, earth, mountains, trees, and rivers to have fellowship between the sacred powers and humans. Taoist philosophy or religion more or less also emerged in the shamanistic context. Various shamanistic dancing movements and healing practices can still be detected in present Taoist religious ceremonies.[29]

In a broad sense, the word *shaman* refers to any magician, sorcerer, medicine man, or ecstatic priest. They are found to have existed in nearly all the primitive societies of India, Persia, Europe, China, and Babylonia. This broad definition of the word engendered some unnecessary confusion. In a more strict sense, however, the word is restricted to religious leaders in Siberia and Central Asia, and they possess a special technique of ecstasy. Etymologically the word *shaman* comes from the Tungusic *saman*. In most areas of Central and North Asian, the traditional magico-religious life centered on the shaman. This strict sense of the word with a special emphasis on a technique of ecstasy demarcates the shamans from other magicians and medicine men in primitive societies.[30]

In ancient China, long before the Classical Period (700–220 BCE), chieftains ruled and guided each tribe. These chieftains were generally not only rulers but also shamans. These shaman chieftains were said to possess extraordinary powers to fight against floods and natural disas-

---

29. Eva Wong, *Taoism* (Boston: Shambhala, 1997) 3.

30. Mircea Eliade, *Shamanism: Archaic Techniques of Ecstasy,* trans. Willard Trask (London: Routledge & Kegan Paul, 1964) 3–5.

ters, as well as to talk to natural objects and travel across the sky and beneath the earth to procure knowledge. According to various legends in China, there was this legendary chieftain, named Yü, who was no ordinary mortal. In fact, he did not have a mother; he came out directly from the body of his father whose name is Kun. Kun was also a shaman. Shun, a tribal leader, asked Kun to fight against a flood, but Kun failed to do so. Kun was severely punished, and his dead body was left on a mountain side. Somehow, when Kun was mysteriously revived, he turned into a brown bear. This bear opened up his own belly and brought forth his son, Yü. As soon as he was born, he changed himself into a bear. Throughout his life, he had both shapes: Sometimes, he looked like a human, and other times, he looked like a bear. He walked by shuffling—known as bear's gate. A thousand years after the legendary times of Yü, many priests in the Chou dynasty (1122–256 BCE) still dressed in bearskins and shuffled their feet as they danced around the gate of power in order to commemorate the Great Yü.[31]

Yü followed and continued the work of his father. He was very successful and surpassed his father's ability because of his exposure to the mythical book *Shui-ching* (*The Book of Power over Waters*). Regularly, he traveled to the stars for the purpose of learning from the celestial spirits. The dance of "the Pace of Yü" carried him to the sky, and this dance is still preserved in many religious Taoist texts. The Pace of Yü has been practiced by generations of Taoist priests, Chinese mystics and sorcerers, as well as many martial artists.[32]

According to legends, Yü was not only able to take forms of other animals but also to communicate with them, who in return revealed their secrets to him. For instance, he saw a tortoise when the flood waters retreated. The shell of the tortoise disclosed the nature of flux and *change* in the world. The *tortoise-shell reading* became the basis of divination in China. As a matter of fact, seeing the reality as Change (*I*) and divination via tortoise shells became the two pivotal elements in the *I Ching*. Furthermore, the oldest way of divination was the tortoise shell reading, which was replaced by reading the yarrow (milfoil) stalks of a divine plant due to complexity and impracticability of the tortoise shell reading.[33]

31. Ibid., 11–12.

32. Ibid., 12–13.

33. Yu-lan Fung, *A History of Chinese Philosophy*, trans. Derk Bodde (Princeton:

The legendary Yü unequivocally fits into Mircea Eliade's classification of a shaman in *Shamanism*. Some of the key characteristics of a shaman according to Eliade include the following: 1) journey through the sky and underground, 2) the dance of power, 3) ecstasy and sudden revelation, 4) conversation with animals, 5) power over some elements such as floods, 6) healing, and 7) knowledge and deployment of plants.[34] These features describe also the activities of the legendary Yü. In ancient Chinese culture, there was a group of people, dubbed the *wu,* whose activities truly resembled the features of shamans. Eliade believed that the *wu* of ancient Chinese culture were shamans. The class of *wu* stayed vital to the tribal society, wherein chieftains were rulers and shamans.[35]

Shamanism in ancient China began a new stage when it entered a literary society at the beginning of the Chou dynasty (1122–256 BCE). Kings and nobles at this time hired shamans as advisers, diviners, and healers. Shamanism developed into an institution wherein they exercised their duties. Shamans who were hired by the state and individuals had to fulfill their functions. Failing to perform their functions often resulted in death. As a matter of fact, according to the historical records of the Chou dynasty, many so-called shamans failed to procure extraordinary powers even though they were dressed in bearskins and practiced the Pace of Yü.[36]

The following are the duties of shamans during the Chou dynasty. The first duty was to invite spirits to visit the earthly sphere and reside temporarily in human bodies. The ceremony of invoking the spirits on shamans began with a dance, which resulted in a trance, and this state allowed the spirits to enter the shaman's body.[37] This is dissimilar to the concept of "demon-possession," of which many Pentecostal Christians nowadays speak, and whereby demons can abuse and mistreat the bodies of the possessed as in the case of Matt 8:28–34. The case of the shaman's trance is the state of consciousness necessary for the visitation of the

---

Princeton University Press, 1952) 1:379–80; J. Y. Lee, *Embracing Change,* 32; Wilhelm, "Introduction," liv.

34. Eliade, *Shamanism,* 6, 181–84.

35. Wong, *Taoism,* 13–14.

36. Ibid., 14.

37. See Jung Young Lee, *Korean Shamanistic Rituals* (New York: Mouton, 1981) 40–80. Dancing and inviting spirits are the two main elements of Korean shamanistic rituals known as *gut.*

spirits, whereas in the case of possession, the spirits enter the bodies of the possessed, which in turn engenders the trance. According to Eliade, the shaman's invocation of the spirits stays different from sorcerers and psychic mediums whose magic depends on possession.[38] Moreover, according to I. M. Lewis, the spirit-possession of shamans truly differs from those of other spirit mediums because the possession of the shaman remains *controlled*. The shamans has the power to control the spirits insofar as they can call up the spirits at will and do perform their rituals in a "controlled" mode and behavior that are accepted by a local culture and ethos.[39]

The next main duty of the shamans during the Chou dynasty was to interpret dreams that are deemed to be carriers of omens. Often, even dreams of nonshamans were seen as messages of the spirits. Ancestors' spirits sometimes speak to their family members in dreams, which can be correctly decoded by shamans who can enter the higher realms. In a shamanic ritual, shamans summon the spirits of the dead.[40]

The third main task of the shamans of the Chou dynasty was to find omens in nature and correctly construe them. By carefully observing strange movements of nature, shamans can predict an immediate future or ask common people to engage in certain types of action in order to eschew some disasters and misfortune. Most shamans in the Chou dynasty were very familiar with the *I Ching* and served as diviners.[41]

The fourth pivotal task was to invoke rain. Especially in the agricultural society, nothing is more vital than rain. In this regard, the ceremony for rain has been an integral part of Chinese religious ritual, and today Taoist priests still perform this ceremony. Dancing and singing are essential parts of the ceremony. The Chinese word for spirit (*ling*) comprises three radicals: 1) rain, 2) chanting (picture of three mouths), and shaman. The whole ideogram depicts a shaman who tries to persuade the heavenly powers to send rain.[42]

The fifth essential task of the shaman was to perform healing. In the earliest times, healing was predominantly performed by the shamaness. According to many oral traditions, the shamaness held a green snake in

---

38. Eliade, *Shamanism,* 6.

39. I. M. Lewis, *Ecstatic Religion* (London: Routledge, 1989) 57.

40. Wong, *Taoism,* 15.

41. Ibid., 15.

42. Ibid.

her right hand and a red snake in her left hand. With these hands, she climbed into the mountains to find the herbs that could heal a sick and dying person. The ancient Chinese in general thought that illness was engendered by malevolent spirits invading human bodies. So it was a job of the shamaness to exorcise the maleficent spirits from the body of a sick person.[43]

The sixth duty of the shamans during the Chou dynasty was celestial divination, which remained very popular during the second half of the Chou dynasty. Harmony in the skies meant prosperity, peace, and harmony on earth. Hence, in order to procure peace and prosperity, one had to study the movements of stars and follow the celestial way, also known as the will of heaven. Thus, shamans were hired to study the skies and construe celestial events.[44]

THE SHAMANIC LEGACIES IN LATER DEVELOPMENTS OF TAOISM

Shamanism gradually declined in the mainline society of the Chou dynasty; however, pockets of shamanic culture continued to be strong in the valley areas of Yang-tze River and the southeastern coast. The three feudal kingdoms (i.e., Ch'u, Wu, and Yüeh) occupied these areas. People residing in the land of Ch'u kept their beliefs in the spirits while more and more people of the northern kingdom were abandoning the shamanic beliefs by developing literacy. As a matter of fact, both founders of the *Tao-chia* (philosophical Taoism), namely Lao-tzŭ[45] and Chuang-tzŭ, came from the feudal kingdom of Ch'u where the most dominant religious form was shamanism.

People in the feudal kingdoms of Wu and Yüeh, farthest to the east and below Yang-tze River were kept away from the mainline culture of the Chou Dynasty. Incantations and mantras were employed to ward off harmful spirits and enemies by the shamans of the Chou dynasty, who also used talismans to bring peace and harmony. Eventually, these talismanic scripts became an important part of Taoist sorcery and magic.

---

43. Ibid., 16.

44. Ibid.

45. See JeeLoo Liu, *An Introduction to Chinese Philosophy* (Malden: Blackwell, 2006) 131–32. There is still a big debate whether Lao-tzu was a real historical person or not. According to the *Shi-chi* (Historical Records) by Ssu-ma Ch'ien, Lao-tzu was a historical figure who was from the state of Ch'u.

Even long after the kingdoms of Yüeh, Wu, and Ch'u, the shamanic characteristics of these kingdoms continuously influenced Chinese culture.

The most obvious absorption of shamanic practices into Taoism was found in the magical and religious side of Taoism (C. *Tao-chiao*) which came to surface in the Han dynasty (206 BCE—220 CE).

Very similar to the shamans in Yüeh, Taoist magicians during the Han employed *incantations and talismans* in order to fight against malevolent and harmful spirits. Taoist priests nowadays still practice this magic.[46]

Other shamanic legacies were found in the Han dynasty. The Taoists during this era practiced their flight to the stars, danced the Pace of Yü, as well as journey through the underground. The Han Taoist mystic Tung-fang Shuo was well-known for his shamanic underground journey. Even today, we see the practice of the underground journey in Taoists ceremonies in order to save dead souls who have been abducted by evil spirits.[47]

Harvey Cox: Shamanism and Asian Pentecostals

In 1995, the Harvard Theologian Harvey Cox published a groundbreaking work, entitled *Fire from Heaven*. In this monograph, Cox explores the Pentecostal-Charismatic movement, which is the fastest-growing Christian movement in the world. The most distinctive and salient doctrine of this global movement remains "baptism in the Holy Spirit."[48] Today, no less than five-hundred-million Christians belong to this movement.[49]

46. Wong, *Taoism*, 17.

47. Ibid., 17.

48. Frank Macchia, *Baptized in the Spirit: A Global Pentecostal Theology* (Grand Rapids: Zondervan, 2006) 11–60. See also K. D. Yun, *Baptism in the Holy Spirit*, 23–44.

49. David Barrett, George Kurian, and Todd Johnson, *World Christian Encyclopedia: A Comparative Survey of Churches and Religions in the Modern World*, 2nd ed. (New York: Oxford University Press, 2001). According to this Encyclopedia, the combined number of both Pentecostals and Charismatics in 2000 is about 523,777,004. For more information, see Table 1–1. For the estimated figures of previous years, see Vinson Synan, "Pentecostalism: Varieties and Contributions," *PNEUMA: The Journal of the Society for Pentecostal Studies* (1986) 43–44; Daniel Albrecht, *Rites in the Spirit: A Ritual Approach to Pentecostal/Charismatic Spirituality* (Sheffield, UK: Sheffield Academic Press, 1999) 27–28; Harvey Cox, "Pentecostalism and the Future of Christianity," *TIKKUN* 9.6 (1994) 43; Koo Dong Yun, *Baptism in the Holy Spirit* (Lanham: University Press of America, 2003) xi.

In chapter 11 of *Fire from Heaven,* Cox finds a connection between shamanism and Asian Pentecostals. Cox avers that shamanism provides a common element in the midst of diverse Asian cultures and religions. Underneath the so-called high religions such as Confucianism and Buddhism, there is shamanism. Shamanism will never die in Asia because it is too deeply embedded in Asian cultures. Moreover, shamanism exemplifies a more basic and universal form of religious expression that can be found almost everywhere.[50]

Cox defines a "shaman" as a person "whose power comes directly from the supernatural world rather than through the medium of a traditional ritual or body of esoteric knowledge."[51] In this sense, the shaman stands at the polar opposite of the priest. Most shamans perform their ceremonies in a trancelike state, which can be reached with certain music, chanting, drumming, or incantation. These shamans exist to help overcome human pain, disease, and demon possession.[52]

The Pentecostal movement in Asia, Cox argues, has been a synthetic process including both the sources from the Christian traditions (e.g., the Bible and Western theology) as well as those from pre-Christian, indigenous Asian religions. Cox writes, "In my opinion, what one finds in the Yoido Full Gospel Church of Seoul [in South Korea] involves a massive importation of shamanic practice into a Christian ritual."[53] The Yoido Full Gospel Church is well-known as the single largest congregation in the world today. As said by Dr. Young-hoon Lee, current Senior Pastor of the Yoido Full Gospel Church, this Church consisted of more than 755,000 members, as of January of 2009.[54] In this Church, Cox finds some shamanistic practices, such as ecstatic trances, demon possession, and exorcism.[55] Moreover, by raising their hands, these Korean Pentecostals worship "Hananim," the name of the Christian God in Korea. As I pointed out in chapter 1 of this book, the name "Hananim"— meaning *One Sovereign Lord*—comes from traditional Korean shaman-

---

50. Harvey Cox, *Fire from Heaven: The Rise of Pentecostal Spirituality and the Reshaping of Religion in the Twenty-first Century* (Cambridge: Da Capo, 1995) 226–27.

51. Ibid., 225.

52. Ibid., 226.

53. Ibid.

54. Young-hoon Lee, *The Holy Spirit Movement in Korea: Its Historical and Theological Development* (Oxford: Regnum, 2009) 99.

55. Cox, *Fire,* 225.

istic roots. In this regard, Cox points out the fact that it is not clear at times whether these Pentecostals in the Yoido Full Gospel Church are worshipping either the *shaman* God or the *Christian* God.

Cox tells of the two main reasons for the Yoido Church's rapid growth. First, it has been a center for spiritual and physical healing. Without much doubt, many physical and spiritual healings as well as supernatural miracles took place in the Yoido Church. Second, it absorbed many shamanistic practices in its worship.[56] As a matter of fact, Korean Pentecostalism has afforded a setting where thousands of Koreans can now exercise their old-time shamanistic rituals in the name of Christianity. In so doing, these Korean Christians can now practice their traditional, indigenous spirituality and at the same time eschew the association with shamanism that has been often persecuted and despised by the ruling class.

After reading *Fire from Heaven*, I was deeply impressed and surprised by Professor Cox's acute and poignant analyses of Korean Pentecostalism as well as other Asian Pentecostal groups. Cox is correct that many Asian Pentecostals integrated certain rituals of their indigenous folk religions. Cox is also correct in that millions of Asian Pentecostals have retrieved *primal speech* (ecstatic utterance or glossolalia), *primal piety* (mystical experience, trance, and healing), and *primal hope* (the unshakable expectation of a better hope) through the Pentecostal movement. As Cox saw, many of these primal elements have been underscored and practiced by shamanism and religious Taoism (C. *Tao Chiao*).[57]

I would argue, however, that Professor Cox explores indigenous Asian religions and Pentecostalism from the *sangjeok* viewpoint that is formal and archetypal. The *sangjeok* dimension of the Spirit has been present and active in all cultures and at all times. Christianity does not monopolize primal speech, primal piety, and primal hope. Other indigenous Asian religions teach these forms of primal spirituality. For instance, Cox regards glossolalia (speaking in tongues) as a form of "ecstatic utterance," which is also found among many Tibetan Buddhist monks and Hindu holy men.[58] As Cox points out, this *sangjeok* dimen-

---

56. Cox, *Fire*, 221–22.

57. Ibid., 81–83.

58. Ibid., 91.

sion stays truly "cosmic" insofar as it is known as the "universal grammar" and "elementary forms."[59]

What Cox does not explore much in *Fire from Heaven* is the *muljeok*
dimension of the Spirit that is material, particular, and categorical. By
contrast, most Pentecostals in South Korea want to underscore almost
exclusively the *muljeok* dimension of the Spirit that is Christological and
Lukan-Pentecostal. They say, "We know the Spirit through Jesus Christ
and the Christian Bible." The *muljeok* dimension of the Spirit discloses
divergences or diversity of the Spirit. As the Spirit takes more and more
particular and tangible shapes in order to reveal its nature to earthly
human beings, it naturally brings forth diverse and even different contextual concepts and appearances. For example, as I discussed before,
an East Asian pneumatology (e.g., *chiology*) observes more continuity
between the divine spirit (*ch'i*) and the human spirit (*ch'i*), whereas many
Western theologians (e.g., Karl Barth) tend to underscore discontinuity
between them. Therefore, from the *muljeok* perspective, one sees more
diversity and difference between them.

Moltmann's Spirit of Life and *Ch'i* in Taoism

One can readily find some similarities between Moltmann's construal
of the Holy Spirit and *ch'i* insofar as both Yahweh's *ruach* (Spirit) and
ch'i are understood as the power of life that interpenetrates all existing
things. In accordance with Jürgen Moltmann, Yahweh's *ruach* possesses
both transcendental and immanent aspects. As the immanent efficacy,
the Holy Spirit is "the power of life in all the living."[60] Moltmann writes,
"When we think about the *ruach*, we have to say that God is in all things,
and all things are in God—though this does not mean making God the
same as everything else."[61] Furthermore, the Spirit can also be construed
as space because *ruach* is related to *rewah*, meaning breadth. In other
words, God's Spirit also refers to God's Space, in which all living beings
can grow and unfold (Ps 31:8; Job 36:16).[62] As both the Spirit of life and
space, the Holy Spirit stays ubiquitous and interpenetrates all things.

59. Ibid., 82.
60. Moltmann, *Spirit of Life*, 42.
61. Ibid.
62. Ibid., 43.

In Taoism, *ch'i (Qi or Ki)* is also understood as "the life force, vital breath, [and] inner pneuma of all existence."[63] As the life force, *ch'i* interpenetrates not only the living being but also all natural objects. Chapter 43 of the *Tao Te Ching* states, "The softest thing in the world dashes against and overcomes the hardest; that which has no (substantial) existence [*ch'i*] enters where there is no crevice. I know hereby what advantage belongs to doing nothing (with a purpose)."[64] The formless, unsubstantial *ch'i* penetrates into all existing entities. Moreover, this *ch'i* sustains the structure of the universe.[65]

Ch'i is inherent in all four areas of life: the body, nature, the sky, and society, which equally stems from the true all-encompassing Tao. There is no structural difference between *ch'i* in humans and *ch'i* in nature. *Ch'i* existing in the four areas of life varies with different density and velocity. *Ch'i* can be either too thick or too thin; it can also flow too fast or too slow. Traditional Chinese medicine specified the movements of *ch'i* in the body. The yin and yang system expatiates on various activities of *ch'i*.[66]

Any entity including a human being can deviate from its inherent harmony given by the Tao. Typically, one's excessive activity causes this deviation. For example, a physical over-exercise a day can cause harm to one's body because she did it too much. Greed, fear as well as earthquakes are engendered by the derailment of *ch'i*. When the flow of *ch'i* is blocked, it results in irregularity and disharmony in oneself and nature. One needs to reopen this blockage by acupuncture, moxibustion, mediation, and prayer.[67]

In addition to the universal presence of the Spirit, both Moltmann and Taoism also accept the continuity between the Spirit of God (the Primordial *ch'i*) and the spirit (*ch'i*) of existent things. In contrast to most modern Protestant theologians (including Karl Barth) who separated the two, Moltmann teaches the continuity between the two. It is the same Spirit of God who is present in humans, living creatures, and nature.

63. Livia Kohn, "Chinese Religion," in *The Human Condition*, ed. Robert Neville (Albany: State University of New York Press, 2001) 23.

64. *The Sacred Books of China: The Texts of Taoism*, trans. James Legge (New York: Dover, 1962) 87.

65. See Paul Chung, "The Mystery of God and Tao in Jewish—Christian—Taoist Context," in *Asian Contextual Theology for the Third Millennium*, 243–66.

66. Kohn, "Chinese Religion," 24.

67. Ibid., 24–26.

God's Spirit of Creation and God's Spirit of redemption are the one and the same.

Each force (*ch'i*) exemplifies a manifestation of the Tao without an active break from the pure, shapeless Tao. *The Primordial ch'i (yuanqi)* was part of the Tao before creation (substantial existence). According to chapter 42 of the *Tao Te Ching*, the Tao is the One! The One produces Two; Two produces Three; Three produced all things.[68] All things originated from the Tao, which is one, and all things endeavor to return to the origin. In the philosophical framework of Taoism, there is a clear continuity between the Tao and the manifested *ch'i*.

The theology of the Donghak movement in Korea as well found continuity between the "Utmost Energy" (God) and the spirit in a human body. Jae Woo Choi (CE 1824–1864), the key leader of the Donghak Movement, promulgated the notion that the "Utmost Energy" represents the creative energy that is pantheistically immanent in human bodies as well as cosmos-nature. The Donghak incantation, which functioned like the Lord's Prayer in Christianity remarks, "Oh Utmost Energy, I'm praying for your advent here and now. Wait on God and everything goes well. Don't forget God at any time and you get to know All. To wait on means that *the divine spirit is inside the body*, the energization is outside the body, and everyone knows the truth which cannot be relocated."[69] This active energy of the Spirit is not only inherent in human body, and it can also provide harmony and peace in cosmos as well as physical healing and prophecy.

The Spirit's Discontinuity in Barth's Theology

Many modern European theologians and philosophers overemphasized the transcendental aspect of the Holy Spirit at the expense of the Spirit's immanent side. One step further, they insisted on the discontinuity between God's Spirit and human spirit. Karl Barth is a prime example of these thinkers, but Moltmann argues that the Spirit is both the Spirit of creation and the Spirit of the church. As Stanley Samartha points out previously, the Scriptures do not ask Christians to control or restrict the presence and work of the Spirit, but ask them to discern the Spirit(s).

---

68. *The Sacred Books of China: The Texts of Taoism*, 85.

69. Kyoung Jae Kim, "The Cosmotheandric Vision in the Third Millennium," *Exchange* 28.4 (1999) 351–63.

Karl Barth speaks of discontinuity between the Holy Spirit and human spirit. In his lecture "The Holy Spirit and Christian Life" (1929), Barth points out the radical difference between God's Spirit and human spirit because there is no continuity between Creator and creatures.[70] In several places in *Church Dogmatics*, even though Karl Barth accepts the fact that the Holy Spirit dwells in believers, he repeatedly underscores that the divine Spirit always remain distinct from human spirits. Barth writes, "A point that we should remember in what has been said already is made quite explicit here: the Spirit is not identical, and does not identify with ourselves. When Paul uses the term πνεῦμα (*pneuma*) in his anthropology he is not saying that the Holy Spirit either wholly or partially, either originally or subsequently, is part of man's own essence. . . . He [the Holy Spirit] is absolutely other, superior."[71]

Barth reiterates the difference between the Holy Spirit and human spirit in *Evangelical Theology*: "There are also *other* spirits, those created good by God, such as the spirit natural to man. Moreover, there are demonic, erring, and disruptive spirits of annihilation which deserve nothing else than to be driven out. *But none of these are the sovereign power of which we speak.* Of none of them, not even of the best among them, can it be said that where they are, there is freedom."[72]

The Spirit's Presence in Other Faiths

In view of pneumatologies of Jürgen Moltmann and Stanley Samartha, it would be very hard to refute the presence of the Holy Spirit in other faiths. In terms of exterior criteria, these people meliorate ethical virtues such as love, kindness, and generosity through their religious practices. In terms of interior criteria, they find inner peace, serenity and restfulness in their religious devotion. In terms of social dimensions, Samartha points out that these people of other faiths also promote renewed communities that go beyond prejudice and limitation of each religious tradition so that they can perceive peace between religions. These people of other faiths, moreover, exhibit ecological sensitivity by revering the whole nature that includes both spiritual and material entities.

70. Moltmann, *Spirit of Life*, 6.

71. Barth, *Church Dogmatics*, I/1:454.

72. Karl Barth, *Evangelical Theology: An Introduction* (Grand Rapids: Eerdmans, 1963) 53. Italics are mine.

In *Discerning the Spirit(s)*, the Pentecostal theologian Amos Yong endeavors to retrieve Pentecostal/charismatic elements in discerning the works of the Holy Spirit. Traditionally, for most Pentecostals, *speaking in tongues* (glossolalia) was known as "the initial-physical evidence" of Spirit baptism (an encounter with the Spirit). Yong points out many other charismata (charisms) that can serve as the signs of the presence of the Spirit. For example, there are the Pauline charisms (1 Cor 12:8–10): message of wisdom, message of knowledge, faith, gifts of healing, miraculous powers, prophecy, discernment of spirits, speaking in tongues, and interpretation of tongues. In addition, Yong wants to underscore other phenomenological signs of the Spirit's presence, such as dreams, visions, holy dance, shouting and chanting. Phenomenologically speaking, even many of these "Pentecostal/charismatic" signs are often detected in other non-Christian religions.[73]

Even in the Hebrew Bible, God's Spirit not only came upon Israelites but also non-Israelites. Balak, a Moabite ruler, asked Balaam to anathematize the Israelites, but Balaam instead blessed the Israelites according to Yahweh's order. Numbers 24:2 (NRSV) remarks, "Balaam looked up and saw Israel camping tribe by tribe. Then *the spirit of God came upon him*."[74] Balaam was neither an Israelite nor a Moabite, but the God's Spirit came upon him. Hence, he saw visions and made prophetic utterances.[75]

In the New Testament, God also worked with Cornelius prior to his conversion in Acts 10. That he received a vision and utterance antecedently should be accepted as the preparatory work of the Holy Spirit. In terms of a narrow definition of Christian, Cornelius was a non-Christian when he received the vision from the Spirit in Acts 10.[76] Moreover, in Acts 10:44, the Holy Spirit came upon the Gentile audience at Cornelius' house in the middle of Peter's sermon. It is logical to think that the Gentiles at that time underwent neither conversion nor (water) baptism (Acts 10:47). From a sacramentalist's standpoint, the Spirit had

---

73. Amos Yong, *Discerning the Spirit(s): A Pentecostal-Charismatic Contribution to Christian Theology of Religions* (Sheffield: Sheffield Academic Press, 2000) 223–27. Yong speaks of 3 tiers of discernment process: 1) phenomenological-experiential, 2) moral-ethical, and 3) theological-soteriological. See 250–55.

74. *Italics* are mine.

75. Cf. Michael Welker, *God the Spirit*, trans. John Hoffmeyer (Minneapolis: Fortress, 1994) 96–98.

76. Cf. Clark H. Pinnock, *Flame of Love: A Theology of the Holy Spirit* (Downers Grove, InterVarsity, 1996) 201.

come upon them even before they became Christians. On the basis of the previous verses, one may conclude that the Holy Spirit is also present and active in non-Christians.

Although it would be hard to negate the presence and activity of the Spirit in other faiths, one should still raise the questions concerning the degree and purity of the Spirit's presence. As Taoists mention the deviated *ch'i*, Christians also speak of evil/demonic spirits, which bring about estrangement and destruction, instead of bringing and preserving peace, unity, harmony and life. Despite the fact that discerning spirits appears very challenging, it is still doable by focusing on interiority, exteriority and sociality of the Spirit as Samartha engaged in this task throughout his life.

Chiological Perspective on World Religions

At this juncture, I want to delve into the reality of the Spirit from a chiological perspective. By "pneumatological perspective" I mean that a person tries to understand the *Pneuma* from the viewpoint of the third Person of the Godhead (i.e., Holy Spirit), mostly derived from the biblical and traditional Western theological traditions. On the contrary, the chiological perspective goes beyond the biblical and traditional Western theologies by adding "irregular" and "other" voices of God in East Asia. The reality of the Pneuma has been construed with *ch'i*, which is a Chinese counterpart to the English term "spirit." The *chiological* perspective endeavors to understand the reality of the Spirit, expressed in the East Asian religious classics such as the *I Ching* and *Tao Te Ching* in addition to biblical and Western theological traditions.

God is a God of all peoples. All life and breath originate from God (Gen 2:7). In this sense, all people are children and heirs of God who is not a racist (Rom 2:11) and loves all of his children, even when they are rebellious. To this extent, our God has not neglected but has communicated with 'other' children, such as Chinese, Korean, and Japanese in East Asia. God's qualities have been revealed since the beginning of creation to all people via general revelation and Pneumatological cosmic presence (Rom 1:20). Hence, the chiological approach (with a critical analysis) affirms God's action and revelation embedded and detected in the East Asian cultures including their religions.

Ch'i as the Essence of All Beings Including I, Tao, and T'ai-chi (the Great Ultimate)

The *I Ching* teaches that the essence of *I* (Change), Tao, and Great Ultimate is *ch'i* and that *ch'i* refers to the source and substance of the creation. Chang Tsai (1020–1077 CE) argued that *ch'i* was synonymous with the Great Ultimate (or the Great Void, *T'ai-hsü*). In addition, when *ch'i* condensed, it became visible things, and when *ch'i* disperses, it became invisible things, lost shapes, and ultimately went back to the Great Void or the Great Ultimate.[77] In this chiological perspective, all things and all beings that include spiritual and non-spiritual beings consist of *ch'i*. *Ch'i* remains the source and substance of all beings.

Mencius (371–289 BCE) believed that the universe was made of *ch'i* with various densities. For example, the grosser and heavier *ch'i* constituted the earth, and the lighter and more refined *ch'i* became the sky. Human beings stayed between the two. These various densities of *ch'i* also applied to a human person. The human body was constitutive of the grosser *ch'i*, and the human heart was constitutive of the refined *ch'i*. Yet the human blood stayed in-between.

How do I translate the Chinese word *ch'i* (or the Korean *ki*) in English? Or the reverse question will be like this: How do I translate the English word *spirit* (or Spirit) in Chinese and Korean? The best answers will be *spirit* and *ch'i* although there is no exact translation. The Chinese word *ch'i* has been translated as "energy," "vital energy," "pure energy," "force," "material force," "spirit," "vapor," "breath," "air," and so forth. Clearly, many similarities exist between the two words. Because of these similarities, I often use those two terms, spirit and *ch'i*, as synonyms. When I see the word *pneuma* in the English horizon, I use the word *spirit*, but when I descry the word *pneuma* in the East Asian horizon, I use the word *ch'i*.

The biblical statement that God is spirit (John 4:24) remains consonant with the chiological statement that the Great Ultimate (even Tao or Change) is *ch'i*. Both the Christian Bible and the *I Ching* construe the essence of the Ultimate being (i.e., God or Tao) as spirit (or *ch'i*). In the *I Ching*, *ch'i* is also the essence of *T'ien* (Heaven), which is often translated as God. Truly, we need to pay special attention to the fact that both the

---

77. For Chang Tsai, the Great Void is a synonym of the Great Ultimate.

New Testament and the *I Ching* regard the essence of the divine being as *spirit* (*ch'i* in Chinese).

The Sangjeok Dimension and Muljeok Dimension of the Spirit

Many scholars deploy over-simplistic categories with respect to the question of the universal presence or ubiquity of the Holy Spirit in other religious faiths and non-Western cultures. In my opinion, the primary question of this sort should not be whether the Holy Spirit is present there or not because the Spirit of God is omnipresent. Rather, we should ask, "In what ways does the Spirit manifest Herself in other faiths?" Moltmann, in *The Spirit of Life*, rightly pointed out the two different aspects of the Holy Spirit, namely, 1) the Spirit of Creation, and 2) the Spirit of Redemption. I, however, call for the other categories (i.e., *sangjeok*—formal, and *muljeok*—material) in order to underscore the multi-faceted dimensions of the Holy Spirit.

Aristotle (c. 384–) speaks of four causes in order to elucidate existing things. In other words, for a thing to exist, it necessitates the four conditions. The first cause is known as *the material cause*, which asks, "What is it made of?" For instance, bronze is the matter of a bronze statue. The second cause is known as *the formal cause*, which asks, "What is the form or pattern of a thing?" To give an example, H2O is the pattern of water. The third is *the efficient cause*, which inquires, "What is the immediate origin of the movement or rest?" For example, a father is a cause of a child. The fourth is *the final cause*, and it asks, "What is the purpose of an existing thing?" The final purpose of exercising is health.[78]

Paul Tillich in *Systematic Theology* also speaks of the formal and material dimension of reality, especially in relation to faith that is defined as "the state of being grasped by an ultimate concern."[79] Formally speaking, faith remains universal to all humans insofar as every person faces an ultimate concern. But materially speaking (in content), faith becomes manifest in Jesus Christ.[80]

The Chinese word which best describes the English word "formal" is *hsiang* (C. 象, K. 상). In the *I Ching,* this word is often used to denote

78. Richard McKeon, ed., *The Basic Works of Aristotle* (New York: The Modern Library, 2001) 240–41.

79. Paul Tillich, *Systematic Theology* (Chicago: The University of Chicago Press, 1963) 3:130.

80. Ibid., 3:131.

the four emblems, namely, 1) old yang, 2) young yang, 3) old yin, and 4) young yin. On the contrary, the Great Sung Neo-Confucianist Shao Yung (1011–77 CE) regarded the eight trigrams as *hsiang*.[81] Like many other Chinese words, this word also has multiple meanings, such as image, symbol, emblem, pattern, archetype or even "idea" in Plato's invisible world, although the most literal meaning of this word is an "elephant." Hence, when I use the word "formal," it refers to pattern, tendency, generality, archetype, vagueness, and emblem more in the Chinese sense. Accordingly, for me, the *formal* dimension (K. *sangjeok*) of the Holy Spirit portrays general pattern and tendency as well as universally equivocal and archetypal manifestations of the Holy Spirit. For instance, when a Confucian mother has affection towards her child, I see a formal aspect of the work of the Holy Spirit.

The Chinese word which best expresses the English word "material" is *wu* (C. 物, K. 물). Whereas the *formal*, universal dimension (K. *sangjeok*) of the Holy Spirit became manifest in other religious faiths and cultures as love, joy, peace, patience, kindness, goodness, faithfulness, gentleness, and self-control, the *material* dimension (K. *muljeok*) of the Holy Spirit was fully expressed on the Cross of Golgotha. With the Crucifixion, the love of God became concrete, visible, and paradigmatic, and now it is categorized and specified in detail. In other words, the *sangjeok* dimension of the Spirit speaks of a *cosmic* pneumatology, whereas the *muljeok* dimension tells of a *Christological* and *Pentecostal* (Acts 2) pneumatology.

I postulate that the Holy Spirit, from a chiological perspective, has been present and working in other faiths and cultures in terms of the *formal* dimension, long before the arrival of Western Christian missionaries. Nevertheless, the *material* dimension was still missing in the indigenous religions in East Asia until the arrival of Christianity. The "formal" works of the Holy Spirit have been confirmed by the teachings of the traditional East Asian religions. For instance, many fruits of the Holy Spirit (Gal 5:22) have been also underscored by Confucianism, such as *jen* (love or benevolence), *i* (righteousness), *li* (propriety or kindness), *hsin* (good faith or faithfulness), and *chih* (wisdom). Plus, the great Korean Neo-Confucian Yi Yulgok (1536–1584) spoke of love as a main manifestation of *ch'i* (the Chinese counterpart to "spirit"). In addition, the three treasures (C. *san bao*) of Taoism (i.e., compassion, modera-

---

81. Fung Yu-lan, *History of Chinese Philosophy*, 2:457.

tion, and humility) can be regarded as the "formal" manifestations of the Holy Spirit. *Hsi Tz'u* in the *Ten Wings* (*Shih I*) teaches that the foremost manifestation of Tao is kindness (love).[82] Moreover, exorcism has been not only the practice in the New Testament and many Charismatic and Pentecostal congregations, but has been a major part of traditional Korean shamanism—the oldest Korean religion before the introduction of Confucianism and Buddhism. Many Korean theologians still consider the exorcism of shamans as a work of the Holy Spirit, who derives out evil, unclean spirits (K. *gui-shin*). In other words, some works of shamans confirm the *formal* aspect of the Spirit.

This does not imply that I am calling for a simple pluralism. Simply accepting other religions as legitimate ways to God as well as salvation devoid of critical examination becomes pernicious. We still need the works of Christian missionaries to people of other faiths inasmuch as indigenous people in East Asia need to be exposed to the *muljeok* material dimension of the Holy Spirit, i.e., the Spirit of Jesus Christ. When the material side of the Spirit became manifest on the Day of Pentecost in Acts 2, the reality of the Spirit turned out to be fuller and more palpable. In other words, with the Pentecost, the Spirit was no longer vague and equivocal; rather, the presence of the Spirit has grown to be more concrete, personal, and categorical.

The *sangjeok* formal manifestations of the Holy Spirit in other religions and cultures in the past remained unclear, implicit, subtle and delicate, so it was hard to detect these workings of the Spirit. Only careful observation saw these subtle works of the Spirit in the traditional East Asian religions. It became even more difficult and challenging especially when these manifestations were distorted and corrupted by the selfish interests of political and religious leaders. A good example of the religious distortion was that many Chinese emperors became not only the Lord of Earth but also the Lord of Heaven (i.e., God). Another good example was found during the first half of the twentieth century in Japanese State Shintoism, which divinized their emperors in order to augment their nationalist and imperialist agendas. This type of distortion, however, has also seen in Christian ecclesial communities insofar as many Christian communities wanted to monopolize and domesticate the Spirit exclusively in the church without realizing God is "bigger" than the church.

82. *The I Ching* (The Wilhelm/Baynes translation) 298–99. See chapter 5, sections 2 to 5.

The *material* dimension of the Holy Spirit is fully embodied on the Day of Pentecost in Acts 2. The name of Jesus Christ was proclaimed (Acts 2:21) by Peter when he was filled with the Holy Spirit. We see the examples of the fruit of the Holy Spirit in the act of love and kindness (*jen* in Chinese) in Acts 2:45: "Selling their possessions and goods, they gave to anyone as he had need" (NIV). Many verses in Acts 2 speak of charismata—the gifts of the Holy Spirit (e.g., Acts 2:4; 2:22). Liberation is another embodiment of the Spirit (Acts 2:18–19) inasmuch as slaves and women were empowered to prophesy. Moreover, a genuine community was created by the material works of the Holy Spirit (Acts 2:42-45). The material dimension of the Holy Spirit includes Christological, moral, charismatic, liberative, and communal elements.[83]

In terms of degree, clarity, depth and breadth, the presence of the Spirit was sublimated to be fuller, richer, deeper, wider, and clearer. The clear and paradigmatic *material* dimension of the Spirit was bestowed on all peoples on the Day of Pentecost.

The *muljeok,* material dimension of the Spirit in the New Testament also bears "Christological" and "Lukan-Pentecostal" characteristics. The Cosmic Spirit (or *Ch'i*) is embodied in the life of Jesus Christ. This Cosmic Spirit manifested itself as personal and tangible *content*. The earthly life of Jesus Christ demonstrated the fruit of the Spirit such as love, joy, peace, patience, kindness, goodness, faithfulness, gentleness, and self-control (Gal 5:22). Now, humans can see the original formless *ch'i* or the formless pneuma in a concrete and categorical way. In this regard, Jesus Christ is the *Christological* embodiment (K. *che,* C. *ti*) of the Spirit.

The *muljeok,* material dimension of the Spirit is also concretized at the Pentecost in Acts 2. Hegel criticized Aristotle's view of "spirit" as *abstract thought*—thought that thinks or objectifies itself.[84] In opposition to Aristotle's view, Hegel wanted to recover the universal and concrete dimension of "spirit." At the Pentecost depicted in Acts 2, the numinous and abstract Spirit of God became universally concrete. This fullness of the Spirit brings missing pieces of our picture of God the Spirit. Here, at the Lukan Pentecost, the Spirit is revealed in fuller, paradigmatic manifestations. One of the main themes in the Book of Matthew is "ful-

83. See Kirsteen Kim, *The Holy Spirit in the World: A Global Conversation* (Maryknoll: Orbis, 2007) 168.

84. Michael Welker, *God the Spirit,* 290.

fillment." In fact, Matt 5:17 states, "Do not think that I have come to abolish the Law or Prophets; I have not come to abolish them but to *fulfill* them."[85] Jesus did not come to eliminate Judaism but to fulfill and correct what was missing and mistaken. In an analogous way, the Holy Spirit at the Pentecost in Acts 2 did not come to abolish other cosmic *sangjeok* works of the Spirit but to fulfill and correct what has been missing and mistaken in other faiths.

Another important point concerning the Lukan Pentecost in Acts 2 is that it epitomized a "meta-event" (or meta-narrative) with its "universal" implication. In other words, there have been many "other pentecosts," as many Jews in the Hebrew Bible and ancient East Asians have experienced the outpourings and powers of the Spirit/spirit, but they have stayed more or less local and partial. What separated the Lukan Pentecost from "other pentecosts" was its universality and full efficacy of the Spirit.

Conclusion

When we look at world religions from a chiological perspective, it is hard to argue against the presence and activities of the Holy Spirit in other faiths and cultures. In light of both the fruits (e.g., love and peace) and gifts of the Holy Spirit (e.g., healing and glossolalia), we detect the activities of the Spirit in other faiths. As we have seen in this chapter, both Moltmann and Samartha avow the activities of the Holy Spirit in other religions. This, however, does not imply that the Holy Spirit has been completely and fully present in traditional East Asian religions (e.g., Taoism and Confucianism) devoid of the Spirit of Christ. The Spirit (*ch'i*) of these indigenous East Asian religions stayed *sangjeok* formal insofar as it was still incomplete, equivocal, and vague. In this sense, we saw a great need for the works of the modern Western Christian missionaries who could bring a more refined and fuller pneumatology. This Christian pneumatology, although it is still distorted by the selfishness of certain individuals within the church, brings the *muljeok* material dimension of the Holy Spirit.

In order to grasp a holistic (wholistic) picture of the reality of the Spirit, we need to go beyond the Judeo-Christian traditions rooted in the Bible and Western church. God created all people; in this regard, all peo-

---

85. *Italics* are mine.

ple including East Asians are God's children. A parallel can also be found in the great Chinese Neo-Confucian Chang Tsai's statement in the *Hsi Ming* (Western Inscription): Heaven (*Ch'ien*) and Earth (*K'un*) are my father and mother. Therefore, my nature is that of the two Commanders— Heaven and Earth. All people are my blood brothers (and sisters), and all creatures are my companions. In other words, all people are from the same origin—the common parents.[86]

It is hard to envisage that God the Father (Mother) neglected and ceased communication with God's own children. Even human parents would not do that! In this sense, we accept "general revelation" and "pneumatological activities" of the Spirit in other faiths. Matteo Ricci (1552–1610 CE), an Italian Jesuit missionary to China, recognized the general, formal works of God in Chinese Confucianism, and H. G. Underwood (one of the first Protestant missionaries to Korea at the end of the nineteenth century) insisted that God (Christian) was already working on indigenous Korean people before the arrival of Western missionaries.[87] For this reason, in order to have a more holistic picture of God's works on God's own people, we need to move from the "pneumatological" perspective to the "chiological" perspective that incorporates "other religious testimonies" in addition to the biblical and Western Christian testimonies.

86. See Yu-lan Fung, *History of Chinese Philosophy*, 2:493.
87. H. G. Underwood, *Call of Korea*, 91.

Bibliography

Albrecht, Daniel. *Rites in the Spirit: A Ritual Approach to Pentecostal/Charismatic Spirituality*. Sheffield: Sheffield Academic Press, 1999.

Athanasius. *The Letters of Saint Athanasius*. Translated by C. R. B. Shapland. London: Epworth, 1951.

Baird, Forrest, and Walter Kaufmann, editors. *From Plato to Derrida*. Upper Saddle River: Prentice Hall, 2000.

Barrett, David, et al. *World Christian Encyclopedia: A Comparative Survey of Churches and Religions in the Modern World*. 2nd ed. New York: Oxford University Press, 2001.

Barth, Karl. *Church Dogmatics* I/1. Translated by G. W. Bromiley. Edinburgh: T. & T. Clark, 1936.

———. *Church Dogmatics* IV/1. Translated by G. W. Bromiley. Edinburgh: T. & T. Clark, 1956.

———. *Church Dogmatics* IV/2. Translated by G. W. Bromiley. Edinburgh: T. & T. Clark, 1958.

———. *Evangelical Theology: An Introduction*. Translated by Grover Foley. Grand Rapids: Eerdmans, 1963.

Best, Ernest. *A Critical and Exegetical Commentary on Ephesians*. Edinburgh: T. & T. Clark, 1998.

Bevans, Stephan B. *Models of Contextual Theology*. Maryknoll: Orbis, 2002.

Bradshaw, Timothy. *Trinity and Ontology*. Edinburgh: Rutherford House, 1988.

Braaten, Carl, editor. *The Theology of Wolfhart Pannenberg*. Minneapolis: Augsburg, 1988.

Bruce, F. F. *The Gospel of John*. Grand Rapids: Eerdmans, 1983.

Burgess, Stanley M. *The Holy Spirit: Eastern Christian Traditions*. Peabody: Hendrickson, 1984

Chai, Ch'u, and Winberg Chai, editors. *I Ching: Book of Changes*. Translated by James Legge. Seacaucus: University Books, 1964.

Cheng, Chung-ying. "*Li* and *Ch'i* in the *I Ching*: A Reconsideration of Being and Non-Being in Chinese Philosophy." *Journal of Chinese Philosophy* 14 (1987) 1–38.

Ching, Julia. *The Religious Thought of Chu Hsi*. Oxford: Oxford University Press, 2000.

Choe, Byeong-heon. *Seongsan Myeong Gyeong*. Translated by Deberniere Torrey. Korean Christian Classics Series IV. Seoul, Korea: KIATS, 2010.

Chung, David. *Syncretism: The Religious Context of Christian Beginnings in Korea*. New York: SUNY, 2001.

Chung, Dai-wi. "Christianity and the Religious World of East Asians: The Principle of Three Religions as One." In *Asian Contextual Theology for the Third Millennium*, edited by Paul Chung et al., 269–83. Eugene: Pickwick, 2007.

Chung, Edward Y. J. *The Korean Neo-Confucianism of Yi T'oegye and Yi Yulgok*. Albany: State University of New York Press, 1995.

Chung, Paul. *Constructing Irregular Theology: Bamboo and Minjung in East Asian Perspective*. Leiden: Brill, 2009.

————. *Karl Barth: God's Word in Action*. Eugene: Cascade, 2008.

Chung, Paul, et al., editors. *Asian Contextual Theology for the Third Millennium: A Theology of Minjung in Fourth-Eye Formation*. Princeton Theological Monograph Series 70. Eugene: Pickwick, 2007.

Cox, Harvey. *Fire from Heaven: The Rise of Pentecostal Spirituality and the Reshaping of Religion in the Twenty-First Century*. Cambridge: Da Capo, 1995.

————. "Pentecostalism and the Future of Christianity." *TIKKUN* 9 (1994) 43.

De Bary, Wm. Theodore, editor. *Sources of Chinese Tradition*. Vol. 1. New York: Columbia University Press, 1960.

De Bary, Wm. Theodore, and Irene Bloom, editors. *Sources of Chinese Tradition: From Earliest Times to 1600*. Vol. 1. 2nd ed. New York: Columbia University Press, 1999.

Descartes, René. *Meditations on First Philosophy*. Translated by John Cottingham. Cambridge: Cambridge University Press, 1986.

Dunn, James D. G. "Spirit, Holy Spirit." In *Dictionary of New Testament Theology*, 3:689. Grand Rapids: Zondervan, 1978.

Earle, William James. *Introduction to Philosophy*. New York: McGraw-Hill, 1992.

Ekken, Kaibara. *The Philosophy of Ch'i: The Record of Great Doubts*. Translated by Mary Evelyn Tucker. New York: Columbia University Press, 2007.

Eliade, Mircea. *Shamanism: Archaic Techniques of Ecstasy*. Translated by Willard Trask. London: Routledge & Kegan Paul, 1964.

Foucault, Michel. *Discipline and Punish: The Birth of the Prison*. Translated by Alan Sheridan. New York: Vintage Books, 1997.

————. *The Order of Things: An Archaeology of the Human Sciences*. New York: Pantheon, 1970.

Franke, John. *Barth for Armchair Theologians*. Louisville: Westminster John Know, 2006.

Fung, Yu-lan. *A History of Chinese Philosophy*. 2 vols. Translated by Derk Bodde. Princeton: Princeton University Press, 1952–53.

Gadamer, Hans-Georg. *Truth and Method*. 2nd ed. Translated by Joel Weinsheimer and Donald Marshall. New York: Continuum, 1989.

Gelpi, Donald. *The Conversion Experience: A Reflective Process of RCIA Participants and Others*. New York: Paulist, 1998.

————. *The Divine Mother: A Trinitarian Theology of the Holy Spirit*. New York: University Press of America, 1984.

————. *Experiencing God: A Theology of Human Emergence*. New York: Paulist, 1978.

Griffin, Michael. "Some Fusions and Diffusions of Horizon in a Gademerian Reading of *A Passage to India*." *Literature and Theology* 12.2 (1998) 172–73.

Hick, John. *An Interpretation of Religion: Human Responses to the Transcendent*. New Haven: Yale University Press, 1989.

Hiddleston, Jane. *Understanding Postcolonialism*. Stocksfield: Acumen, 2009.

Huang, Alfred. *The Complete I Ching*. Rochester: Inner Traditions, 1998.

Huang, Siu-chi. "Chang Tsai's Concept of Ch'i." *Philosophy East and West* 18 (1968) 225–26.

The I Ching or Book of Changes. Translated by Richard Wilhelm and Cary Baynes. Princeton: Princeton University Press, 1977.

Jenson, Robert W. "Jesus in the Trinity: Wolfhart Pannenberg's Christology and Doctrine of the Trinity." In *The Theology of Wolfhart Pannenberg*, edited by Carl E. Braaten. Minneapolis: Augsburg, 1988.

Kalton, Michael C. *The Four-Seven Debate*. Albany: SUNY, 1994

Kärkkäinen, Veli-Matti. *The Doctrine of God: A Global Introduction: A Biblical, Historical, and Contemporary Survey*. Grand Rapids: Baker Academics, 2004.

———. *An Introduction to the Theology of Religions: Biblical, Historical and Contemporary Perspectives*. Downers Grove: InterVarsity, 2003.

———. *Pneumatology: The Holy Spirit in Ecumenical, International, and Contextual Perspective*. Grand Rapids: Baker Academic, 2002.

Kasper, Walter. *The God of Jesus Christ*. Translated by Matthew J. O'Connell. New York: Crossroad, 1984.

Kim, Grace Ji-sun. "A Global Understanding of the Spirit." *Dialogue and Alliance* 21 (2007) 17–31.

———. *The Holy Spirit, Chi, and the Other: A Model of Global and Intercultural Pneumatology*. New York: Palgrave Macmillan, 2011.

Kim, Kirsteen. *The Holy Spirit in the World: A Global Conversation*. Maryknoll: Orbis, 2007.

Kim, Kyoung-jae. "The Cosmotheandric Vision in the Third Millennium." *Exchange* 28.4 (1999) 351–63.

Kim, Seung-tae. "Japan's Policy of Christianity and Japanization of Korean Church." Paper presented as part of the symposium "Indigenization of Christianity in China and Korea" at Shanghai University, China, 7–8 November 2009.

Knitter, Paul. *Introducing Theologies of Religions*. Maryknoll: Orbis, 2002.

Kohn, Livia. "Chinese Religion." In *The Human Condition*, edited by Robert Neville, 10–31. Albany: State University of New York Press, 2001.

Kraft, Charles H. *Christianity in Culture: A Study in Dynamic Biblical Theologizing in Cross-Cultural Perspective*. Maryknoll: Orbis, 1979.

Kwok, Pui-lan. *Postcolonial Imagination & Feminist Theology*. Louisville: Westminster John Knox, 2005.

Lakeland, Paul. *Postmodernity: Christian Identity in a Fragmented Age*. Minneapolis: Fortress, 1997.

Land, Steven. *Pentecostal Spirituality: A Passion for the Kingdom*. Sheffield, UK: Sheffield Academic Press, 1997.

Lee, Jung Young. *Embracing Change: Postmodern Interpretation of the I Ching from a Christian Perspective*. Scranton, PA: University of Scranton Press, 1994.

———. *Korean Shamanistic Rituals*. New York: Mouton, 1981.

———. *The Trinity in Asian Perspective*. Nashville: Abingdon, 1996.

Lee, Sang Hyun. *From a Liminal Space: An Asian American Theology*. Philadelphia: Fortress, 2010.

Lee, Young-hoon. *The Holy Spirit Movement in Korea: Its Historical and Theological Development*. Oxford: Regnum, 2009.

Legge, James, translator. *The Chinese Classics* 1. Hong Kong: Hong Kong University Press, 1970.

———. *The Sacred Books of China: The Texts of Taoism*. New York: Dover, 1962.

Lewis, I. M. *Ecstatic Religion*. London: Routledge, 1989

Lindbeck, George. *The Nature of Doctrine: Religion and Theology in a Postliberal Age*. Philadelphia: Westminster, 1984.

Liu, JeeLoo. *An Introduction to Chinese Philosophy: From Ancient Philosophy to Chinese Buddhism*. Oxford: Blackwell, 2006.

Lonergan, Bernard. *Method in Theology*. New York: Herder & Herder, 1972.

Macchia, Frank. *Baptized in the Spirit: A Global Pentecostal Theology*. Grand Rapids: Zondervan, 2006.

Martin, Ralph P. *Ephesians, Colossians, and Philemon*. Interpretation: A Bible Commentary for Teaching and Preaching. Atlanta: John Knox, 1991.

Marx, Karl. *Theses on Feuerbach*. Vol. 11, *Writings of the Young Marx on Philosophy and Society*. Translated and edited by L. D. Easton and K. H. Guddat. Garden City: Anchor Doubleday, 1967.

McCormack, Bruce. *Studies in the Theology of Karl Barth: Orthodox and Modern*. Grand Rapids: Baker Academic, 2008.

McKeon, Richard, editor. *The Basic Works of Aristotle*. New York: The Modern Library, 2001.

Mencius. Translated by D. C. Lau. London: Penguin, 2003.

Miller, L., and Stanley Grenz, editors. *Fortress Introduction to Contemporary Theologies*. Minneapolis: Fortress, 1998.

Molloy, Michael. *Experiencing the World's Religions: Traditions, Challenge, and Change*. 5th ed. New York: McGraw Hill, 2010.

Moltmann, Jürgen. *Experiences of God*. Translated by Margaret Kohl. Philadelphia: Fortress, 1980.

———. *The Source of Life: The Holy Spirit and the Theology of Life*. Translated by Margaret Kohl. Minneapolis: Fortress Press, 1997.

———. *The Spirit of Life: A Universal Affirmation*. Translated by Margaret Kohl. Minneapolis: Fortress Press, 1992.

———. "Theological Proposals towards the Resolution of the Filioque Controversy in Lukas Vischer." In *Spirit of God, Spirit of Christ: Ecumenical Reflections on the Filioque Controversy*, edited by Jürgen Moltmann, 164–73. London: SPCK, 1981.

Niebuhr, H. Richard. *Christ and Culture*. New York: Harper & Row, 1951.

Pannenberg, Wolfhart. "An Autobiographical Sketch." In *The Theology of Wolfhart Pannenberg*, edited by Carl E. Braaten. Minneapolis: Augsburg, 1998.

———. *Jesus—God and Man*. 2nd ed. Louisville: Westminster John Knox, 1977.

———. *Systematic Theology*. Vol. 1. Translated by Geoffrey Bromiley. Grand Rapids: Eerdmans, 1991.

———. *Systematic Theology*. Vol. 2. Translated by Geoffrey Bromiley. Grand Rapids: Eerdmans, 1994.

Paul, Richard, and Linda Elder. *Critical Thinking*. 2nd ed. New Jersey: Prentice Hall, 2006.

Peirce, Charles Sanders. *Collected Papers,* edited by Charles Hartshorne and Paul Weiss. 8 vols. Cambridge: Harvard University Press, 1931 ff.

Peters, Ted. *God as Trinity: Relationality and Temporality in Divine Life*. Louisville: Westminster John Knox, 1993.

Pinnock, Clark. *Flame of Love: A Theology of the Holy Spirit*. Downers Grove: InterVarsity, 1996.

Rosato, Philip J. *The Spirit as Lord: The Pneumatology of Karl Barth*. Edinburgh: T. & T. Clark, 1981.

Said, Edward. "In Conversation with Neeladri Bhattacharya, Suvir Kaul, and Ania Loomba." In *Relocating Postcolonialism*, edited by David Theo Goldberg and Ato Quayson. Oxford: Blackwell, 2002.

———. *Orientalism*. New York: Pantheon, 1978.

Samartha, Stanley. "The Holy Spirit and People of Other Faiths." *Ecumenical Review* 42 (2004) 250–52.

———. "The Holy Spirit and People of Various Faiths, Cultures, and Ideologies." In *The Holy Spirit*, edited by Dow Kilpatrick, 33–34. Nashville: Tidings, 1974.

Schmitz, E. D. "Knowledge, Experience, Ignorance." In *The New International Dictionary of New Testament Theology*. Translated and edited by Colin Brown. Grand Rapids: Zondervan, 1976.

Seol, Chung-su. "Studies on H. G. Underwood's Understanding of *Ha-na-nim*." PhD diss., Beijing University, 2009.

Sherman, Steven B. *Revitalizing Theological Epistemology: Holistic Evangelical Approaches to the Knowledge of God*. Princeton Theological Monograph Series 83. Eugene: Pickwick, 2008.

Simpson, E. K., and F. F. Bruce. *Commentary on the Epistles to the Ephesians and the Colossians*. The New International Commentary on the New Testament. Grand Rapids: Eerdmans, 1973.

St. Augustine. *On the Trinity*. A Select Library of the Nicene and Post-Nicene Fathers 3. Grand Rapids: Eerdmans, 1956.

Synan, Vinson. "Pentecostalism: Varieties and Contributions." *PNEUMA: The Journal of the Society for Pentecostal Studies* (1986) 43–44.

Tao Te Ching. Translated by Stephen Mitchell. New York: Harper Perennial, 2006.

Taylor, John V. *The Primal Vision*. London: SCM, 1963.

Thompson, John. *The Holy Spirit in the Theology of Karl Barth*. Allison Park, PA: Pickwick, 1991.

Tillich, Paul. *Systematic Theology*. 3 vols. Chicago: The University of Chicago Press, 1951–63.

Tracy, David. *Plurality and Ambiguity: Hermeneutics, Religion, Hope*. New York: Harper & Row, 1987.

Waardenburg, Jean Jacques. *Classical Approaches to the Study of Religion: Aims, Methods and Theories of Research*. The Hague: Mouton, 1973.

Weber, Max. *The Religion of China: Confucianism and Taoism*. Translated by Hans Gerth. New York: The Free Press, 1951.

Welker, Brian. *The I Ching or Book of Changes: A Guide to Life's Turning Points*. New York: St. Martin's Griffin, 1992.

Welker, Michael. *God the Spirit*. Translated by John Hoffmeyer. Minneapolis: Fortress, 1994.

Wilhelm, Richard. "Introduction." In *The I Ching or Book of Changes*. xlvii–lxii. Translated by Richard Wilhelm and Cary Baynes. Princeton: Princeton University Press, 1977.

Wittgenstein, Ludwig. *Philosophical Investigations*. Translated by G. E. M. Anscombe. 3rd ed. New York: Macmillan, 1953.

Wong, Eva. *Taoism*. Boston: Shambhala, 1997.

Yong, Amos. *Discerning the Spirit(s): A Pentecostal-Charismatic Contribution to Christian Theology of Religions*. Sheffield, UK: Sheffield Academic Press, 2000.

Yun, Koo Dong. *Baptism in the Holy Spirit: An Ecumenical Theology of Spirit Baptism*. Lanham: University Press of America, 2003.

———. "Pentecostalism from Below: Minjung Liberation and Asian Pentecostal Theology." In *The Spirit in the World: Emerging Pentecostal Theologies in Global Context*, edited by Veli-Matti Kärkkäinen, 89–114. Grand Rapids: Eerdmans, 2009.

Index